KU-603-839

# The Concept of Poverty

# The Concept of Poverty

*Working Papers on Methods of Investigation
and Life-Styles of the Poor in Different Countries*

*Edited by*

Peter Townsend

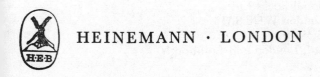 HEINEMANN · LONDON

Heinemann Educational Books Ltd
LONDON EDINBURGH MELBOURNE
SINGAPORE JOHANNESBURG
TORONTO AUCKLAND
IBADAN HONG KONG
NAIROBI NEW DELHI

ISBN 0435 82890 8

© Heinemann Educational Books 1970
First published 1970

Published by
Heinemann Educational Books Ltd
48 Charles Street, London W1X 8AH
Printed in Great Britain by
Morrison & Gibb Ltd, London and Edinburgh

# Contents

# Acknowledgements

It was at the initiative of the International Committee on Poverty Research that a conference was planned to take place in April 1967 at the University of Essex, with the object of encouraging the international exchange of methods of studying poverty, and raising the quality of study. Mr Henning Friis, as chairman of this committee, also chaired the conference, and Mlle A. A. de Vos Van Steenwijk, the committee's secretary, played an important part in planning its proceedings. A full list of the participants is given on pp. 251–253.

A grant towards the cost of the conference and the preparation of papers was made by the Joseph Rowntree Memorial Trust. This Trust has done much in recent years to promote research into poverty, and was already financing a series of studies of poverty in Britain directed by Professor Brian Abel-Smith and myself.

I am indebted to Brian Abel-Smith for continuous help and advice throughout the period covering the organization of the conference and the preparation of the text for publication. The contributions to this volume by him, Adrian Sinfield, Dennis Marsden, Christopher Bagley and myself, give some indication of the programme of work which the research team in Britain has planned. The secretary to the Department at the time of the conference, Mrs Wendy Morgan, did most to organize it efficiently and she typed many of the original papers. Miss Sue Best, the present secretary, has helped to prepare much of this volume for the press. Rarely can a University Department have been blessed with work as accurate and good-natured as by these two people. I am also grateful to Pat Healey and Walter Jaehnig for their unremitting help at proof stage.

# Introduction

In the mid-1950s a number of studies appearing in Britain showed that despite post-war social reform, high taxation and low levels of unemployment there was poverty among old people, fatherless families, the unemployed and the sick. Up to that stage few people in any advanced industrial society believed that, following the 1939 war, substantial poverty remained. Indeed, even Professor Kenneth Galbraith referred to 'pockets' of poverty in his provoking analysis of *The Affluent Society*. By 1960 public assumptions were transformed. Michael Harrington's *The Other America* was published in 1959 and official studies in the United States showed that, according to new definitions which became widely accepted, more than a fifth of the population were living in conditions of poverty. In 1964 the American war on poverty was launched and throughout the early 1960s in many parts of Europe problems of squalor, deprivation and want were gradually acknowledged.[1] In Britain two Government studies of pensioners[2] and families with children[3] found substantial numbers living below subsistence standards which society had approved.

1. See, for example, OECD, *Low Income Groups and Methods of Dealing with their Problems*, Papers for a Trade Union Seminar, Supplement to the Report, Paris, 1966; De la Gorce, P., *La France Pauvre*, Paris, Bernard Grasset, 1965; Klanfer, J., *L'Exclusion Sociale*—based on and including papers for the second conference on Handicapped Families, Aide à Toute Détresse, UNESCO, Paris, 1964; Czeh-Szombathy, L. and Andorka, R., *A Budapesti Nyugdijasok Helyzete es Problemai* (Situation and Problems of the Pensioners of Budapest), Budapest, Central Statistical Office, 1965; Friis, H., and Manniche, E., *Enlige Ældre* (Old People in a Low-Income Area of Copenhagen), Copenhagen, Danish National Institute of Social Research, 1961; Østergård, F., *De Ældres Levevilkår* (Living Conditions of the Elderly, Vol. I., Incomes), Copenhagen, Danish National Institute of Social Research, 1965; Blume, O., *Die Situation der Kinderreichen Familien in Stuttgart* (Large Families in Stuttgart), City of Stuttgart, 1965; Blume, O., *Die Obdachlosen in Köln* (The Homeless in Cologne), Goettingen, Schwarz, 1960; Diena, L., *Borgata Milanese* (Shanty Towns in Milan), Milan, 1963; Durlacher, G. L., *De Laagstbetaalden* (The Lowest-paid), Amsterdam, Stichting, 1965. For a comprehensive review see Sinfield, A., 'Poverty Research in Britain and Europe', paper prepared for conference at the Bureau of Social Science Research, Washington, Nov. 1967 (publication forthcoming).
2. *Report of the Enquiry into the Financial and Other Circumstances of Retirement Pensioners*, London, HMSO, 1966.
3. *Circumstances of Families*, London, HMSO, 1967.

In all countries there was a grave lack of information about the conditions in which millions of poor people lived. A two-fold conceptual problem also arose, which sooner or later social scientists would have to resolve. On the one hand, the subsistence concept, invented and worked out in England by Charles Booth and Seebohm Rowntree in the late nineteenth century, was coming under fire as providing a basis for defining poverty.[4] In societies which were changing fast it seemed reasonable to suppose that human needs were changing too. The subsistence concept seemed too static, somehow locked up in the distant youth of the grandparental generation.

On the other hand, the dire needs of the poor nations had also come to the forefront of public awareness and the paradox of poverty in America, judged by one standard, and poverty in the developing countries, judged by other standards, had somehow to be explained. Despite the frustrating lack of information an intellectual framework, consistent cross-nationally as well as through time, had to be created into which new information could be fed.

It was in this situation that a British team embarked in 1963 on a series of studies financed by the Joseph Rowntree Memorial Trust,[5] and that social scientists decided in the same year to set up the International Committee on Poverty Research to hold meetings, assist the communication of research findings and stimulate new research. After two previous meetings in Paris, a conference was sponsored by the International Committee and held in the University of Essex in Colchester, England, in 1967. The papers included in this book are selected from its proceedings and subsequently revised.[6]

This book aims to make some contribution to a resolution of the conceptual problem. The chapters by Peter Townsend and Martin

4. Seebohm Rowntree did in fact develop a more generous human needs standard, but the subsistence standard was extremely influential both in shaping views about the nature and extent of poverty in different countries and in supplying a basis for the payment of social insurance or public assistance. For criticisms see, *Poverty: Ten Years After Beveridge*, Planning, No. 344, 1952; Townsend, P., 'Measuring Poverty', *British Journal of Sociology*, June, 1954; Townsend, P., 'The Meaning of Poverty', *British Journal of Sociology*, September, 1962; and Rein, M., in this volume.
5. A series of pilot studies and a preliminary national survey were financed. See, for example, Marsden, D., *Mothers Alone*, London, Allen Lane, 1969; Land, H., *Large Families in London*, London, Bell, 1970. The fieldwork for the national survey was completed early in 1969.
6. A full list of the participants is given on pp. 251–253.

Rein make the case for a relative concept of poverty and deal both with the cross-national and developmental aspects of poverty.

The next four chapters by J. C. McKenzie, Brian Abel-Smith and Christopher Bagley, Peter Townsend and Alvin Schorr, then plunge into some of the problems that are involved in obtaining indices of poverty and translating general concepts into operational definitions. Alvin Schorr is deliberately controversial in stressing the effect on all other aspects of life of bad housing.

The remainder of the book is devoted to the theme of poverty in relation to the social structure. S. M. Miller and Pamela Roby show that the conditions of the poor can best be understood as a special feature of social stratification. Herbert Gans suggests that in studying the life-styles of the poor we should pay particular attention not only to ways in which behaviour deviates from middle-class norms but to norms and aspirations which are resistant to change. We should, he contends, try to create experimental situations to find how people respond to new opportunities. Leopold Rosenmayr then considers the social development of youth and argues that formalized teaching, instruction and information is of great importance in ameliorating poverty. Dorothy Wedderburn discusses the special problems of the aged in three countries, the United States, Britain and Denmark, and concludes that there is least evidence of poverty among the aged in Denmark. Otto Blume reports data from Germany which suggest that poverty among the aged in rural areas is at least as extensive and in some ways more severe than among the aged in urban areas. Adrian Sinfield calls attention to the uneasy and complex relationship between the labour market and social security in the causation of poverty, while Dennis Marsden reveals some of the special problems of meeting the needs of fatherless families by the methods of public assistance. Finally, Vilhelm Aubert shows the difficulties of keeping isolated communities in touch with the rapidly changing conditions of an advanced society.

Although several of the authors are well-known for their writing on social policy, this is not a theme deeply pursued in this volume. The authors are agreed in believing that the most constructive contribution to the development of policy will occur as a result of a more penetrating analysis of the nature of the problem of poverty—and that will be possible only with a radical change and improvement in methods of investigation.

PETER TOWNSEND

# 1. Measures and Explanations of Poverty in High Income and Low Income Countries: The Problems of Operationalizing the Concepts of Development, Class and Poverty*

## Peter Townsend

A fifth of the population of the United States, the wealthiest nation in the world, were officially described in 1964 as living in conditions of poverty.[1] Yet the United States, with only 6 per cent of its population, accounts for nearly a third of the world's Gross National Product in real terms. This is nearly twice as much as all the so-called developing countries put together, excluding China.[2] Moreover, some families in the United States with ten times the real income per person of that in the poorest developing countries are adjudged to be in poverty.[3]

Can this paradox be explained? Is there a coherent theoretical framework which will relate statements about poverty in affluent

* I am indebted to the following for their valuable comments on a first draft: Johan Galtung, Roland Robertson, Werner Landecker, Herbert Gans, Jeremy Tunstall, John McKenzie, N. N. Franklin and Adrian Sinfield.

1. Economic Report of the President of the United States for 1964, Washington D.C., US Government Printing Office, 1964; Orshansky, M., 'Counting the Poor: Another Look at the Poverty Profile', *Social Security Bulletin*, Vol. 28, January, 1965.
2. See, for example, Lagos, G., *International Stratification and Underdeveloped Countries*, Chapel Hill, University of North Carolina Press, 1963, p. 4.
3. The poverty line used by the US Social Security Administration in 1963 ranged from $1,500 a year for a person living alone to about $700 a head for large families. See Orshansky, M., *op. cit.* Despite difficulties in comparing these amounts with income per person in developing countries (see in particular the difficulties in estimating GNP listed by Russett, B. M., *et al*, *World Handbook of Political and Social Indicators*, New Haven and London, Yale University Press, 1964, pp. 149–151) it is clear that the line represents a standard of living which is several times greater than the average standard in the poorest countries.

with that in developing societies? The view taken in this chapter is that needs which are unmet can be defined satisfactorily only in terms relative to the society in which they are found or expressed. Distinctions hitherto made between 'absolute' and 'relative' poverty, or between 'basic' and 'cultural' needs are argued to be unreal upon analysis. Needs which are believed to be absolute or basic can be shown to be relative. Poverty must be regarded as a general form of relative deprivation which is the effect of the maldistribution of resources. This will be the theme of the chapter.

The view put forward is therefore that the description, analysis and explanation of poverty in any country must proceed within the context of a general theory of stratification as applied to social systems and sub-systems on a continuum ranging from the household or family at one extreme through local communities and national societies to world society at the other. But this is easier said than done. If good theory is to be developed, three groups of studies upon which a great deal of attention has been recently concentrated need to be deliberately related. These are (a) studies of differences between countries in their degree of development or modernization, which help us to understand their poverty; (b) studies of the form of social stratification within countries; and (c) studies of the scale and nature of poverty in advanced industrial societies. We are still at a very early stage in our understanding of the manifestations and causation of poverty and for historical reasons some of the most relevant work in the social sciences has been undertaken in isolated compartments. The relationship between the concepts of development, class and poverty will be explored in this chapter for heuristic purposes. I will start by looking at stratification internationally and consider the implications for a theory of poverty of recent comparative work on development. I will then endeavour to show how a population might be ranked in strata or classes according to the distribution of resources so that the relationship of the poor to the rest of society can be better understood. Finally I will illustrate the kind of analysis which is necessary to explain poverty in developing as well as advanced industrial societies.

## Development and International Social Stratification

The comparative study of total societies has been given considerable impetus in recent years because of the emergence of new nation-states, the interests of the big powers in geographical spheres of influence and the promotion of 'development' by the United Nations to combat 'world poverty'. The very existence of the United Nations and of many other international agencies, such as UNESCO, ILO and FAO, promotes comparison and national self-consciousness and has had a profound influence as much upon academic pursuits as upon social and political perspectives. The United Nations has itself begun to issue extremely valuable compendia of national statistics. One study examined the relative standing of 74 countries according to income, health, nutrients and food consumption and literacy.[4] In recent years a growing number of cross-national economic, political and social studies have been published.[5]

One consequence of cross-national comparison is, as Table 1 suggests, that a basis for explanation and for practical policy-making can be laid. Not only may 'stages' of economic and social development be hypothesized; at any one time nation-states can be ranked according to their economic activity, social structure and possession of different resources. Some countries are wealthier, or have a larger population, a lower mortality rate, relatively more men under arms and more young people in higher education than others. Their position in the world economic order, or their power or prestige, can be regarded as superior. Social scientists have seized upon the possibilities offered by modern methods of data-collection to present ambitious comparisons between countries as a basis for theories of development.

Some of the efforts being made in this direction by social scientists may be misplaced, however. There are various problems in producing theories of development. There is the uneven quality of basic information; the unconscious ideological or technical bias in the selection of those parts of the economic and social systems of

4. United Nations, *Report on the World Social Situation*, New York, 1961.
5. See, for example, Ginsberg, N., *Atlas of Economic Development*, Chicago, 1961; Lerner, D., *The Passing of Traditional Society*, The Free Press, Glencoe, Ill., 1958; Deutsch, K. W., 'Social Mobilization and Political Development', *American Political Science Review*, Vol. 55, September, 1961; Miller, S. M., 'Comparative Social Mobility', *Current Sociology*, Vol. 9, 1960; Almond, G. A., and Coleman, J. S., *The Politics of the Developing Areas*, Princeton, Princeton University Press, 1960; Cutright, P., 'National Political Development: Measurement and Analysis', *American Sociological Review*, Vol. 28, April, 1963; Russett, B. M., *et al, op. cit.*; and Drewnowski, J., and Scott, W., *The Level of Living Index*, United Nations Research Institute for Social Development. Report No. 4, Geneva, September, 1966.

## TABLE 1

### Stages of Economic and Political Development (Russett et al)

| Stages | Numbers of countries | GNP per person (1) | Per cent of population which is urban (living in towns 20,000+) | Per cent of population which is literate | Numbers in higher education per 100,000 population | Inhabitants per physician | Per cent of population voting in major elections | Numbers of radios per 1,000 population |
|---|---|---|---|---|---|---|---|---|
| I 'Traditional Primitive' Societies | 11 | 56 | 6 | 13 | 27 | 46,100 | 30 | 12 |
| II 'Traditional Civilizations' | 15 | 87 | 10 | 24 | 86 | 22,200 | 49 | 20 |
| III 'Transitional' Societies | 31 | 173 | 21 | 42 | 165 | 5,400 | 41 | 56 |
| IV 'Industrial Revolution' Societies | 36 | 445 | 34 | 77 | 386 | 1,600 | 69 | 157 |
| V 'High Mass-Consumption' Societies | 14 | 1,330 | 45 | 98 | 650 | 900 | 78 | 352 |
| **Selected Nations** | | | | | | | | |
| I Laos | | 50 | 4 | 17 | 4 | 100,000 | — | 8 |
| Libya | | 60 | 18 | 13 | 49 | 5,800 | — | 63 |
| II Nigeria | | 78 | 10 | 10 | 4 | 32,000 | 40 | 4 |
| Thailand | | 96 | 8 | 68 | 251 | 7,500 | — | 6 |
| III Philippines | | 220 | 13 | 75 | 976 | 5,600 | 55 | 22 |
| Mauritius | | 225 | 27 | 52 | 14 | 4,500 | — | — |
| IV Hungary | | 490 | 37 | 97 | 258 | 650 | 93 | 231 |
| Puerto Rico | | 563 | 32 | 81 | 1,192 | 2,200 | 73 | — |
| V West Germany | | 927 | 55 | 98 | 528 | 798 | 87 | 319 |
| France | | 943 | 30 | 96 | 667 | 1,014 | 89 | 282 |
| United Kingdom | | 1,189 | 67 | 98 | 460 | 935 | 78 | 289 |
| United States | | 2,577 | 52 | 98 | 1,983 | 780 | 64 | 948 |

(1) Estimates converted at current exchange rates into US dollars.

*Source*: Russett, B. M., and Alker, H. R., Deutsch, K. W., Lasswell, H. D., *World Handbook of Political and Social Indicators*, New Haven and London, Yale University Press, 1964.

different countries which are felt to be relevant to 'development'; the difficulty of deciding what *weight* should be given to different parts of the economic and social system at different stages of development; and finally the difficulty of deciding whether there are definite stages of development and whether different nations follow roughly the same or widely different paths of development. First, basic information—essential statistics are just not available for some developing countries; no population census has yet taken place in Afghanistan, for example. The lack of statistics about some matters means, of course, that these matters get too little attention in national and international discussion. When statistics do exist for developing countries, they are often unreliable. Population statistics for Nigeria, for example, have recently been revised upwards and are still recognized to be subject to a considerable margin of error. Such difficulties as these are very great and must not be underestimated. Perhaps the random sample survey has been insufficiently exploited in some countries, especially in Africa and Asia.[6]

As well as the lack of quantitative information over many aspects of social and economic life there is, second, the problem of selecting the criteria according to which comparisons between countries can be made. It can be argued that there is a kind of bias in the selection of the variables which are felt to be relevant to development. The criteria of comparison which are adopted in all studies tend to favour western-style 'consumption' societies. Non-monetary resources other than the distribution of agricultural land tend to be overlooked. Cinema attendance and ownership of radios take precedence over measures of direct participation in local cultural events. Urbanization rates have more significance than living space or playing space for children. Unpaid services reciprocated within the family and the community do not feature among the indicators of 'development'. Neither is there a place for measures of social integration, such as low prevalence, say, of individual isolation. One author notes that 'recreation, funerals, religious services, domestic service and indigenous medicine, provided outside the market sector in a peasant economy and sometimes included in national income and sometimes not, ought to be fully included in a comparison with a country where these items are automatically

6. See, for example, Mitchell, R. E., 'Survey materials collected in the Developing Countries: Sampling, Measurement and Interviewing Obstacles to Intra- and Inter-National Comparisons', *International Social Science Journal*, Vol. XVII, No. 4, 1965.

part of income because they are within the market factor'.[7] All the factor analyses and regression equations in the world cannot make good the crudity of the information that is available, nor objectify the western-style cultural and economic ideology that underlies the whole approach.

Whether development is defined restrictedly in terms of economic variables alone or broadly to cover economic, social and political variables there is a problem not only of selecting the variables, but also of relating variables of different weight, many of which may not be quantifiable. If a broad definition is adopted, how would the indicator for higher education, as in Table 1, for example, be weighed with that for number of inhabitants per physician? A broad definition has been employed on behalf of the United Nations Research Institute for Social Development by Drewnowski and Scott. They compiled a 'level of living index'. This is summarized in Table 2. The index represents an attempt to produce an operational definition of social development. Level of living is defined as 'the level of satisfaction of the needs of the population assured by the flow of goods and services enjoyed in a unit of time'. The authors give equal weight to the component indices. They recognize that this is arbitrary and candidly say that any method of weighting is one dependent upon value judgements.[8] However, perhaps they are also reluctant to conceptualize the kind of society that would be highly 'developed' and analyse how strongly certain factors and policies contribute towards the achievement of it. In addition to the failure to deal with weighting one of the weakest features of the index is the distinction that is drawn between 'basic human needs' or 'necessities' and 'higher needs' or 'comforts'. It would be very difficult to define the shelter, whether in terms of cubic footage or of facilities, needed by a family, without taking account of social norms about the sharing of beds and rooms by people of different sex, age and consanguinity. It would be difficult to define nutritional needs without taking account of the kinds and demands of occupations and of leisure time pursuits in a society. Recent sociological and other studies have shown how tenuous are definitions of absolute needs.[9]

7. Usher, D., *Rich and Poor Countries: A Study in Problems of Comparisons of Real Income*, London, Institute of Economic Affairs, 1966, p. 17.

8. Drewnowski, J., and Scott, W., *op. cit.*, pp. 17–22.

9. See, for example, Townsend, P., 'The Meaning of Poverty', *British Journal of Sociology*, September, 1962; Franklin, N. N., 'The Concept and Measurement of "Minimum Living Standards" ', *International Labour Review*, April, 1967.

TABLE 2

*Level of Living Index* (Drewnowski and Scott)

| Components | | Types of Indicators |
|---|---|---|
| I Basic physical needs | 1. Nutrition | (intake of calories and protein per head) |
| | 2. Shelter | (degree of overcrowding; structural facilities) |
| | 3. Health | (proportion of deaths at young ages; proportion of population with access to adequate medical care) |
| II Basic cultural needs | 4. Education | (proportion of children enrolled at school: pupil teacher ratio) |
| | 5. Leisure and Recreation | (number of hours free from work per head per year; daily newspapers per 1,000 population; radio and TV sets per 1,000 population) |
| | 6. Security | (violent deaths per million population per year; proportion of population covered by unemployment and sickness insurance and old age pensions) |
| III Higher needs | 7. Surplus income | (income in excess of cost of meeting basic needs) |

*Source:* Drewnowski, J., and Scott, W., *The Level of Living Index*, United Nations Research Institute for Social Development, Report No. 4, Geneva, September 1966, pp. 44–45.

A final problem that is involved in ranking countries according to certain criteria and comparing them is that of appearing to represent 'stages' of development. Let us consider certain lesser objections before turning to a fundamental objection. At what point can a society be called 'developed'? Is there a logical continuum through all stages or are there discontinuities or thresholds which separate quite different kinds of economic and social activity? It can be argued that societies in Stages I and V (see Table 1) are so different in their resources and organization that it may be difficult to find common criteria of comparison. To meet this objection it has been suggested that it may be more appropriate to outline 'short span' operational criteria to apply to groups of societies within limited ranges. A series of overlapping measures would still permit detailed study within a general theory of development.

Even if a continuum of development is assumed, the path of development is by no means smooth or consistent. Let us consider certain problems of detail. Through the various stages of development, as crudely represented in Table 1, there seems to be a rapid increase in GNP per person and in the proportions of the population that are urbanized, literate and receiving higher education, while there is a sharp decrease in the number of persons depending on a single physician. In the broadest terms these and other variables 'form a quite consistent cluster indicating the state of a nation's economic growth'.[10] But there are marked deviations, as the lower half of the table shows. For its GNP per person and its low rate of urbanization Thailand has remarkably high rates for literacy and higher education, and the ratio of physicians to population is relatively favourable. The difference between the Philippines and Mauritius in the proportion of the population receiving higher education is enormous and, at the next stage of development, that between Puerto Rico and Hungary is also large. The special situation in the Philippines and Puerto Rico no doubt owes much to prolonged American cultural domination. But these examples in themselves show that profiles of achievement vary and may be difficult to explain.[11]

Rather than throwing doubt on the hypothesis of a continuum of development it has been suggested that disequilibrium in ranking may indicate high rates of development for the societies in question.[12]

10. Russett, B. M., *et al, op. cit.*, p. 288.
11. In a valuable analysis of a large number of Afro-Asian and European nations Robertson and Tudor have shown that rank disequilibrium (i.e. the extent to which a nation, or unit, is high-ranking on some dimensions, e.g. income and education, and not on others, e.g. newspapers) is in practice common among the nations of the world; that this disequilibrium tends to be greatest for those nations in the middle or the upper-middle of the total ranking (mainly but not entirely in correspondence with a simple mathematical model); but that some nations, like Malaysia and Turkey, diverge strikingly from 'expected' degrees of disequilibrium. They call for further study of such rank divergence. Robertson, R., and Tudor, A., 'The Third World and International Stratification: Theoretical Considerations and Research Findings, *Sociology*, January, 1968.
12. Galtung, J., and Höivik, T., 'On the Definition and Theory of Development with a View to the Application of Rank Order Indicators in the Elaboration of a Composite Index of Human Resources,' UNESCO, Warsaw, December, 1967.

The effort of trying to restore equilibrium is thought to result in increased growth. This theory has prompted intensive study of the effects of investing disproportionately in one sector of the economy, or institution such as, higher education. However, the correlation between GNP per person and higher education enrolment, unlike that between GNP per person and primary and secondary education or literacy, is quite low.[13]

But the more we study stages, component variables and the weighting of component variables of development, the more we are led to question the assumptions that are made about the nature of development. Not only is it difficult to fit certain countries in any continuum, even if it is presumed that some of them miss certain stages of development entirely. It is also difficult to treat two countries as being so independent of each other that the second can be said to represent the predictable future state of the first. It is like suggesting that as an inevitable result of economic growth the poorest man in the United States or Britain will one day live and behave just like the richest man in that society. In each case a simple connection is overlooked. The privilege of the one and the deprivation of the other are directly related.

Rostow, for example, posits five stages of development (rather like the five stages adopted from Russett *et al* in Table 1): traditional society, pre-conditions for take-off, take-off, the drive to maturity and the age of high mass-consumption[14] as if societies which had entered the final stage had achieved it largely without help and as if societies in the first two stages had never experienced anything different. Yet any attempt to document these stages from world history encounters awkward facts. India was de-industrialized. In Africa the slave trade plundered social resources long before colonialism did so again. In Latin America the high civilizations of the Incas and Aztecs were obliterated. Many of the societies now acknowledged to be highly developed were capitalized at the expense of those which have remained underdeveloped. In many important respects it would be fair to conclude that the structure of underdevelopment has been created by centuries of association with the mercantile and colonialist nations. It would be naïve in the extreme not to recognize that western countries may have much to gain economically and politically even today from the poverty

13. Russett, B. M., *et al, op. cit.*, p. 288.
14. Rostow, W. W., *The Stages of Economic Growth, A Non-Communist Manifesto*, Cambridge, Cambridge University Press, 1962.

of the so-called developing countries though they may also have a lot to lose by policies of exploitation. Theories of development may unwittingly safeguard western ideology.[15]

The relationships between societies must therefore be seen in terms of a system of international social stratification. Lagos, for example, has defined the situation of developing countries as one of *atimia*, meaning that the evolution of an international stratified system with economic, power and prestige relations has 'ended in a loss or lowering of status of the underdeveloped nations'. In contradiction to the formal status that they are presumed to enjoy according to international equalitarian ideology they have low real status. Their international relations can be regarded as 'systems of action oriented to enhance the real status of the nation in a stratified world, dominated by the values of wealth, power and prestige'.[16] Economic relations can also be studied in this way and societies grouped in strata according to their resources and economic behaviour.

In relation to a system of stratification there are three conceptions of development. First, all societies advance equally and uniformly; mobility is nil and the form of stratification remains constant. Second, some societies are mobile; they improve their rank *vis-à-vis* others but the form and dispersion of stratification remains constant. Third, there is a convergence of rank; more societies may cluster in the middle ranks or the form of stratification may change in that the number of ranks may be reduced. Most theories of development implicitly adopt the first of these conceptions.

Development is usually interpreted as a process maximizing economic growth, and GNP per person the indicator of that growth. GNP per person is often used also as a measure of comfort or well-being. But it is a measure of production rather than of welfare. The United States has the largest GNP per person but has neither the highest life expectancy nor the lowest infant mortality rate. By selecting GNP per person as the ultimate criterion of advanced development and international status a distorted view of the world is presented. The selection of such a measure inevitably discriminates against the developing countries; for example, agricultural products and consumption from the land tend to be

15. This theme is elaborated trenchantly and caustically in one of the best critical analyses of theories of development by Frank, André G., 'Sociology of Development and Underdevelopment of Sociology', *Catalyst* (State University of New York in Buffalo), No. 3, Summer, 1967.
16. Lagos, G., *op. cit.*, pp. ix–x.

under-reported.[17] But the question of favouring industrial as compared with agricultural economies is perhaps an incidental one. Precedence is given to economic institutions and the products from the economic system. Other national activities and achievements, such as the redistribution of wealth, the development of social services, the integration of racial minorities and the minimization of violent acts against the person, are correspondingly accorded smaller value. The narrowly economic view of development can, of course, be challenged. Development can be conceived alternatively as a process achieving balanced economic and social well-being.[18] This demands the formulation in detail of social objectives and of criteria by which indicators of degrees of success in attaining objectives may be combined. At the least it means that societies low in rank according to GNP may be ranked higher in social development than, say, the United States and West Germany.

The implications of all this for the study of world poverty are far-reaching. Some societies are desperately poor more because wealthier societies are continuing to follow policies of protecting their own special interests than because the poor societies lack technology and special skills which they need to learn or be taught to develop. What we need to study are the different systems which control the accumulation and unequal distribution of resources: trade, overseas investment, political relations and military alliances and campaigns. The degeneration or depression of regions, nations and sections of nations into conditions of deprivation can then be traced. The 'stages of growth' theory of development implies that the poverty of poor nations is relieved as their economies grow. It

17. For some of the difficulties in the valuation of subsistence output, see Prest, A. R., *Public Finance in Underdeveloped Countries*, London, Weidenfeld and Nicolson, 1962, Appendix 1, 'The Valuation of Subsistence Output'.
18. See, for example, Drewnowski, J., *Social and Economic Factors in Development*, United Nations Research Institute for Social Development, Report No. 3, Geneva, February, 1966. Attempts have been made to distinguish development from 'modernization'. Lagos, for example, regards the modernization of a society as the process of insuring 'a regular flow of innovations within its social system'. Lagos, *op. cit.*, p. 243. Nettl and Robertson have argued that 'modernization' is the crucial concept, to which the concepts of development and industrialization should be subordinated. 'Modernization is the process whereby national élites seek successfully to reduce their atimic status and move towards equivalence with other 'well-placed' nations. The goal of equivalence is not a fixed but a moving target...'. Nettl, J. P., and Robertson, R., 'Industrialization, Development or Modernization', *British Journal of Sociology*, Vol. XVII, No. 3, September, 1966.

implies that the poverty of traditional societies is natural and encourages them to be patient until the preconditions for take-off and industrialization are established. Yet this is no more convincing than the corresponding theory, which held widespread currency throughout the West in the decade or more following the second world war, that poverty *within* societies is gradually eliminated as their economies grow. For the United States provides living testimony of the falsity of this proposition.

### Poverty in Advanced Industrial and Developing Societies

The Council of Economic Advisers presented an annual report to the President of the United States in 1964 which showed that at constant prices the number of families in poverty in the United States had been reduced from 32 to 20 per cent between 1947 and 1962.[19] The Social Security Administration estimated that the figure had declined from 22 to 18 per cent between 1959 and 1964.[20] But these measures are plainly inconsistent when the bases are compared either with those used in other countries or with conceptions of poverty adopted in the United States 20 years or 50 years previously. In an interesting attempt to apply *contemporary* standards of 'minimum adequacy' to the circumstances of different years Ornati found little change in the number of poor between 1947 and 1960 (falling from 28 to 27 per cent). He pointed out that when 1960 *standards* were applied to the 1930s, 'it appears that more people three decades ago were "poor" than were considered to be poor at the time. And, quite evidently, if we were to use the standards of thirty years ago and project them forward to today, we would find that "poverty" had decidedly dwindled'.[21] In England, without applying explicit controls in relation to changing social conditions and wages, Seebohm Rowntree in fact revised his poverty line upwards when he sought to compare the scale of poverty in York in 1936 and 1950 with that when he first studied the city's population in 1899.[22] But his revisions

19. *The Economic Report of the President together with the Annual Report of the Council of Economic Advisers*, January, 1964.
20. *Economic Report of the President of the United States*, 1964.
21. Ornati, O., *Poverty Amid Affluence*, New York, The Twentieth Century Fund, 1966.
22. 'In 1899 Rowntree's standard for a family of five approximated to 79 per cent of average manual earnings; in 1936 it was 69 per cent and in 1950, 60 per cent'. Abel-Smith, B., and Townsend, P., *The Poor and the Poorest*, London, Bell, 1965, p. 16.

fell midway between price and wage increases and, accordingly, he found smaller proportions in poverty at successive dates than he would have found if a strictly relative standard had been used. It could be argued that while his first survey took account of the growth of need from pre-industrial conditions to industrial society, his second and third surveys failed to acknowledge to an adequate extent the further growth of need. In both countries, relative conceptions of poverty may come to be properly worked out by social scientists and accepted by government.

The United States Social Security Administration measure of poverty is of greater purchasing value than the United Kingdom 'national assistance' standard[23] but has an approximately similar relationship to average wage levels. Both standards represent very much higher living standards than those experienced by the mass of the populations of the poorest developing countries. When measures of poverty are devised for the populations of these countries they are sometimes found to represent higher standards of living than can be secured by *average* wage rates. For example, Professor E. Batson, Director of the School of Social Science and Social Administration, University of Cape Town, devised a Poverty Datum Line which furnished 'the barest minimum upon which subsistence and health can theoretically be achieved'. When applied at the time to Kenya and Tanganyika it was found to be higher than average wages. The Tanganyika Territorial Minimum Wages Board found that it exceeded average cash earnings of African workers and preferred to adopt other criteria as guidelines for recommendations about minimum wages.[24] There are other examples of the misapplication of western standards of need to the deprived nations, and there are few reliable studies of the components of living standards. Standards of need tend to be unrealistic and lack a consistent theoretical perspective. They are not worked out in relation to the nations to which they are applied. Rarely in agricultural societies are non-monetary resources adequately investigated and assessed. We must conclude that two standards of poverty are required, 'nation-relational' and 'world-relational', which are both conceived in terms of systems of national and international stratification.

23. Abel-Smith, B., and Townsend, P., *op. cit.*, pp. 16–20.
24. *Report of the Territorial Minimum Wages Board, Tanganyika*, Dar es Salaam, printed by the Government Printer, 1962. See also, United Nations, *Assistance to the Needy in Less-Developed Areas*, Department of Economic and Social Affairs, New York, United Nations, 1956, pp. 19–21.

## The Form of Stratification Within Countries

There are important forms of stratification within societies which need to be delineated as precisely as forms of international stratification. Yet there is astonishingly little attempt to provide exact measurement. It is rather significant, for example, that many of the indicators used in comparing societies are expressed in averages or per 1,000 population.[25] The equalization of resources is given very little attention and is certainly not regarded as the hallmark of a highly developed society. Yet it could be so regarded if a 'convergence' rather than an 'infinitely hierarchical' or 'stages of growth' theory of development is preferred.

There are different kinds of variations in income distribution within countries. There are regional variations which are extremely important in some countries, such as Nigeria, Pakistan, Italy, and Yugoslavia.[26] There are also variations according to occupation, education and dependency. In general, some societies can be said to have a more equal distribution of income than others, as Table 3 shows, but there are few income data for the poor countries and considerable doubt has been cast on the validity of the data relating to income distribution for some of the wealthier countries.[27] Moreover, the Gini index of inequality, which furnishes the basis for Table 3, is extraordinarily crude and conceals some types of 'skewed' distribution. In both advanced and developing countries there are few official data about the 'incomes' of those who are not tax-paying wage or salary earners.

It is particularly difficult to compare the different layers of wealth or of income of different countries. The data which are available are rarely comprehensive in the sense that they cover entire national populations; they are insufficient in the sense that they are based on narrow definitions of income and of wealth, and they are over-generalized in the sense that different types of income units and households and a wide range of income levels are often lumped together in analysis. Table 4 gives another example of the rough

25. Of the 75 indicators used in Russett, *et al*, *World Handbook of Political and Social Indicators*, only three are measures of dispersion.
26. According to the Government of Pakistan's *Third Five Year Plan*, the top 5 per cent of income earners had 22 per cent of total income in Karachi in 1959–60, compared with 14 per cent and 11 per cent respectively in rural West Pakistan and East Pakistan.
27. See, for example, Titmuss, R. M., *Income Distribution and Social Change*, London, Allen & Unwin, 1962.

TABLE 3

*Income Distribution after Taxes: Gini Index of Inequality*
(Russett *et al*)

| Country | Index of Inequality | Year | Per cent of income earned by the top 10 per cent of earners |
|---|---|---|---|
| West Germany | 0·432 | 1950 | 34 |
| Guatemala | 0·423 | 1948 | 43 |
| Ceylon | 0·407 | 1953 | 37 |
| Denmark | 0·396 | 1952 | 29 |
| El Salvador | 0·393 | 1946 | 43 |
| Netherlands | 0·388 | 1950 | 33 |
| Sweden | 0·388 | 1948 | 29 |
| United States | 0·373 | 1956 | 29 |
| India | 0·350 | 1956 | 33 |
| United Kingdom | 0·318 | 1955 | 26 |
| Norway | 0·313 | 1950 | 26 |
| Australia | 0·277 | 1956 | 30 |

*Source:* Russett, B. M., *et al, World Handbook of Political and Social Indicators*, New Haven and London, Yale University Press, 1964, p. 247.

results that are all that can be obtained from existing data. The 5 per cent of persons with highest incomes had 37 per cent of total income in Mexico, 31 per cent in Ceylon, 29 per cent in Argentina and the Philippines, but around 20 per cent in the United States, Denmark, India and the United Kingdom. By contrast the 60 per cent of persons with lowest incomes had around a third of total personal income in the United States, the United Kingdom and India but only 25 per cent in the Philippines and only 21 per cent in Mexico. While there is some support from Tables 3 and 4 for the conclusion that incomes tend to be distributed more unequally in the low than in the high income countries there are some interesting puzzles in the statistics and the pattern is by no means consistent.[28] It should be stressed that important variations are concealed by sweeping comparisons of the kind that have so far

28. There are alternative estimates for income distribution in India which are much closer to those for Ceylon. Government of India Planning Commission, *Report of the Committee on Distribution of Income and Levels of Living*, Part I, February, 1964, Statement 2, p. 27.

TABLE 4

*Percentage of Total Personal Income received by the Five Per Cent of Persons in the Population with Highest Incomes and by the Sixty Per Cent with Lowest Incomes*

| Country | Five per cent with highest incomes | Sixty per cent with lowest incomes |
| --- | --- | --- |
| Mexico, 1957 | 37 | 21 |
| Ceylon, 1963 | 31 | 28 |
| Philippines, 1961 | 29 | 25 |
| Argentina, 1961 | 29 | 30 |
| Puerto Rico, 1953 | 23 | 30 |
| United Kingdom, 1951–2 | 21 | 33 |
| India, 1953–7 | 20 | 36 |
| Denmark, 1952 | 20 | 30 |
| United States, 1950 | 20 | 32 |

*Sources:* United Nations, *Economic Survey of Asia and the Far East 1966, Part 1, Aspects of the Finance of Development*, March, 1967; United Nations, Economic Commission for Europe, *Economic Survey of Europe*, 1956; Ohja, P. D., and Bhatt, V. V., 'Pattern of Income Distribution in an Underdeveloped Economy: A Case-Study of India,' *The American Economic Review*, Vol. LIV, No. 5, September, 1964; Reyes, P. S., and Chan, T. L., 'Family Income Distribution in the Philippines', *The Statistical Reporter*, Vol. 9, No. 2, 1965, p. 30; United Nations, *Economic Bulletin for Latin America*, Vol. 11, No. 1, April, 1966.

been made in international studies and more sophisticated studies are badly needed.[29]

The origins of social inequality and conflict between classes have always been of central concern to sociology. But *variations* between societies in the form and degree of inequality are poorly documented. This applies not just to inequality of money incomes, but to assets and other types of resources as well. Why are some élites in poor countries as rich as or richer than the élites of the wealthiest countries in the world? Why is there greater equality, at least according to

29. See, for example, Lydall, H., and Lansing, J. B., 'A Comparison of the Distribution of Personal Income and Wealth in the United States and Great Britain', *American Economic Review*, Vol. XLIX, March, 1959; and Wedderburn, D., 'The Financial Resources of Older People: A General Review', in Shanas, E., Townsend, P., Wedderburn, D., Friis, H., Milhøj, P., and Stehouwer, J., *Old People in Three Industrial Societies*, New York and London, Atherton and Routledge, 1967.

some criteria, in Norway than in the United States, and more in Tanzania than Nigeria? Why in particular is the proportion of the population living at relatively depressed levels apparently much larger in some societies than in others, even when their Gross National Product is approximately the same? Despite a gross lack of information certain statements can be made about the theoretical possibilities.

FIG. 1

*Illustrations of Principal Social Strata in Four Countries*

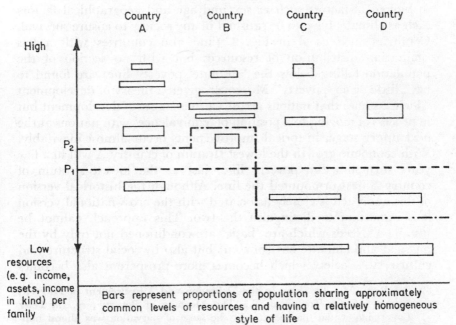

Bars represent proportions of population sharing approximately common levels of resources and having a relatively homogeneous style of life

Fig. 1 illustrates the ways in which social stratification may be related to the distribution of resources and hence to poverty, and both stratification and poverty may depend, therefore, for explanation upon a common general theory. The figure is intended to illustrate a number of features of stratification (a) the number of strata or 'classes' may vary between societies (five in countries A and B, four in C and three in D); (b) the strata may or may not be bunched around a common means of resources, even when national 'wealth' is equivalent (compare country A with country B and country C with country D); and (c) the 'distance' between some or all strata may be small or large. That is, the difference in resources between two sections of the population which are sufficiently large and sufficiently distinct in type and extent of resources to justify treatment as separate strata may be relatively large or relatively small.

How can poverty be conceived in relation to these different models of stratification? One commonly held view of poverty is represented by the line $P_1$ in Fig. 1. This view is concordant with the 'infinitely hierarchical' or 'stages of growth' theory of development. It is that there are basic human needs which, apart from variations attributable to biological factors such as sex and age and geographical factors such as climate, have to be satisfied in any society to ensure survival. Countries such as B in Fig. 1 (and also countries with a less egalitarian distribution of resources but with no section of the population falling below the 'absolute' poverty line) are found to have little or no 'poverty'. Moreover, given a theory of development which assumes that nations are at various stages of development but in process of moving to a position of 'equivalence' with nations at the next upper stage, historical improvements occur almost inevitably. With economic growth the lowest stratum of country A will in a few years surmount the poverty line, just as the lowest stratum of country B has surmounted the line. Although the historical version of this approach is closely associated with the cross-national version it is important to distinguish the two. This approach cannot be sustained. Needs which are 'basic' are conditioned not only by the physical and climatic environment but also by social structure and culture.[30] A society which becomes more prosperous also becomes

30. See Rein, M., 'Problems in the Definition and Measurement of Poverty', in this volume; Townsend, P., 'The Meaning of Poverty', *op. cit.* Peter Laslett has shown that poverty in the sense of starvation was almost non-existent in pre-industrial Britain, although sporadic in pre-industrial France. ' "The starving peasantry" is a common phrase. . . . Perhaps starving should not be taken to mean actually dying of lack of food; rather badly fed and clothed, wretchedly housed in hovels, miserable in general. . . . The crises in the villages of the Beauvaisis came at irregular intervals: 1625, 1648–53, 1693–4 were some of the dates. The parish registers of these communities, and of the churches of the city of Beauvais itself, would show a sudden rise in burials; double or even treble the normal would be entered. Towards the first peak in mortality, marriages would drop and conceptions would go down too. . . . By the time the second peak in mortality came, for these crises were often though not always double-headed, the poor would be eating grass of the fields and offal from dung-heaps in the streets, dying perhaps more often from the effects of things like this and from the onset of endemic diseases than

more complex and imposes new needs on its members. For example, by legislating for compulsory education or a higher school leaving age a country makes new demands upon parents and their resources. Or again, the types of occupation or styles of living followed in a society will determine the kinds and amounts of nutrients that individuals require.

An alternative view is represented by the line $P_2$ in Fig. 1. That section of the population whose resources are so depressed from the mean as to be deprived of enjoying the benefits and participating in the activities which are customary in that society can be said to be in poverty. This is *not* the same thing as saying that the poor are the 10 per cent or 20 per cent in every society with the least resources (though this statement offers a useful point of departure for empirical analysis); for it is at least conceivable that some of the families included, at least in societies with a more egalitarian distribution of resources, might not be deprived of sharing activities which are customary. The frame of reference in adopting this approach can be regional, national or international. The poor do not necessarily form a single coherent 'class' or stratum and this question, like the number of classes or strata in different societies, must be treated as a matter for empirical investigation. Not only may there be different groupings which have few links but there may be 'travellers'—such as the temporary unemployed or sick— circulating between strata. A frequently forgotten fact, too, is that a large proportion of the population has at some time in life belonged to the lowest stratum. The proportion of the population who have ever been in poverty is of course far larger than the proportion in poverty at any single time.

To what extent can each stratum be said to 'cohere'? In almost every population there are families who are difficult to place in class categories. They have high income and low assets, or they have a mixed educational, occupational and social background. There are men, for example, with virtually no education who have been

---

from starvation as such. . . . Nearly all the English registers which have been studied so far yield entirely negative conclusions; they contain no examples of harvest years where a conspicuous rise in burials was accompanied by a corresponding fall in conceptions and marriages. We may here be faced with a sociological discovery of the first historical importance, that our country in the seventeenth century was already immune from these periodical disasters, whereas France was not'. Laslett, P., *The World We Have Lost*, London, Methuen, 1965, pp. 107–114.

339.46

50017431

unskilled manual labourers and who live simply and yet have become company directors or even Cabinet Ministers. Similarly, there are men from rich families and with university degrees who live from hand to mouth in city slums. In recent years contributions have been made to stratification theory which have important implications for research into poverty. Werner S. Landecker has developed certain ideas about class and status crystallization advanced by Gerhard A. Lenski.[31] The basic idea is that inconsistency in class or status according to different criteria may explain certain types of individual and social behaviour. On the basis of interviews with a random sample of 700 individuals in Detroit the population was ranked according to four characteristics: occupation, income, education and ethnic-racial descent. The object was to measure class crystallization, or 'the degree of equivalence among the ranks held by a given person in each of the four rank systems. For this purpose every rank of each individual was represented by the midpoint of its percentile range; this midpoint was designated as "status score". By inverting a measure of dispersion among his four status scores, a "crystallization score" was computed for each person. The actually obtained scores range from a minimum of 10 for the most amorphous to a maximum of 98 for the most crystallized status. When used in the aggregate, individual scores provide a basis for measuring crystallization as a property of an entire class system, or of particular levels within it.'[32] Table 5 shows the form of the four ranking systems.

The work on status-crystallization has begun to develop into an important sub-field of research, and status inconsistency, or rank disequilibrium, has been held to account in part for such things as psychomatic disorders, aggressiveness and suicide.[33] But there are

31. Lenski, G. E., 'Status Crystallization: A Non-Vertical Dimension of Social Status', *American Sociological Review*, Vol. 19, August, 1954; Lenski, G. E., 'Social Participation and Status Crystallization', *American Sociological Review*, Vol. 21, 1956. Also his recent major work, Lenski, G. E., *Power and Privilege*, New York, McGraw-Hill, 1966.

32. Landecker, W. S., 'Class Crystallization and its Urban Pattern', *Social Research*, Vol. 27, 1960, pp. 313–315. Also see, Landecker, W. S., 'Class Crystallization and Class Consciousness', *American Sociological Review*, Vol. 28, 1963.

33. See, for example, Jackson, E. F., 'Status Consistency and Symptoms of Stress', *American Sociological Review*, Vol. 27, 1962; Kelly, K. D., and Chambliss, W. J., 'Status Consistency and Political Attitudes', *American Sociological Review*, Vol. 31, 1966; Gibbs, J. P., and Martin, W. J., 'A Theory of Status Integra-

major difficulties. First, the choice of dimensions, such as the four in Table 5, is arbitrary and plainly more suitable for America than for, say, Norwegian, Tibetan or Afghan society. Second, ranking on some dimensions usually assumes consensus about status and recent evidence calls into question the extent of such consensus.[34] Third, the systematic work of describing each rank dimension has not yet been done. As one critic remarks: 'We should first understand individual indicators before combining them into complex indices'.[35] For each of the dimensions in Table 5, occupational status, income distribution, years of education and ethnic-racial status needs to be traced even for one nation in a lot more detail before it can be regarded as appropriate. Further research might show that different dimensions might properly be divided into different numbers of ranks. And if that were to be justified there would be the problem of determining equivalence or inconsistency of rank, quite apart from the problem of weighting the different dimensions overall. A separate problem of determining equivalence of rank arises when a population is distributed very differently across two or more rank dimensions. All this suggests the extreme primitiveness, and weakness, of models such as that illustrated in Table 5.

Finally, status is insufficiently distinguished from class, partly ⟨ because objective dimensions (e.g. income and years of education) are combined rather haphazardly with subjective dimensions (e.g. occupational and ethnic-racial status).[36] Class is only one form of

tion and its Relationship to Suicide', *American Sociological Review*, Vol. 23, April, 1958. Galtung, J., 'A Structural Theory of Aggression', *Journal of Peace Research*, Vol. 1, 1964. Jackson, E. F., and Burke, P. J., 'Status and Symptoms of Stress: Additive and Interaction Effects', *American Sociological Review*, Vol. 30, August, 1965. Galtung, J., 'Rank and Social Integration: A Multidimensional Approach', in Berger, J., Zelditch, M., and Anderson, B., *Sociological Theories in Progress*, Vol. I, Houghton Mifflin, Boston, 1966. Footnote 4 in the last-named paper provides a full list up to 1963 of the literature.

34. Young, M., and Willmott, P., 'Social Grading by Manual Workers', *British Journal of Sociology*, 1956; Bott, E., *Family and Social Network*, London, Tavistock, 1957.

35. Mitchell, R. E., 'Methodological Notes on a Theory of Status Crystallization', *Public Opinion Quarterly*, Vol. 28, Summer, 1964.

36. Landecker has reviewed the alternative hypotheses of 'class structure' and 'status continuum' as best describing social stratification in the United States. He concludes that neither takes precedence over the other 'but rather that each is appropriate to a different portion of the total system of stratification'. But he gives so little information about the social structure of the

## TABLE 5

*Approximately Equivalent Rank Levels in Four Rank Systems\**
(Landecker)

| Status percentiles | Occupational rank system† | Income rank system (annual) | Educational rank system (in years completed) | Ethnic-racial rank system‡ |
|---|---|---|---|---|
| 91–100 | A | $8,000 and over | 15 and over | English |
| 81–90 | B | $6,000–7,999 | 13–14 | Scandinavian French |
| 71–80 | B | $5,000–5,999 | 12 (diploma) | Scottish Finnish |
| 61–70 | C | $4,000–4,999 | 12 (others) | German |
| 51–60 | C | $4,000–4,999 | 11 | Irish |
| 41–50 | C | $3,000–3,999 | 10 | Greek Italian |
| 31–40 | D | $3,000–3,999 | 9 | Polish |
| 21–30 | D | $3,000–3,999 | 8 | Hungarian Russian |
| 11–20 | D | $2,000–2,999 | 7 | Negro |
| 1–10 | E | $1,999 or less | 6 and less | Mexican Hillbilly |

\* Upper and lower percentile limits of each rank are rounded to the nearest tenth percentile.

† Major occupations illustrative of each level are the following:
  A banker, engineer, industrialist, physician, school principal;
  B building contractor, electrician, newspaper reporter, registered nurse, toolmaker;
  C auto mechanic, bricklayer, policeman, secretary, real estate agent;
  D barber, machine operative, salesclerk, truckdriver, typist;
  E dockworker, gas-station attendant, janitor, maid, waiter.

‡ The ethnic-racial categories listed constitute major examples. Each status decile is represented by its largest component if the latter fills more than half of that decile; otherwise it is represented by its two largest components.

*Source:* Landecker, W. S., 'Class Crystallisation and its Urban Pattern', *Social Research*, Vol. 27, 1960.

stratification which helps to explain other forms. There are, of course, forms of stratification which no one would incorporate into 'class' conceptualization. For example, all individuals can be ranked according to their degree of dependence or independence of persons

sample and the economic position of individuals and households in it that the question must be considered to be open. Landecker, W. S., 'Class Boundaries', *American Sociological Review*, 1960.

around them (for help in the household, care in illness, financial support and so on). Again, rankings by intelligence or health and strength are at least to some extent socially determined but are also difficult to align with class; there are wide variations, especially within families. But because of lack of consensus about status ranking it may be more satisfactory to conceive of class either as a single objective dimension or as a series of objective dimensions all related to a common unit of measurement. Some of the latest evidence suggests that the more traditional concepts of social class membership and minority group status are superior explanatory concepts to that of status-crystallization.[37]

The concept of social class is poorly operationalized. Marx's definition of class in relation to the control and use of the powers of production could be said to have been modified by Weber in relation to the processes of production, distribution and exchange. In a sense he extended the concept from ownership or lack of capital to the ownership or lack of economic advantages in general, including those of the commodity and labour markets. A number of sociologists have recently attempted to bring this approach up to date. Lockwood, for example, has pointed out that the 'work situation', or the social relations consequent upon the division of labour which separate manual from non-manual workers as well as 'market situation' has to be weighed.[38] Differences in security of employment, promotion opportunities and retirement benefits, for example, are now important. But this modification may not be sufficient. Industry does not provide the framework for the whole of society. Other institutions, particularly education, the social services and the fiscal system, contribute far more than they did to the definition of class. This fact has yet to be absorbed into current sociological theory, though some sociologists have recognized its importance.[39] If Marx failed to explain social inequalities satisfactorily in terms of economic developments modern sociology has also failed take full account of the same developments.

Basically there has been an increase in the numbers of different *kinds* of resources which might be given the description 'economic' in the widest sense and upon which individuals in modern society

37. Kelly, K. D., and Chambliss, W. J., *op. cit.*
38. Lockwood, D., *The Blackcoated Worker*, London, Allen & Unwin, 1958, p. 15.
39. Titmuss, R. M., 'The Social Division of Welfare', in his *Essays on the Welfare State*, Allen & Unwin, 1958; Miller, S. M., and Rein, M., 'Poverty and Policy', in Becker, H. S. (ed), *Social Problems*, New York, John Wiley, 1966.

draw. Also, more individuals draw upon these resources in different measure. The alignments of class position may no longer be so uniformly horizontal. This suggests how the work on status-crystallization can be adapted for alternative use. We are ripe for a major empirical study of class, using the concepts of 'resources' and 'total rank' or 'crystallization'. Such a study also opens the way logically to the description and analysis of 'total' and 'partial' poverty. In the development of a theory of poverty at least four concepts seem to be crucial: 'resources', 'total rank', 'deprivation' and 'constancy of rank'. I shall explain these in turn.

## Resources

First, *resources*. Income as normally defined in industrial countries is insufficient to describe economic position. A memorandum of dissent in Britain by a minority of the Royal Commission on Taxation pointed out the narrowness of the definition of income used by the Board of Inland Revenue. 'In fact no concept of income can be really equitable that stops short of the comprehensive definition which embraces all receipts which increase an individual's command over the use of society's scarce resources—in other words, his "net accretion of economic power between two points of time".'[40] In all societies, and particularly those which have large numbers of farmers and smallholders or peasants, there are people with small monetary incomes but substantial income in kind and vice versa. There are people with the same wage or salary but widely different income or income in kind from employers' fringe benefits. There are people too with equal access in principle but not in practice to the public social services. The wealth dispensed by government and employer is, to adapt Charles Reich's phrase, 'the new property'.[41] There are in fact a variety of resources which are distributed unequally. An attempt to identify them in five groups is illustrated in Figure 2.

1. *Current cash income* may be defined as all regular sources of cash receipts, including wages and salaries, income from rents, dividends and interest, social security benefits and pensions.

2. *Capital assets* include cash and deposits in banks and the post

40. *Report of the Royal Commission on Taxation*, Cmd. 9474, London, HMSO, 1955, p. 8.
41. Reich, C. A., 'The New Property', *The Yale Law Journal*, Vol. 73, No. 5, April, 1964.

office, holdings of stocks and shares, the value of property in businesses, land and buildings (counting owner-occupied housing and household facilities and possessions of every kind, including gardens). Capital assets also include educational qualifications, since sizeable if very rough estimates can be made of the financial value to the individual of each additional year spent at school beyond the school leaving age and of the years in higher education.[42] By finding from individuals the number of years' schooling they have had it would be possible to compute, if only very crudely, the value to them of their education.

3. *Employment benefits* include current provision of income in kind such as housing, cars and travel, education, meals and entertainment. But they might also be defined to include the cash equivalent of occupational facilities providing comfort, safety, technical support and freedom from noise.

4. *Social service benefits* include the value of benefits in kind from public sources—health and welfare, education and housing.[43]

5. *Private income in kind* includes gifts of food and clothing from relatives and friends, produce from the land and gardens and help with outings, holidays and education.

A research team investigating poverty in the United Kingdom from the University of Essex and the London School of Economics is experimenting with resource 'indicators' of this kind. None of these dimensions are easy to operationalize in practice and methods of defining and measuring the resources commanded by families are still imprecise.

## Total Rank

Second, *total rank*. It is clear from the argument that individual persons or households might be ranked differently according to the

42. Bowen, W. G., 'Assessing the Economic Contribution of Education', in *Higher Education* (Robbins Report), Appendix 4, Cmnd. 2154–IV, London, HMSO, 1963; Schultz, T. W., *The Economic Value of Education*, New York, Columbia University Press, 1963; Abrams, M., 'Rewards of Education', *New Society*, Vol. 4, No. 93, July 9, 1964.

43. Where information could not be collected in sufficient detail about individuals, estimates would have to be made on the basis of previous studies of the redistributive effect of the social services. See, for example, Nicholson, J. L., *Redistribution of Income in the United Kingdom in 1959, 1957 and 1953*, London, Bowes and Bowes, 1965; *Economic Trends*, Nos. 109, 124 and 154, November, 1962, February, 1964 and August, 1966.

five types of resources. In a modern society like Britain there might be, for example, two fatherless families with identical cash incomes. One might live in a slum house in a city at a high rent. The children might attend a slum school and local medical (including hospital) facilities might be impoverished. The other family might live in a new town, renting a new council house at a low rent, the children attending a new school with good facilities and with young, forward-looking teachers, and local medical facilities might be excellent. The real overall standard of living of the two families would be widely different.

FIG. 2

*Rank Distribution of Different Types of Resources as Percentage of Mean*

| Per cent of mean | A | B | C | D | E |
|---|---|---|---|---|---|
| 50+ | 1 | 1 | 1 | 1 | 1 |
| 25–49 | 2 | 2 | 2 | 2 | 2 |
| ±24 | 3 | 3 | 3 | 3 | 3 |
| −25–49 | 4 | 4 | 4 | 4 | 4 |
| −50+ | 5 | 5 | 5 | 5 | 5 |
|  | cash income | capital assets (incl. housing) | value of employment benefits | value of public social services | private income in kind |

Let us consider a simple formal example. Suppose that on two rank-dimensions, namely cash income and capital assets, the population could be divided not into five but into three groups, those having a high, middle and low share of these resources. What would be the possible combinations? Table 6 shows that there are nine. If we treat total rank as the sum of ranks on each dimension then we would end up with five separate ranks or 'classes', viz.:

| HH | $3+3$ | $=6$ |
|---|---|---|
| MH, HM | $2+3$ or $3+2$ | $=5$ |
| MM, HL, LH | $2+2$ or $3+1$ or $1+3$ | $=4$ |
| ML, LM | $2+1$ or $1+2$ | $=3$ |
| LL | $1+1$ | $=2$ |

Rank agreement would represent the extent to which the number of units (persons or households) which are ranked the same on both dimensions approaches the total number of units. If rank agreement in a society is high then few individual units will be found in classes 5 and 3 above (i.e. MH and HM, or ML and LM). There would be little 'criss-cross', that is, individuals with one rank in common with individuals at another level of total rank. Alternatively, the more numerous these classes are the more justification there is for separately identifying, say, an 'upper' as well as a 'lower' middle class or stratum.

TABLE 6

*Distribution of Two Resources*

| | Cash Income | | |
|---|---|---|---|
| Assets | High | Middle | Low |
| High | HH | HM | HL |
| Middle | MH | MM | ML |
| Low | LH | LM | LL |

There is no need to illustrate further the formal possibilities. Galtung and others have developed useful definitions of rank disequilibrium, congruence and so on.[44] But there are conceptual difficulties. If income were bunched around a common mean but capital assets widely distributed the problem of representing total rank (even on these two dimensions alone) would be immensely difficult. It would be wrong to ignore resources which are equally distributed, but difficult in practice to express total rank if the individual dimensions vary in the depth of their 'vertical' distribution, or stratification. This suggests that the *equivalence* in form of every dimension has to be validated. Finally, if both income and capital assets are normally distributed it may nevertheless be difficult to assume that they have equal weight. We can quite easily imagine societies with roughly the same total income but with a widely different valuation of assets. Or, to refer again to Table 6, ML may *not* be equivalent in total rank in practice to LM. All this suggests that the *weighting* of each dimension has to be validated.

It is doubtful whether the multi-dimensional approach to stratification of Lenski, Landecker and others can be developed very far

44. See Galtung, J., (1966) *op. cit.*, and also Galtung, J., 'International Relations and International Conflicts: A Sociological Approach', a paper presented to the Sixth World Congress of Sociology, Evian, September, 1966.

without introducing some considerable changes. Perhaps two crucial limitations need to be accepted. There are analytical advantages to be gained, as Weber taught, from distinguishing carefully between the concepts of class and status, or between the objective and subjective (even if collectively subjective) criteria of stratification. One depends on behaviour and style of life, as determined fundamentally by the resources that are commanded by different families and individuals. The other has more the quality of personal assessment of that behaviour and style of life, deriving from the prestige in which people are held by virtue of their social position. So far as class is concerned I have tried to argue that there is much to be gained by operationalizing the concept in terms of distribution of resources.

A second limitation that might be placed on the multi-dimensional approach to stratification is that there should be satisfactory criteria by which the individual dimensions can be weighted, or alternatively that all the individual dimensions should be re-definable on one general dimension. The five dimensions suggested in Fig. 2 can at least in principle be translated into a common value—cash income. There are a number of difficulties but by tentatively re-defining certain assets, for example, in terms of annuity values, interest and rent equivalents, it may be possible to minimize them.

The concept of 'total rank' offers one means of operationalizing the concepts of 'total' and 'partial' poverty. If 5 in Fig. 2, for example, were found to represent a justifiable category of poverty then individual units ranked consistently 5 in A, B, C, D and E would be defined as in total poverty. Thus a family with very low cash income, no assets and living in a privately-rented slum flat, having bad and insecure working conditions, making relatively little use of the social services or using relatively low quality services, and having little or no private help and support, would be treated as living in total poverty. By contrast, a family with good cash income, good working conditions and facilities, and making more than average use of the public social services, might nonetheless be fairly regarded as living in partial poverty, by virtue of having few or no assets and living in a slum house.

## Deprivation

Third, *deprivation*. Arbitrary cut off points are shown in Fig. 2 for purpose of illustration. Empirical investigation must, however, justify ranking, in the sense that families or individuals with different total rank must be shown to behave and consume differently. It may be that there are empirical 'clusters' according to the definitions of resources that are adopted.[45] Or at a depressed level of resources families and individuals may be excluded from participation in common social activities and enjoyments. The Essex-London School of Economics research team are experimenting with a 'deprivation' index, based on a list of activities and customs which are common for a majority of the population of the United Kingdom: for example, not having summer holiday away from home; neither staying over-night with relatives or friends, nor having them to stay in the course of a year; not holding a birthday party for children; not having a meal or a snack with friends at home or outside the home in the course of a month; missing a meal sometimes or often in the course of a fortnight; not eating fresh meat as much as twice a week. Such a list could be devised for any society. We assume that the deprivation index will not be correlated uniformly with total resources at the lower levels and that there will be a 'threshold' of resources below which deprivation will be marked.

## Constancy of Rank

Finally, *constancy of rank*. Resources grow and diminish and change their form and a population does not remain in rigid ranks. Some people may maintain their total rank-position for long periods but the fact that most people have known relatively good and relatively bad times in the course of their lives is commonplace. A wage-earner with several children will have a much poorer standard of living while all the children are dependent upon him than he will in middle-life when they have grown up. Just as there are slow cycles of boom and slump in family experience there are also temporary windfalls of wealth and plunges into the abyss, through short-term unemployment and sickness. There are not two permanently exclusive categories of the population, the rich or the comfortably off and the poor. A small proportion of the population may have been poor all their lives. But a large proportion may have had occasional or sustained but not continuous experience of poverty. It is therefore important to build some measure of the stability of family resources into a conception of poverty. Empirical investiga-

45. Methods of distinguishing class boundaries have been discussed by Landecker, W. S., 'Class Boundaries', *op. cit.*

tion, again, will show how much of a time-lag there is before a family newly arrived 'at the bottom' exhibits the same deprivation behaviour as one which has been there for two years or more.

## The Analysis of Poverty in Low Income Countries

In what ways can the foregoing approach to development and stratification help in explaining how poverty arises and is perpetuated in low income and high income countries? I shall concentrate here on poverty in low income countries. The accelerating collapse of colonialism since the war, the spread of post-colonial nationalism, the geometric rise of population in many countries and the fumbling moves towards a world order have all played their part in arousing the public's interest in the problems of development and modernization. The early pages of this chapter have described the response to the need that has been felt for information and an interpretative framework. There are many ways in which comparisons such as those illustrated in Table 1 can be extended—not just additional single indicators like marriage rates, numbers of children per woman of childbearing age and so on but carefully worked out types of family and community groupings, value-systems, patterns of ritual and political systems. Immensely valuable work is now going on but much of it is of a rather elementary kind, being a mixture of slightly haphazard description with a few comparisons of single indices of the kind I have given, rather than solidly integrated analyses of different social and economic structures. It is important to have separate concepts of social and economic development (or at least a well integrated concept of social and economic development) to help redress present western ideological bias in the selection, application and interpretation of indicators. But it is important also to remember that a set of statistical indicators can only provide part, if a helpful part, of an overall interpretative framework. I shall try to suggest how certain concepts and measures might be applied in analysing poverty in low-income countries.

Let us reconsider first the theme of development. Table 1 carries the implicit assumption that if a nation can climb up a stage or two this represents progress. Differences in achievement at a moment in time can be represented as earlier and later stages of development. (Some of the same overtones attach to the upper strata in a system of social stratification: if an individual can advance himself by his own efforts through social mobility this represents progress.) As

discussed above (p. 10) a view of development can be very misleading both analytically and ideologically (though, of course, value
can be wrung out of detailed structural comparison). It is like
conducting a cross-sectional survey among the middle-aged population, choosing persons aged from 35 to 55 to interview and putting
forward a theory of what it is to go through middle-life on the basis
of the results. Yet those aged 35 will spend their next 20 years living
through the 1970s and early 1980s in very different social conditions
from what the 55-year olds experienced in the 1950s and 1960s. The
*process* of what might variously be called socialization, maturation,
ageing or life-development is not the same.

This difference is much more sharply accentuated in the case of
development. Compared with individuals of different age living
within a single society, total societies cannot be said to be so power-
fully controlled and influenced by the common social framework or
common social history. Peter Laslett's account of pre-industrial
society, *The World We Have Lost,* can be compared with any account
of a modern low income or 'under-developed' society. The starting-
points, as well as the rate of change or economic escalation, along
the road of industrialization or modernization are different. Yet
there are sufficient isolated points of similarity to make us pause—
the predominant subsistence agriculture, the extreme contrast in
wealth between the upper class or élites and the mass of the population, and the high mortality rates.

Both high and low income countries are a mixture, though to a
differing degree, of traditional and modern elements. In many low
income countries the most startling visual and physical contrasts are
cheek by jowl—American cars and primitive rickshaws, Sandhurst-
trained Nigerian Army officers and street beggars, Government
offices in new skyscrapers and corrugated-roofed shanty towns. Yet
in all high income countries there are strong traces of the past—
villages, landed estates, rural preservation societies, folk-dancing,
religious and political rituals, social courtesies. These images are
suggested for a deliberate theoretical purpose. Too often extreme
analytic polarizations have plagued our attempts to compare
different societies—'modern' and 'primitive', 'developed' and 'underdeveloped', 'industrial' and 'agrarian'. We are encouraged to feel
that they are so far removed at either end of a long spectrum, like
chalk and cheese, that there is little that is alike (and the divergent
history of anthropological theory and fieldwork, on the one hand,
and of sociological theory and field work on the other, help to

preserve the illusion). Almost inevitably corresponding ideas of superiority and inferiority are encouraged, however much they may be denied or qualified.

All this expresses, in effect, profound scepticism of the value of much sociological theory of industrialization, modernization and development.[46] Like Rostow's theory of stages of economic growth, both the historical and contemporaneous evidence about different societies tends to be insufficiently sought and digested.[47] There are primary relationships (e.g. between parents and grandparents within the family) and traditional customs and practices which are an important part of modern society. Every modern society has a traditional one inside it. As Professor Almond has argued, we need dualistic models *rather than* monistic ones and developmental *as well as* equilibrium models if we are to understand differences between societies and the processes of social and political change.[48] More constant reference needs to be made to empirical reality by theorists than it has in the past.[49] Like development, world poverty cannot adequately be explained or understood, therefore, by applying any of the 'stages of growth', 'diffusionist' or 'structural differentiationist' models of development.

## Nationalism and Development

There are certain factors which are of particular value in revealing the present direction being taken by low income societies, which help also to explain the existence of poverty among them. Why is nationalism rampant? Whether we look at the republics of Latin

46. A good example of the failure of latter-day functionalists, for example, to adapt theoretical models of change to the increasing volume of historical and contemporary evidence is the section on 'Changing Family Relations' in Smelser, N. J., 'Processes of Social Change', in Smelser, N. J. (ed), *Sociology: An Introduction*, New York, John Wiley, 1967, pp. 720–722.

47. See, for example, the criticisms of Hoselitz, Parsons and others in Frank, A. G., *op. cit.*

48. Almond, G. A., and Coleman, J. S. (eds), *op. cit.*, pp. 20–25.

49. Such reference will also help to moderate over-enthusiastic attempts to adapt formal techniques in economics to the construction of sociological theories of development. It would be wrong to make out that there is a 'positive' sociology which can 'predict' development in any strict sense. We can only hope to show specific probable connections between variables within a general descriptive context, as Leibenstein and others have argued. See, for example, Leibenstein, H., 'What Can We Expect from a Theory of Development', *Kyklos*, Fasc 1, Switzerland, 1966.

America, the new African states, at India or Indonesia, or even China, nationalism is strong and dynamic—though of course it takes a number of different forms. It is a response conditioned by contact with western countries. It is not the nationalism of old States like Ethiopia, Liberia, and the former kingdom of Dahomey in Africa, or of the Mogul Empire in India. Old-style nationalism was founded on submission to a common ruler, who was recognized to occupy a position at the apex of a social and political hierarchy. The adoption of political equality, with elaboration of the individual's legal and social rights, distinguished modern nation-states from preceding monarchies. Nationalism almost seems to be a requirement if the States are to survive and if economic aims are to be achieved. What does it do?

First, negatively, it provides antagonists, enemies. Once independence is achieved the foreign dominating power is no longer an easy scapegoat of frustrated aspirations. Colonial powers nurture nationalism in their final stages, but once they disappear from the scene they lose conviction as scapegoats and something has to take their place. The existence of adversaries, opponents, or antagonists helps to define the separateness of the new society. All this follows from the familiar distinction between in-groups and out-groups in sociology. Yet the ideology of independence conceals membership of the system of international stratification, which partly controls the distribution and value of resources.

Second, positively, nationalism gives a common meaning to the interests of its peoples. It provides wider loyalties than those just to clans, tribes, ethnic or linguistic groups and helps to integrate what might otherwise be a diverse anarchy. It defines the rights of citizens. Shrill nationalism is in part an over-anxious response to the possibilities of fragmentation. These possibilities are real enough. Recently we have had examples from Tanzania and the Sudan as well as in Nigeria of breakaway movements: in many developing countries there are several ethnic communities and other divisive elements, antagonistic religious orders, clans and fraternities, castes and classes, and a striking division between urban and rural communities. Yet governments which are disposed to promote nationalism are disinclined to have attention called to the hierarchy of privilege and deprivation inherited from colonialism and the unequal distribution of resources among ethnic groups.

Thirdly, by promoting loyalties to the nation as a whole rather than just to the clan, the family or the local community, nationalism gives the impression of facilitating the transition to modernity. Changes are easier to introduce, and to justify. The individual's aims and interests are identified with those of the nation as a whole. His efforts and his sympathies can be harnessed to the State. In particular this means that he can be associated with plans for economic expansion. The difficult task of redistributing resources in favour of the poor can be made to seem no longer necessary. Such plans for development can be represented as coexistent with nationalist ideology and sentiment. If they are fulfilled they are believed sooner or later to bring about a general rise in levels of living. Nationalism can in some ways be represented as indispensable to the actual achievement of higher standards of living, while largely continuing existing stratification, or, more related to the concept of poverty put forward in this chapter, the hierarchy of privilege and deprivation.

When we remember that the great majority of people in the low income countries are engaged in subsistence agriculture and live in villages which are relatively self-contained economic units, we can begin to understand the almost inevitable link between nationalism and economic development. Some writers see its function as the *transference* of primary loyalties from the village or kinship group to the larger society[50] but, in keeping with the *dualistic* approach I described earlier, I believe it is better viewed both as a broadening or an extension of loyalties and a means of safeguarding the security of élites and enhancing their status, by consolidating political and social control and establishing their independence of foreign dominating powers.

## Social and Political Élites

The withdrawal of the occupying power completely transforms the lives of some nationals. Although some may have held high positions formerly, others suddenly find themselves projected from subordinate positions as, say, clerks or itinerant students into positions of power. There is a tendency to take over the salaries, the attitudes of superiority and even to some extent the styles of life of colonial administrators. Some new leaders are very youthful. This is not social mobility: it is 'pitchfork' upward mobility. The former administrative hierarchy has an inheritance effect.

Contact with high income countries also has many subtle effects.

50. For example, Hoselitz, B. F., 'Nationalism and Economic Development', in Feinstein, O. (ed), *Two Worlds of Change*, New York, Doubleday Anchor Books, 1964, pp. 256–257.

Here is the new state comparing itself not only with its neighbours in the third world but with former colonial powers and other heavily industrialized countries. The international agencies reinforce a system of social stratification among nations, with nominal equality of status but wide, and widening,[51] inequality of wealth. The humbling ratios of the kind described in Table 1, average incomes, mortality rates and literacy rates, are brought embarrassingly into the light of day. Small wonder that one response of the low-income country is an over-assertive nationalism and a determination to insist on the rights of national equality. Status at international meetings and in the dealings with advanced countries is jealously watched. Wherever possible political and administrative leaders emulate their counterparts in western countries. Moreover, many of them have been educated in the United States or Europe and when they become lawyers, business managers, doctors, administrators and political leaders they expect broadly commensurate living standards. Long periods without contact with family and community of origin also lead some of them to a kind of dissociation of attitude which tends to confirm the seclusion of élites rather than élites attempting to pursue policies of social integration. Traditional control of ethical values is weakened. Again, before independence there is often a cluster of, say, African or Asian élites gathering around the European administrators, traders and settlers, expecting to take over the same positions.

All this results in the extreme wealth and exceptionally high salaries of many élites. If there is greater inequality of wealth in low income than in high income societies (and this remains to be firmly established) then it may be primarily the result of prolonged contact with colonial or high income countries. The wealth and power of some élites, as in India, may have been 'artificially' maintained or increased before independence, and afterwards emulation of élites in high income countries, combined with trading, political and professional contacts, may perpetuate the disparity. A year after independence Dahomey spent 60 per cent of its budget on the salaries of Government personnel. In Nigeria, as the Morgan Report on Wages and Salaries revealed, Ministers and managing directors were recently drawing between £3,500 and £10,000 while unskilled workers in the State sector were earning an average of £50 to £60

51. Economic inequality between countries is in certain senses widening. See Myrdal, G., *Economic Theory and Underdeveloped Regions*, London, Methuen University Paperbacks, 1963.

a year. The latter, of course, were better off than many peasants and agricultural workers.

On top of their salaries Ministers were given houses specially built at a cost of £32,000 each. They also pay no electricity, telephone or water charges; they get a basic car allowance of £80 a month and when on an official trip they are also paid 1s. 3d. a mile. In addition they get cheap petrol from Public Works Department pumps . . . Senior Civil Servants and officials of Corporations fare little worse.[52]

In other societies the remuneration of élites is less generous but still substantial. The virtues of national loyalty and of the need to consolidate new administrative, commercial and industrial institutions have to be paraded constantly before the people through propaganda and agitation. A staff of manufacturers and manipulators of nationalist symbols is required to implement the consolidation of national identity. The tendency is usually to develop strong centralized leadership and one-party states, with trade unions (or the military) as business partners of the government, and as agencies of increasing production, and, generally to discourage the institutionalization of opposition or protest groups and factions.[53]

The social characteristics of the élites, tend, therefore, to place them apart from and on top of the mass of the people. The middle class tends to be small. One additional reason for this is that before independence and in some states long afterwards commercial activity has been in the hands of alien groups: for example, Indians in South and East Africa, Indians and Chinese in South-East Asia and Lebanese and Jews in North Africa. Table 7 gives a vivid illustration of the comparative wealth of Europeans and Asians in Africa and shows how small are the middle income groups. The number of African income-units with much less than £120 a year is, of course, underestimated in the table. Many families working on the land pay no tax.[54]

52. Bulloch, J., 'Nigerian Anger at Leaders' Rich Living', *Sunday Telegraph*, 21st June 1964, quoted by Davies, I., *African Trade Unions*, Harmondsworth, Penguin Books, 1966, pp. 127–128.
53. Davies, I., *op. cit.*
54. The differences between the races in South Africa are even more extreme. In 1959–60 only 16 of the 43,780 persons in South Africa having an income of more than $5,600 were Africans. Only one of the 5,938 persons with an income of more than $14,000 was African. It is estimated that the income *per capita* of the European population since the war has been more than ten times as much as that of the African population. United Nations, *Economic Survey of Africa: Vol. 1, Western Sub-Region*, 1966, p. 178.

Kenya and the Congo the figure ranges from a fifth to a third.[57] Less than 20 per cent of the population of India and Ceylon and only 10 per cent of that of Pakistan is categorized as urban.

But the relative advantage of the urban wage-earner should be kept in mind. It is not simply the fact that he obtains a disproportionate share of increases in national income and has, by African standards, a good income. Many undertakings give him well-cooked and balanced meals and some issue rations to his family as well. When so large a part of the population is malnourished, high productivity depends on giving special privileges to the wage-earning class.[58] Standards of living in agricultural regions may even be depressed so that an urban wage-earning class may be established.

## Poverty and Development

The structural developments I have described have the effect of introducing a more hierarchical, or similarly hierarchical, form of social stratification, with the consequence of increasing, or at least perpetuating, poverty. There is the rural poverty of large sections of the population who live on the margins of dietary sufficiency and some of whom struggle for survival. The arrival of nationhood, the extension of systems of communication and the growth of urban areas contributes to the deepening of their poverty. But what are conditions like? There are great difficulties in establishing the true resources and in particular the nutritive content of the diet of many peoples in the agricultural regions. The Food and Agriculture Organization has made recommendations that the average daily calorie intake for a man should be around 3,000. Most experts consider that fewer than 2,500 represents under-nourishment, under

---

57. Coleman, J. S., 'Sub-Saharan Africa', in Almond, G. A., and Coleman, J. S., *The Politics of the Developing Areas*, Princeton, Princeton University Press, 1960, pp. 271–275.
58. Employers estimate that productivity can rise by as much as 30 per cent, and that labour turnover and absenteeism are reduced to small dimensions by providing meals to workers and families. Drogat, N., *The Challenge of Hunger*, London, Burns and Oates, 1962, pp. 52–53. Nonetheless, this kind of paternalism is not universal. Many urban workers depend solely on wages only, and these wages are insufficient to obtain adequate diets. See, for example, the description of men working from Nairobi on the Kenya-Uganda railway, some of whom had no midday meal and little to eat in the mornings. UNESCO, *Social Aspects of the Industrialisation and Urbanisation of Africa to the South of the Sahara*, 1956, p. 152.

2,000 acute shortage and around 1,500 famine. But while the food supply in Bolivia, Chile, Peru and Ecuador does not reach 2,000 calories a day, Josue de Castro, for example, argues that this is in fact supplemented to a greater extent than is usually assumed by home production and 'natural' foodstuffs which are peculiar to particular areas.[59] In the period immediately before the harvest, when stocks of food are low, the intake drops in some areas of Africa below 1,000 calories a day. Where the diet appears to be on the borderline of sufficiency, as among the Senoufo, special account may have to be taken of the quite frequent festival days. The average daily ration here was found to rise as a result from 2,586 calories a head to 2,750. In one fertile district on the lower Senegal river a careful year's investigation by one team from the Organization for Research into Food and Nutrition in Africa showed an average daily intake per person of 2,175 calories.[60] These are the kind of problems that arise in attempting any exact measurement of malnutrition in these areas. Moreover, care has to be taken not to assume that the prevalence of deficiency diseases such as kwashiorkor, beriberi, scurvy, pellagra, glaucoma and anaemia are due solely to a shortage of food. While populations sometimes escape widespread deficiency diseases they can also invite them because of their food customs. Kwashiorkor, which is primarily protein deficiency, may become common because it is believed that rich meats are bad for children, not because there is a scarcity of meat as such. Beriberi would not be so prevalent if highly milled rice was not so popular. And the slender margins of nutritional sufficiency of some people in these areas can be lost in a drought, by the repressive act of an overlord, by the introduction of less nutritious commercial foodstuffs and by the influx of refugees.

The poverty of the people in these agricultural regions is a resigned or compliant poverty, or at least, so it has seemed in the past. With limited social horizons and reference points, it is not surprising that they find it difficult even to conceive of vastly improved standards of living. But the establishment of nation states and the ideology of nationalism are changing all this, and introducing a second form of poverty. There is the miserable poverty of those in the cities and towns whose share of national resources, whose conditions of life and whose opportunities are far below either average real, or average computed, resources. In addition to the

59. de Castro, J., *Hunger in Brazil*, p. 57.
60. Drogat, N., *op. cit.*, pp. 65–80.

shortage of simple foodstuffs the insanitary squalor
conditions is imposed upon them. Knowledge of
parities between élites, regular wage-earners and agr
in standards of living and career opportunities is
colating through to the rural areas. Men and families are a
temporarily or permanently to the towns. The new wage-earners
are jealous of their pay and their security. The movement into the
urban centres is bigger than growth of capacity to provide employment, and population increase makes the problem worse. As a
consequence there are large groups of destitute families and individuals living in shanty towns, many of whom hope they are on
their way up the income and social scales, others of whom, after
continued disappointments, still find compensations in urban life.
When the Moroccan Trade Union was formed in 1955 more than
half its 600,000 members were unable to pay their dues because they
were either under-employed or unemployed altogether. There is the
extreme situation described by Ahmed Mezerna:

> . . . the bands of men, women and children and aged, almost totally
> naked, whom misery and death have pushed towards the cities and who,
> each morning, search the garbage pails, disputing with dogs and cats
> for remnants of food, the rags and the empty tin cans.[61]

In Lima, Peru, hordes of poor wait for the city scavengers to unload
the next lorry-loads of refuse. This kind of poverty is a direct and
inevitable consequence of the overall social structure—a creation of
relative wage-earning prosperity, which is concentrated in the cities,
of subsistence farming in the rural regions, of 'pedestal' élites and
of nationalist ideology.

## Accounting for Poverty

The thesis of this chapter has been that systems of international social
stratification and social stratification interact to produce poverty.
We started with a puzzle: does it make sense to say there are considerable numbers of people in poverty in the United States when
they can buy far more than the masses of the population in, say,
Asia, Africa or Latin America? I have tried to show that it is in
attempting to give a systematic and comprehensive answer to this

61. Gillespie, J., *Algeria, Rebellion and Revolution*, London, Berin, 1960, p. 69,
   quoted in Davies, I., *op. cit.*, p. 122.

holidays and evenings out. Indicators selected for each country can be compiled into a deprivation index for purposes of measuring the prevalence of poverty in different societies.

Poverty is therefore defined in terms of relative deprivation (understood in an objective and not, as by some sociologists, a subjective sense) and two steps have to be taken to identify it. One is to show exactly how resources are distributed among a population and by what different ranking systems. The other is to show what diets, activities and living conditions are customary in society as a whole from which the poor tend to be excluded. Much more information from both high income and low income countries is required before these steps can be traced in any detail and before theory can be developed very far.

However, the conception of different rank systems of resource distribution, each encompassing sub-systems, allows a start to be made. We can begin to account for differences in the prevalence of poverty in different societies. Although no strictly comparative measure has been applied it would seem from the surveys which have been carried out that a rather higher percentage of the population of the United States than of the United Kingdom are in poverty.[62] The explanation is to be found largely in the systems of resource distribution but partly in the high cost of participating in the activities which are enjoined by the culture. For example, although there appears to be a slightly more egalitarian distribution of capital assets in the U.S. than in the U.K.,[63] there is a more unequal distribution of cash income and much less well-developed public systems of social security, health and welfare. Differential pay structures may be more unequal because productivity has been valued for longer and scientific and technological change has resulted in more unemployment and redundancy and hence a larger proportion of dependency. Differential pay structures may also be more unequal, at least in the south, because of the long history of a substantial coloured minority and the depression of the Negro's status in the value system of society.

The same model can be adapted to account for variations in the prevalence of poverty over time. There is evidence to suggest that at least according to a conventional or normative definition the prevalence of poverty in the United Kingdom increased between

62. Orshansky, M., *op. cit.*; Abel-Smith, B., and Townsend, P., *op. cit.*
63. Lydall, H., and Lansing, J. B., *op. cit.*, p. 66.

1950 and the mid-1960s.[64] Unemployment grew and more persons of working age were excluded from the wage-system. The pay structure seems to have become slightly more unequal.[65] Employment benefits in kind and occupational pension and sick pay schemes expanded rapidly, but did not include millions of manual workers within their scope. Interest and dividend income grew rapidly in the late 1950s, but again, for only a restricted section of the population. Some parts of social security income, especially family allowances, did not keep pace with wage and salary increases during that period. Finally there was a disproportionate increase in dependency. Thus there was a shift in structure of the adult population towards the older age-groups; a revival of the birth-rate together with an increase in the number of families with four or more children, and small increases in the numbers of chronic sick, disabled and handicapped among the middle and older age-groups. All these groups tended to have relatively low incomes. There are, of course, many other factors in the explanation—including external ones, for the internationalization of industry, politics and the professions is doing much to widen the distribution of rewards within any particular society and national sentiment about 'great' powers, sporting prowess and the brain drain helps to maintain pay differentials by increasing the incomes of élites at the expense of the poor.

This approach to theory does, of course, have direct implications for action. Theories which place responsibility for poverty with the individual or with 'the culture of poverty'[66] are rejected. The concept of the culture of poverty concentrates attention upon the familial and local setting of behaviour and largely ignores the external and unseen social forces which condition the distribution of different types of resources to the community, family and individual. The elimination of poverty requires not the reform, education or rehabilitation of the individual or even, bearing in mind a major strategy of the American war on poverty, the creation of more opportunities of upward mobility for the individual. It requires reconstruction of the national and regional systems by which

64. Abel-Smith, B., and Townsend, P., *op. cit.* See also Townsend, P., *Poverty, Socialism and Labour in Power*, Fabian Tract 371, London, Fabian Society, 1967.
65. Industries with low average earnings were not able to increase earnings by up to the average amount during the period 1960–1966, for example. Ministry of Labour, Statistics on Incomes, Prices, Employment and Production, No. 18, September, 1966, pp. 26–27.
66. Lewis, O., *The Children of Sanchez*, New York, Random House, 1961; *La Vida*, New York, Random House, 1966.

resources are distributed, or, alternatively, the introduction of
additional systems which are universalistic and egalitarian. Systems
which are confined either to the rich (like the ownership of land or
of stocks and shares) or to the poor (like public assistance and free
school meals) tend towards privilege on the one hand, and dis-
privilege on the other. They separate society into more rigidly
defined strata.

Given this analysis of poverty there can be no single remedy.
Poverty can be reduced by introducing and strengthening systems
of social security (particularly family allowances, allowances for
fatherless families and pensions for the old and disabled); by
extending (through legislation) employer benefits in kind to all
employees; by developing free community welfare services for all;
but also by restricting the privileges of the prosperous sections of
society—partly by restricting excessively high salaries among élites
and by maintaining a strong system of progressive taxation, but also
diffusing wealth by the elimination of substantial private ownership.
These policies have positive value in breaking down rigid attitudes
about human superiority and inferiority, which is required if the
dominant wage-system is to become more egalitarian. The restraints
placed on élites by, for example, the Tanzanian Arusha Declaration,
suggest one strategy.[67] Poverty is not just a lack of resources required
to live a normal life. It is lack of resources in fact used, and felt to be
rightly used, by the rich.

67. The following are extracts from the resolution agreed by the Tanzanian
    National Executive Committee at Arusha, January, 1967:
      No TANU or Government leader should . . .
      —hold shares in any company
      —receive two or more salaries
      —hold directorships in any privately-owned enterprises
      —own houses which he rents to others.
    A 'leader' was defined to include Ministers, Members of Parliament, senior
    officials, councillors and civil servants of high and medium grade.

# 2. Problems in the Definition and Measurement of Poverty

## *Martin Rein*

The problems of how to define and measure poverty cannot proceed until we clarify the conception of poverty we wish to employ. Three broad concepts of poverty can be identified. Poverty may be regarded as subsistence, inequality or externality. Subsistence is concerned with the minimum of provision needed to maintain health and working capacity. Its terms of reference are the capacity to survive and to maintain physical efficiency. Inequality is concerned with the relative position of income groups to each other. Poverty cannot be understood by isolating the poor and treating them as a special group. Society is seen as a series of stratified income layers and poverty is concerned with how the bottom layers fare relative to the rest of society. Hence, the concept of poverty must be seen in the context of society as a whole. The study of the poor then depends on an understanding of the level of living of the rich, since it is these conditions relative to each other that are critical in the conception of inequality. To understand the poor we must then study the affluent. Externality is concerned with the social consequences of poverty for the rest of society rather than in terms of the needs of the poor. The poverty line should serve 'as an index of the disutility to the community of the persistence of poverty'.[1]

People must not be allowed to become so poor that they offend or are hurtful to society. It is not so much the misery and plight of the poor but the discomfort and cost to the community which is crucial to this view of poverty. We have a problem of poverty to the extent that low income creates problems for those who are not poor. Poverty then consists of social problems correlated with low income. Hence only when income-conditioned problems are randomized can poverty be eliminated. To improve the level of

1. Smolensky, E., 'Investment in the Education of the Poor: A Pessimistic Report', *American Economic Review*, Supplement LV, May, 1966.

living of the poor without reducing disutility to the rest of community, is insufficient.

Each of these concepts presents numerous problems of definition and measurement. Should we define poverty only in terms of economic insufficiency, economic inequality and economic diseconomy, or should the definition be broadened to embrace non-economic variables such as prestige, power and social services? For example, Titmuss has insisted that 'we cannot . . . delineate the new frontiers of poverty unless we take account of the changing agents and characteristics of inequality'.[2] Although the concept of poverty Titmuss holds is that of inequality, he is posing the broader question that poverty is more than the lack of income.

When a more encompassing view of poverty is accepted which extends beyond the distribution of income, two critical issues emerge —where to establish the cut-off points which separate the poor from the non-poor, and which non-economic conditions should be taken into account.

Paradoxically, we measure poverty in subsistence terms, but the programs and policies we have evolved to reduce poverty in America are based on a broader conception of the dimensions of well-being for which no systematic statistical information is available. These include the lack of accepted minima, or inequalities in the distribution of power, education and legal justice. These dimensions of the level of living are not included in the goods and services which make up a minimum personal market basket, on which the measurement of poverty is based, because these items cannot be purchased by the individual with low income in the market. However, little organized effort has been directed at conceptualizing and measuring a conception of poverty which is more closely related to the programs we have developed, or at developing a program to reduce poverty (cash transfers) which is more closely tied to the concept of poverty we employ—the lack of minimum income for subsistence.

However, a small body of literature is being developed which does attempt to spell out the wider dimensions of poverty. Townsend, influenced by Titmuss, defines poverty as inequities in the distribution of five resources,[3] including income, capital assets, occupational fringe benefits, current public services and current private services. A national study of poverty in England based on an empirical

2. Titmuss, R., *Income Distribution and Social Change*, London, Allen & Unwin, 1962, p. 187.
3. Townsend, P., Chapter 1.

investigation of the distribution of these items is now being undertaken by Townsend and Abel-Smith. Miller and Rein, also influenced
by Titmuss, have drawn up a somewhat different list of items which,
in being more responsive to the American context, pays attention
to the political, legal and educational components of well-being.[4]

But broadening the definition only confounds the problem of
where to draw the cut-off points which distinguish those in poverty
from the rest of the population. For a solution to this dilemma we
return again to relative, absolute and disutility conceptions of
poverty. Are we interested in establishing standards which will
enable us to define minimum powers, social honor, environmental
health and justice? Our search for such standards is illusory and no
viable definition can be found which does not depend on inequalities
in the distribution of these resources which comprise our level of
living. Grigsby and Baratz suggest that the cut-off points may be
established at that point or region where the relationship between
income and social and personal problems is statistically randomized.[5]
This formulation of where to establish the division between poor
and non-poor draws on the externality conception of poverty, for it
is concerned with the consequences of being poor or with the bottom
of an income distribution.

The extensive reliance by governmental bodies such as the Office
of Economic Opportunity and the Council of Economic Advisers on
estimates of poverty which are based upon data concerning the cost
of subsistence in the United States suggests that we have what is in
effect an official American definition of poverty. As such, it deserves
the closest scrutiny. This paper examines some of the problems
inherent in the current 'official' definition of poverty. Some attempt
is made to place the analysis in a historical context, although no
systematic historical review is attempted.

## A Subsistence Definition of Poverty

A definition of poverty in terms of subsistence levels of living has
had wide acceptance because it seems to accord with common sense
and appears to be divorced from personal values of either harshness
or compassion. It seeks to describe poverty objectively as lack of the
income needed to acquire the minimum necessities of life. Those

4. Miller, S. M., Rein, M., *et al*, 'Poverty, Inequality and Conflict', *The Annals*,
   September, 1967.
5. Grigsby, W., and Baratz, M., with Rein, M., 'Conceptualization and
   Measurement of Poverty', mimeo.

who lack the necessities to sustain life are by definition poor. But how should 'minimum' be defined? Agreement on the meaning of minimum is crucial to the development of standards which will permit the establishment of a dividing line separating the poor from the non-poor. Much of the history of the study of poverty can be understood as an effort to establish a non-subjective or 'scientific' poverty line, the standard for which was equated with subsistence— the amount needed to sustain life. But like the search for the philosopher's stone, the efforts to discover an absolute and value-free definition of poverty based on the concept of subsistence proved abortive.

Rowntree was the first investigator to attempt a rigorous definition of poverty in subsistence terms. In his classic study of poverty in the city of York, he wrote:

> My primary poverty line represented the minimum sum on which physical efficiency could be maintained. It was a standard of bare subsistence rather than living. In calculating it the utmost economy was practised . . . 'A family living upon the scale allowed for in this estimate must . . . be governed by the regulation, "Nothing must be bought but that which is absolutely necessary for the maintenance of physical health, and what is bought must be of the plainest and most economic description" '.[6]

Thus, a standard of bare subsistence could be supported if all human passions for frivolity, the relief of monotony, and even irresponsibility were ruthlessly suppressed. Only expenditures which provided physical health were permissible. The failure or the incapacity to conduct one's daily affairs according to these severe regulations brought the family into a state of secondary poverty. Secondary poverty existed when income was adequate to maintain a subsistence level, but the family failed to spend its income to purchase the necessities to sustain life and health. According to Rowntree, a defect of moral character or native intelligence rather than an insufficiency of resources, distinguishes primary from secondary poverty. For his definition of 'the minimum necessaries for the maintenance of mere physical efficiency', Rowntree drew upon the research of the American nutritionist, Atwater, who had devised a minimum diet based on research undertaken on American convicts. Atwater estimated minimum caloric intake per day by determining the amount of food which was required to prevent

6. Rowntree, B.S., *Poverty and Progress: A Second Social Survey of York*, London, Longmans, Green, 1941, pp. 102–103.

prisoners from either gaining or losing weight. Estimating variations for men and women and determining the market value of the food which satisfied these minimum requirements, Rowntree arrived at a low-cost food plan which served as the basis for his definition of poverty.[7]

Present procedures for estimating minimum nutritional requirements have progressed beyond these primitive beginnings, but they still depend on a judgement of nutritional need which takes into account both actual consumption patterns and a definition of minimum caloric intake based on an independent assessment of nutritional adequacy. The basic technique is operationalized in the U.S. Department of Agriculture's economy food plan which forms the basis for several subsistence estimates of poverty. But the minimum amount of money needed to achieve minimum nutritional standards tell us nothing about the cost of clothing, shelter and other items necessary to maintain life. Some means of converting expenditure for food into total expenditure is needed. Engels had observed in 1857 that there was an inverse relationship between income and the percentage of total expenditure spent for food. By examining the proportion of the family budget spent for food in various income classes an Engels coefficient[8] can be computed, when multiplied by food expenditure, provides an estimate of the total minimum budget required to keep a family out of poverty.[9]

An alternative to an aggregate estimate of all non-food expenditures through the use of the Engels coefficient is the development of an itemized budget for each consumption item necessary for subsistence—shelter, medical care, clothing etc. This procedure assumes that minimum requirements can be specified for each item and that these can serve as cut-off points separating adequate consumption from inadequate. To illustrate the procedure, we can consider how minimum clothing needs may be defined.

7. Townsend, P., 'The Meaning of Poverty', *British Journal of Sociology*, XVIII, No. 3, September, 1962, pp. 215 ff.
8. For a discussion of the Engels coefficient see Hobsbawm, E. J., 'Poverty', *New International Encyclopaedia of the Social Sciences* (forthcoming).
9. The relationship can be expressed by the following equation: $C = ME$ where C is equal to the cost of total consumption of a household, M equals expenditures for a minimum food basket, and E equals the size of the Engels coefficient. See Taira, Koji, *Country Report No. 6 on Japan*, International Trade Union Seminar on Low Income Groups and Methods of Dealing with their Problems, Social Affairs Division of the Organization for Economic Co-operation and Development.

lly, as will be demonstrated below, even in the minimum food requirements, accepted standards are is fact raised a serious question as to the usefulness of pt to measure an absolute standard of adequacy which subsistence implies.

## A Definition of Poverty Based on Nutritional Adequacy

Poverty is defined by the Social Security Administration (SSA) as nutritional inadequacy. This definition clearly implies some standard for determining the minimum cost of an adequate diet. During the depression the National Research Council undertook intensive work in developing a recommended dietary allowance which served as a basis for defining minimal nutritional requirements for calories and essential nutrients. All foods were sorted into eleven categories on the basis of the nutrients they contained. An estimate was then made of the quantities of food needed in each of these food groups, by individuals of different age and sex. As it turned out, if the recommended quantities of food were purchased in the most economical way and without regard to dietary habits, the cost of the food plan would be extremely low. Stigler, for example, estimated that if the minimum number of calories were purchased in the cheapest bulk market basket, the total cost to purchase the food needed for an adequate diet would come to about \$40 per year in 1944.[13] Even allowing for a tripling of prices since that date, the present cost would come to less than \$120 per annum. Unfortunately, as Stigler sought to demonstrate by this calculation, persons in American society simply do not consume the lowest-cost food items. Thus, a realistic definition of poverty requires that attention be given to actual consumption patterns. 'Even with food,' Orshansky acknowledges, 'social conscience and custom dictate that there be not only sufficient quantity but sufficient variety to meet recommended nutritional goals and conform to customary eating patterns. Calories alone will not be enough.'[14] Yet food alone provides the best basis for measuring minimum requirements; however, the definition must therefore be based on both customary behaviour and expert definition of nutritional adequacy.

12. Orshansky, M., 'Counting the Poor: Another Look at the Poverty Profile', *Social Security Bulletin*, XXVIII, No. 1, January, 1965, p. 5.
13. Stigler, J., 'The Cost of Subsistence', *Journal of Farm Economics*, XXVII 1945, p. 311 ff.
14. Orshansky, M., 'Counting the Poor', *op. cit.*

Reflecting this fact, a household food consumption survey undertaken by the U.S. Department of Agriculture was divided into four levels of cost: economy, low, moderate and liberal. The cost of a standard family food plan is developed at each of these levels. If, however, only prevailing consumption patterns were taken as a standard, without attention to an independent definition of adequacy, there would be no objective way of establishing a cut-off point which distinguishes an adequate from an inadequate diet. When the food plan was developed for each income group, therefore, it was based on expert judgement regarding an acceptable trade-off between nutritional standards and consumption patterns.[15]

The SSA procedure for measuring poverty is based on the cost of USDA's 'economy' food plan, which is adapted to the pattern of food expenditures of those in the lowest third of the income range. It is designed for 'temporary or emergency use when funds are low' and costs about 75–80 per cent of the low-cost plan.[16] It was adopted in about 1960 when a food plan was needed which was consistent with actual food budgets already developed for families receiving public assistance. The existing standards of welfare assistance served to define the food consumption needs of the poor.

In estimating costs, the Department of Agriculture assumed that housewives make average choices within each food group and average prices are paid for each food item in the basket. Each year these average prices are adjusted for changes in the price level. It is further assumed that all family members under the plan prepare all of their food at home, including lunches which they may eat at work.

To determine the minimum total income requirements for a family an Engels coefficient is needed. A Department of Agriculture survey conducted in 1955 was used to determine the proportion of total family income among low-income family units that was spent for food.[17] Actually, three different coefficients were used: 0·27 for two-person families; 0·33 for families of 3 or more; and for unattached individuals, a special estimate based on approximately 80 per cent of the total requirements of a two-person family. The last is based on the assumption that when income is low, the cost

15. Orshansky, M., 'Counting the Poor', op. cit., p. 5.
16. Orshansky, M., ibid, p. 6.
17. US Department of Agriculture, Household Food Consumption Survey, 1955, Dietary Evaluation of Food Used in Households in the United States, Report No. 16, November, 1961.

of living for a single person is only slightly less than for a couple.

The SSA procedure for defining and measuring poverty is especially vulnerable to the criticism that when a choice among alternative estimating procedures was necessary the rationale for selection was arbitrary, but not necessarily unreasoned. The extent and character of this arbitrariness will be examined in four substantive areas: the size of the Engels coefficient; the diversity of nutritional need; the disparity between actual consumption patterns and expert judgement as to the ingredients of an adequate diet, and the insistence on an economical market basket.

## The Size of the Engels Coefficient

The size of the Engels coefficient obviously affects estimates of the extent of poverty. However, an Engels coefficient is not used by the SSA to determine minimum budget requirements for persons living alone. The requirements of an unattached individual living alone are estimated indirectly as a proportion of the expenditures for a couple. The explanation offered is that 'the consumption data are hard to interpret because of the heavy representation of aged individuals not shown separately'.[18] Although this procedure seems reasonable, there appears to be no firm evidence on which to estimate the needs of one aged person as a proportion of the needs of an aged couple. In an early report Orshansky notes that, 'pending further research, the relationship of the cost of living for a single individual to that of a couple must remain something everyone talks about but about which little is known'. The deficiency is serious, because, as Orshansky explains, the correction for single-person households is 'by far the most important adjustment' which is necessary in making an estimate of the budgetary needs of the elderly persons. The extent of poverty among the aged could drop, perhaps sharply, if an estimate of 60 or 70 per cent were used, instead of 80 per cent.[19]

If we consider the size of the coefficient used, even more serious objections can be raised to the procedures followed by SSA. As has been said, the lower the coefficient, the larger the number of impoverished. In estimating the income-food-expenditure relationship Orshansky had available two surveys, the Department of

18. Orshansky, M., 'Counting the Poor', *op. cit.*, p. 9.
19. Orshansky, M., 'Budget for an Elderly Couple: Interim Revision by the B.L.S.', *Social Security Bulletin*, XXIII, No. 12, December, 1960, pp. 28–31.

Agriculture consumption survey of 1955,[20] and a 1960–1 Bureau of Labor Statistics survey of urban families.[21]

The BLS survey found that about 25 per cent of the income of all families regardless of size goes for food, whereas the Agriculture survey found substantial variations by family size and an average expenditure for food of 33 per cent for families with two or more members. The BLS data are based on interviewer estimates of annual outlays for food, while the Department of Agriculture figures are derived from a detailed checklist of foods consumed during the week in which the survey was held. The Social Security Administration used the Agriculture study. Haber criticizes this choice.

> It was suggested [by Orshansky] that the BLS study tended to understate food expenditures; but this would affect ratio figures only if it also tended to overstate or not similarly understate other expenditures. This was not demonstrated and since the study collected data on expenditure in all categories, not just food, there would seem to be an internal check on the relative figures. Furthermore, comparisons of 1950 to 1960–61 BLS studies reflected a decline of 5·6 per cent in the ratio within the same methodology. The earlier USDA figure is almost certain to be overstated.[22]

Re-calculating the poverty cut-off point with a coefficient of 0·30 rather than 0·33 for a four-person urban family and taking into account gross income rather than income after taxes, Haber arrives at a $3,474 poverty line 'for the deceptive economy plan and a truer $4,263 for the low-cost plan', compared with a $3,130 line using Agriculture data.[23]

Rose Friedman also criticizes the 'official' definition of poverty but on different groups. Using estimates based on actual consumption and a higher Engels coefficient, she is able to cut the poverty population in half.

> The nutritive adequacy definition of poverty . . . gives an income of $2,200 as the poverty line for a nonfarm family of four. The cost of food implied by the $3,000 income for a family of four . . . is $5.00 per person per week. The amount actually spent for food, on the average,

20. US Department of Agriculture, *op. cit.*
21. US Bureau of Labor Statistics, *Consumer Expenditures and Income*, Urban US 1960–61. Supplement 3-Part A to BLS Report 237–238. Table 29A, July, 1964.
22. Haber, A., 'Poverty Budgets: How Much is Enough', *Poverty and Human Resources Abstracts*, I, No. 3 (1966), Ann Arbor, p. 6.
23. Haber, A., *op. cit.*, p. 7.

by a family of four with an income of $2,200 was over $6.00 per person
per week, because the fraction of income spent on food at this level
was about 60 per cent and not 33 per cent. It should be emphasized
that the difference between the Council's estimate that 20 per cent of
families were poor . . . and my estimate that 10 per cent were poor
results neither from a different basic criterion of poverty nor from the
use of different data. Both use nutrition to separate the poor from the
not-poor; both use the same standard of nutritive-adequacy; both use
the same statistical data.[24]

It is interesting to speculate on how political realities affect
technical decisions. The first working definition of poverty used by
the Council of Economic Advisors established the extent of American
poverty at about 34 million persons, or roughly one-fifth of the
population. More refined estimates, if they were to be politically
acceptable, had to be consistent with CEA's estimate of the size of
the problem. It was all right for a new definition to change the
character of poverty, but not its size. As a consequence, technical
decisions regarding definition of income or the size of the Engels
coefficient or the choice of a survey on food consumption, all of
which can significantly alter the estimated extent of poverty, have
come to reflect not only our understanding of the meaning of subsistence but also the political views and realities which provide the
framework for professional judgements.

What is important in all these controversies is not who is right
and who is wrong but that even where presumably objective
measures are available, the selection of minimum standards is of
necessity arbitrary. This point is expanded upon in the following
section.

## The Diversity of Nutritional Need

Another example of arbitrariness concerns the adjustments which
are made for different nutritional needs based on age and sex
groupings, but not upon the level of activity. Adequate caloric intake
comes to about 3,000 calories a day for a male age 18 to 64, while a
child under ten requires 1,200 to 1,800 calories. However, the level
of physical activity appears to be as important as age. A farmer, for
example, may require as many as 4,500 calories.[25]

24. Friedman, R. D., *Poverty: Definition and Perspective*, Washington D.C., American
    Enterprise Institute for Public Policy Research, 1965, p. 35.
25. Luck, J., *op. cit.*

Physical fitness is not a precisely definable condition. One has first to ask fitness for what? A bank clerk in the best of health might be unfit to work on a trolley or in a coal mine. A woman able to bear two or three children without endangering her health might well prove unfit for the demands of motherhood in a society where families of seven or eight children were the rule. Secondly, standards of physical fitness vary over time, as well as between country and country . . . class and class.[26]

Townsend estimates that when sedentary and manual occupations are compared, the number of calories needed per hour may differ from 30 to as much as 450. Since age and sex are taken into account in estimating minimal caloric need, one would think that the level of physical activity would be regarded as equally important, the more so because the poor are more likely than the non-poor to be employed in manual and unskilled jobs requiring physical exertion.

Townsend is sharply critical not only of the neglect of activity levels, but also of other factors involved in nutritional standards. In expressing his criticism, he offers an analysis of the formidable barriers to scientifically determined subsistence diets.

There are real difficulties in estimating nutritional needs. The nutritionists have not subtly broken up the different needs of individuals; they have made overall estimates. These estimates are not even based on studies of the intake of persons in different occupations. Beyond a certain minimum (somewhere, perhaps, between 1,000 and 1,500 calories), the number of calories a man needs . . . depends upon the society in which he lives. Even his dietary needs depend upon climate, the kind of housing he lives in, the kind of job he has, and the kind of leisure activities he follows. In other words, estimates of need, even nutritional needs, cannot be absolute; they must be relative to the kind of society in which a man is living.[27]

The estimates of caloric requirements at one time did take into account level of activity, but nutritionists have dropped this variable, perhaps because they were not primarily concerned with the problem of poverty. Caloric estimates lack the scientific rigor which is claimed for them, for they depend on global and aggregate judgements which underestimate the diversity of human need. But endless

26. Lynes, T., *National Assistance and National Prosperity*, Occasional Papers on Social Administration, Welwyn, Codicote Press, 1962, pp. 9–10.
27. Townsend, P., 'The Scale and Meaning of Poverty in Contemporary Western Society', *Dependency and Poverty*, 1963–64, Colloquium Series Paper, Brandeis University, July, 1965, p. 15.

refinement of details is not the appropriate answer to the problem. The standards which emerge will become so complex and detailed as to add new dimensions of unreality. Moreover, there is no way of defining minimum levels of activity for work and leisure, even though caloric needs depend on energy spent.

These criticisms of estimates of caloric levels may seem somewhat overdrawn, since caloric requirements alone can be met quite cheaply. It is achieving a balance of vitamins, minerals, and other nutrients that is most problematic for the poor. Further, disagreements over minimum caloric requirements are not nearly so important as disagreements over what constitutes an adequate diet generally and whether minor deviations from prescribed diets affect performance—the capacity to learn and work. Still further, it is doubtful whether getting more refined estimates would affect the numbers of those in poverty to the same extent as does a change in the estimate of the size of the Engels coefficient. On the other hand, the issue of level of physical activity does highlight value problems by undermining the nutritionist claim for objectivity and by dramatizing the difficulties of measurement.

### The Disparity Between Actual Behavior and Expert Judgement

An examination of actual consumption patterns reveals great variation between low-income families. On the average, families in the $2,999 income group in 1958 were spending more for food per person than the low-cost food plan of the Department of Agriculture calls for, but equally interesting was the fact that 28 per cent of families were spending less than the amount suggested. Some of this spread is due simply to regional variations. In 1959, for example, the United States average weekly food consumption for a family consisting of a mother, father and two children under the age of 12 was $24.00, but expenditures ranged from $19.80 in the South to $26.50 in the Northeast, a difference of 35 per cent.[28]

28. What is often overlooked is that migration between regions seems to affect food costs, because food consumption patterns are not instantly abandoned. A report on nutrition of Negroes states, 'the food habits of Southern Negroes in the North . . . appear to be particularly erratic, with a substantial amount of money being spent to acquire Southern food which has a very limited nutritional value, such as fat-back and grits', Mayer, J., 'The Nutritional Status of American Negroes', *Nutrition Review*, XXIII, No. 6, June, 1965, p. 163. Also see 'Low-Cost Food Plans—New Regional Estimates', *Research and Statistics*, *No. 28*, Social Security Administration, October, 1959.

There were also wide variations in expenditures by the aged. Orshansky estimates that there was a 20 per cent spread in the cost of living for the aged in the 20 largest cities and suburbs of the United States, ranging from $2,641 in Houston to $3,366 in Chicago. How these variations in the cost of living affect the cost of the low-cost food plan is by no means clear. On one hand, it is plausible to argue that at subsistence levels there is much less room for significant variations in actual budgets, and there is therefore little variability in actual expenditures. On the other hand, there are wide variations in actual expenditures for the income group which is expected to follow the low-cost food plan. If we consider one item—consumption of food at home—the range of expenditures seems to be impressively large, from $711 for an elderly couple in Houston to $900 in Boston.

These variations raise questions about the use of a single food plan to estimate poverty. Another reason for skepticism has to do with the fact that the economy food and low-cost plans assume an efficient housekeeper who secures an adequate diet for the family within the cost of the plan. This seems unlikely, partly because the low-income housewife is likely to be a less informed customer and partly because the quality of the food she purchases may be inferior and higher priced in comparison with food purchased by higher-income shoppers. A recent study by the Bureau of Labor Statistics concluded that the poor pay more for food than consumers in higher-income areas, but that food stores do not charge more in low-income areas. It is not that the poor are overcharged, but that they cannot exploit the economics of bulk purchase. For example, the poor tend to buy flour in two-pound rather than five-pound sacks, though 'the price for flour ranged from 14 per cent a pound higher in New York to 35 per cent higher in Chicago when purchased in two-pound sacks'. Similar differentials hold for milk, sugar and other food items.[29]

In light of the above, it is not surprising to learn that many persons who have resources sufficient to live only at the level prescribed by the economy or low-cost food plan will also fail to meet a prescribed minimum diet. But to what extent should the experts be forced to revise their estimates of the cost of a minimum diet to reflect actual consumption patterns? If the budget needed to achieve minimum dietary adequacy is defined as less than what families apparently do spend to achieve this minimum, it is difficult to determine

29. The study did not, however, examine why chain stores tend to stay out of low income areas. *New York Times*, June 12, 1966, p. 56.

whether the experts are wrong in where they have placed the poverty line, or whether the prevailing pattern of consumption is an inappropriate criterion because the poor lack the capacity to consume. More important, to the extent that standards are based on actual consumption, there is a circularity in the analysis.[30] Orshansky in a discussion with the author made a similar observation that there are no extrinsic standards for determining minimum nutritional needs.

## The Economical Market Basket

The cost of the market basket of food items needed to prevent nutritional poverty is computed so that it is the most economic basket possible. The concern for least cost is at conflict with the desire to take account of actual consumption patterns and introduces a note of unreality into the definition of the poverty line. Rowntree recognized this when he observed that 'no housewife without a considerable knowledge of the nutritive value of different food-stuffs and considerable skill in cooking, would be likely to choose a menu at once so economically and comparatively attractive as the one upon which I base my costs'.[31] Orshansky makes the same observation: 'the lower the level of cost, the more restricted the kinds and qualities of food must be and the more skill in marketing and food preparation is required'.[32] But those in poverty clearly have the least skills in marketing, knowledge of nutrition, and resourcefulness in cooking to meet the stringent demands of economy. The failure to meet the nutritional standards set by the poverty budget is assumed to reflect the incapacity of the poor to consume, that is, secondary poverty. If the diet is to be based on actual consumption, and if it is to avoid building into its definition a confusion between primary and secondary poverty, then the standards of economy must be relaxed and a more realistic assumption of human error be accepted. The effect of this intrusion of reality into budgeting will be to raise the poverty level and increase the amount of poverty.

## Summary

I have tried to demonstrate that the subsistence-level definition of poverty is arbitrary, circular and relative. The definition of poverty

30. Orshansky, M., 'Counting the Poor', *op. cit.*, p. 8.
31. Rowntree, B. S., *Human Needs of Labour*, *op. cit.*, p. 112.
32. Orshansky, M., 'Counting the Poor', *op. cit.*, p. 6.

based on nutritional requirements is dependent not only on expert definition but also on actual levels and patterns of living. Thus, no extrinsic standard to measure food adequacy is available and the subsistence definition of poverty is, therefore, circular. But this procedure imposes a number of arbitrary judgements which rob the nutritional approach of its claim that it is based on scientific rigor with minimum attention to value judgements. To take account of customary behavior requires that we know in advance the relevant income group which distinguishes the poor from the non-poor. Thus the procedure for measuring poverty is based on a circular argument from which it cannot retreat. The result is that those who hold different value judgements concerning how stringent or lenient the poverty standard should be, can use the same data to demonstrate that poverty is either a significant or trivial problem. All of the procedures in establishing a trade-off between consumption standards and expert judgement have an arbitrary quality which can be challenged by those who wish to see the standards of poverty defined more harshly or more leniently. On the other hand, the criterion that the budget should be most economical forces the expert to accept an unrealistic assumption of a no-waste budget, and extensive knowledge in marketing and cooking. An economical budget must be based on knowledge and skill which is least likely to be present in the low-income groups we are concerned with. The result is that a stubborn and continuing ambiguity between primary and secondary poverty is built into the very procedures by which the minimum nutritional standard is determined. If we cannot distinguish between the capacity to consume and the adequacy of the resource base for consumption, there is no independent standard for questioning and revising expert judgement.

Almost every procedure in the subsistence-level definition of poverty can be reasonably challenged. The estimates are based on the consumption pattern of the entire low-income third instead of sub-groups of this population. The estimates of nutritional needs take age and sex into account but not physical activity. Average price and average consumption are used as the standard for constructing the low-cost food plan, rather than actual behaviour. The economy food plan is an arbitrary derivative (approximately three-quarters) of the low-cost plan. We must conclude that subsistence measures of poverty cannot claim to rest solely on a technical or scientific definition of nutritional adequacy. Values, preferences, and political realities influence the definition of subsistence. Yet once a biological definition is abandoned and actual consumption is taken into account, no absolute measurement of poverty in subsistence terms is possible.[33] The other conceptions of poverty reviewed at the beginning of this chapter deserve more attention and developments.

33. In the light of these observations it is rather surprising to note Kolko's insistence on the validity of an absolute measure of subsistence. He asserts: 'The maintenance budget is a synthesis of what families actually spend, modified to include what they must have to meet minimum health criteria. It is not a relative or changing standard such as that employed by 'social workers' (who) will call a person "underprivileged" whose scale of living is considerably below the average'. Kolko, G., *Wealth and Power in America*, New York, Frederick A. Praeger, 1962, p. 96.

BIBLIOGRAPHY

Ben. H. Bagdikian, *In the Midst of Plenty: A New Report on the Poor in America*, New York, Signet Books, 1964.

Robert H. Bremner, *From the Depths: The Discovery of Poverty in the United States*, New York University Press, 1956.

Wilbur J. Cohen and Eugenia Sullivan, 'Poverty in the United States', *Health, Education and Welfare Indicators*, February, 1964.

Leo Fishman, *Poverty Amid Affluence*, New Haven, Yale University Press, 1966.

John Kenneth Galbraith, *The Affluent Society*, Boston, Houghton Mifflin Company, 1960.

Nathan Glazer, 'Paradoxes of American Poverty', *Public Interest*, Fall 1965.

Margaret S. Gordon (ed), *Poverty in America*, San Francisco, Chandler Publishing Co., 1965.

Allan Haber, 'Poverty Budgets: How Much is Enough?', *Poverty and Human Resources Abstracts*, Vol. 1, No. 3 (May-June 1966), pp. 5-22.

Michael Harrington, *The Other America—Poverty in the United States*, New York, The Macmillan Co., 1962.

Nat Hentoff, *The New Equality*, New York, The Viking Press, 1964.

Leon H. Keyserling, *Progress or Poverty: The United States at the Crossroads*, Washington, D.C., Conference on Economic Progress, December, 1964.

Helen H. Lamale and Margaret S. Strotz, 'The Interim City Worker's Family Budget', *Monthly Labor Review*, August, 1960.

Robert J. Lampman, *The Low Income Population and Economic Growth*, United States Congress, Joint Economic Committee, Study Paper Number 12, 86th Congress, First Session, December, 1959.

Herman P. Miller, 'Changes in the Number and Composition of the Poor', *Poverty in America*, M. S. Gordon (ed), San Francisco, Chandler Publishing Co., 1965, pp. 81-101.

Herman P. Miller, *Income of the American People*, New York, John Wiley and Sons, Inc., 1955.

Herman P. Miller (ed), *Poverty—American Style*, Belmont, California, Wadsworth Publishing Co., 1966.

Herman P. Miller, *Rich Man, Poor Man: A Study of Income Distribution in America*, New York, Crowell, 1964.

James N. Morgan, David H. Martin, Wilbur J. Cohen, and Harvey E. Brazer, *Income and Welfare in the United States*, New York, McGraw-Hill Book Co., Inc., 1962.

Mollie Orshansky, 'Budget for an Elderly Couple. An Interim Revision by the Bureau of Labor Statistics', *Social Security Bulletin*, December, 1960.

Mollie Orshansky, 'Recounting the Poor—A Five Year Review', *Social Security Bulletin*, April, 1966, pp. 2–19.

Mollie Orshansky, 'Who's Who Among the Poor: A Demographic View of Poverty', *Social Security Bulletin*, July, 1965, pp. 3–33.

Charles E. Silberman, *Crisis in Black and White*, New York, Random House, 1964.

*Economic Report of the President*, Transmitted to the Congress, January 1964 and 1965 together with *The Annual Report of the Council of Economic Advisors*.

*Manpower Report of the President*, and *A Report on Manpower Requirements, Resources, Utilization and Training by the United States Department of Labor*, Transmitted to Congress, March 1964 and March 1965.

# 3. Poverty: Food and Nutrition Indices

## J. C. McKenzie

One of the most difficult problems to deal with is one which a community does not believe exists. Such a statement in many ways summarizes the major difficulties concerning any evaluation of nutritional deficiencies in the affluent society. In developing countries there is no debate as to whether or not people are mal-nourished. This can be obviously and fairly simply demonstrated just by looking at the population and the conditions in which they have to live. In consequence the debate becomes one on the extent of the problem and the best ways of dealing with it. But in the so-called affluent world many are not prepared even to consider whether or not any problem of malnutrition still exists and certainly there is no longer very obvious visual evidence of chronic deficiencies to remind them. In this area, therefore, the major issue becomes one of isolating the key nutrition indices and of indicating in real terms the nature and extent of the problem, if indeed a problem exists.[1] As such this chapter will be concerned primarily with isolating the indices, indicating limitations and pointing out the problems surrounding such measurements. They will be considered in the context of a study to assess whether or not there are any indications of mal-nutrition in the United Kingdom.

### The United Kingdom: A Case Study[2]

The economic and social history of the twentieth century paints a picture of substantial improvement for the community as a whole. Poverty and hardship for large sections of the population in the 1920s and 1930s was replaced in the 1950s and 1960s by full employ-

1. It is possible that this problem of non-awareness is the key issue not only of malnutrition but also of poverty generally and that throughout this paragraph the word 'poverty' might appropriately be substituted for 'malnutrition' and 'nutritional deficiences'.
2. Much of this section of the chapter is based on an Office of Health Economics booklet, *Malnutrition in the 1960s,* June, 1967.

ment and the attractions of a 'boom' economy. I shall review the extent to which the nutritional status of the United Kingdom population has shown a similar improvement over the period. Such an investigation requires the collection and assessment of several types of evidence and I will examine each in turn. Information is required on the food consumption and nutrient intake of the population. Details of clinical examinations are needed to indicate the extent to which health has been affected by differing diets. The results of biochemical tests may be used to indicate the level of nutrient reserves within the body. The study of vital statistics and anthropometric data will demonstrate the impact of dietary variations. Too often in the past attempts have been made to investigate the nutritional status of a community using only one of these methods and unjustified deductions based on these findings have been published. Only after an examination of all these areas and their inter-relationship can an adequate assessment of nutritional status be made.

## Dietary Intake and Nutrient Requirements

Evidence on the dietary intake of the population of the United Kingdom has rested mainly with the National Food Survey. This is a continuous sampling enquiry into the domestic food purchases of private households in Great Britain. A sample is selected by means of a three-stage stratified random sampling scheme. In 1964 the effective response rate was only 52 per cent.[3] The housewife is asked to keep a record of the description, quantity and cost of food which enters the household during one week. Items such as soft drinks, ice cream, alcohol and other items likely to be purchased by the other members of the family are not included.

The energy value and nutrient content of the recorded quantities of food are evaluated using tables of food composition which make allowance for inedible material.[4] The calculated nutrient intake is then compared with the allowances based on British Medical Association recommendations of what is believed to be the quantity of each nutrient required to maintain health.[5] In making this com-

3. *Domestic Food Consumption and Expenditure, 1964*, London, HMSO, 1966.
4. In addition, to allow for loss in cooking and storage, the figure for thiamine is reduced by 15 per cent and for Vitamin C by 75 per cent for green vegetables, and by 50 per cent for other vegetables.
5. It should be noted that these allowances are not minimum requirements to

parison allowances are made for the presence of visitors and for meals eaten outside the home, and in addition a general reduction of 10 per cent in the total intake figure for each nutrient is made to allow for wastage.

TABLE 1

*Energy Value and Nutrient Content of Food Consumption of Certain United Kingdom Households in 1950 and 1964 Expressed as a Percentage of Recommended Allowances*

| Nutrient | Families with 1 child | | | Families with 4 or more children | | |
|---|---|---|---|---|---|---|
| | 1950 | 1964 | Change | 1950 | 1964 | Change |
| Energy Value | 109 | 114 | + 5 | 101 | 101 | − 0 |
| Total Protein | 117 | 112 | − 5 | 94 | 90 | − 4 |
| Calcium | 120 | 118 | − 2 | 92 | 87 | − 5 |
| Iron | 123 | 126 | + 3 | 107* | 110 | + 3 |
| *Vitamins†* | | | | | | |
| Vitamin A | 167* | 211 | +44 | 145* | 176 | +31 |
| Thiamine | 140* | 141 | + 1 | 131* | 122 | − 9 |
| Riboflavin | 126 | 130 | + 4 | 109 | 108 | − 1 |
| Nicotinic Acid | 146 | 154 | + 8 | 123 | 128 | + 5 |
| Vitamin C | 283* | 272 | −11 | 213* | 187 | −26 |

* 1952 figures.
† No details are given for vitamin D as there are no BMA recommended allowances for this nutrient.

*Source:* *Domestic Food Consumption and Expenditure Survey, 1950 and 1964,* London, HMSO, 1952 and 1966.

A number of issues emerge from the figures. The first is that the recommended allowances for protein and calcium are not on average reached by certain sub-groups, *namely,* households with a man and woman and three or more children, or adolescents and children. Similarly, the standard is not reached for protein in other households with adolescents but no children or for protein and calcium

keep a particular individual alive. They are allowances 'believed to be sufficient to establish and maintain a good nutritional state in representative individuals in the groups concerned'. Adjustments are made for age, sex, and activity. British Medical Association, *Nutrition Committee Report,* 1950.

in other households with one or more children. The types of household in which the standards for protein or calcium are not on average reached constitute 48 per cent of the families with children in the sample.

The trend over time also demonstrates a slight decline in standards compared with the period of austerity in 1950. Thus today families with only one child have a lower nutrient intake of protein, calcium and Vitamin C than in 1950. For families with four or more children the intake is lower for protein, calcium and the vitamins thiamine, riboflavin and Vitamin C (Table 1). Additionally, variations between classes are also still substantial and in some nutrients growing (Table 2).

However, the situation may be more serious than these figures suggest, depending on the extent of dispersion around the average. This is particularly important if the average intake comes close to the recommended allowance (Table 3). Thus families with a dietary intake 10 per cent less than the average would be below the recommended allowance for calories, protein and calcium. This problem has long been appreciated by the Ministry of Agriculture.

TABLE 2

*Range in Nutrient Consumption for Different Social Classes in the United Kingdom—1950 to 1964*

| | Difference in percentage points between highest (A1) and lowest (D1) social classes, when the intake of each is expressed as a percentage of the average intake | | | | |
|---|---|---|---|---|---|
| Nutrient | 1950 | 1954 | 1958 | 1960 | 1962 |
| Calories | 6 | −0·5* | 6 | 5 | 3 |
| Protein | 8 | 5 | 12 | 13 | 9 |
| Fat | 12 | 9 | 20 | 20 | 13 |
| Calcium | 16 | 11 | 14 | 19 | 16 |
| Iron | 10 | 7 | 9 | 7 | 9 |
| Vitamin A | 30 | 18 | 32 | 30 | 18 |
| Thiamine | 4 | 6 | 12 | 7 | 9 |
| Riboflavin | 20 | 17 | 21 | 23 | 19 |
| Nicotinic Acid | 7 | 8 | 15 | 14 | 17 |
| Vitamin C | 27 | 50 | 45 | 36 | 44 |
| Vitamin D | 22 | 10 | 11 | 4 | 2 |

* Negative figures indicate higher consumption for social class D1

*Source:* Greaves, J. P., and Hollingsworth, D. F., 1966.

## TABLE 3

*Energy Value and Nutrient Content of Household Food Consumption of Households of Different Social Class in the United Kingdom in 1964 (expressed as a percentage of recommended allowances)*

| Nutrient | CLASS | | | | | | | | |
| --- | --- | --- | --- | --- | --- | --- | --- | --- | --- |
| | A1 | A2 | A11 | B | C | D | | | All House-holds |
| | | | | | | Excluding OAP | | OAP | |
| | | | | | | with earners | with-out earners | | |
| Energy Value | 113 | 110 | 111 | 108 | 105 | 107 | 115 | 114 | 108 |
| Total Protein | 118 | 107 | 110 | 104 | 100 | 103 | 113 | 115 | 104 |
| Calcium | 123 | 114 | 116 | 109 | 104 | 102 | 110 | 115 | 108 |
| Iron | 128 | 118 | 120 | 118 | 116 | 114 | 110 | 101 | 118 |
| Vitamin A | 223 | 210 | 213 | 198 | 168 | 180 | 170 | 156 | 193 |
| Thiamine | 144 | 138 | 139 | 131 | 126 | 130 | 141 | 133 | 131 |
| Riboflavin | 138 | 128 | 130 | 118 | 110 | 112 | 123 | 120 | 116 |
| Nicotinic Acid | 175 | 148 | 154 | 144 | 137 | 144 | 152 | 144 | 143 |
| Vitamin C | 329 | 278 | 291 | 239 | 219 | 204 | 237 | 207 | 236 |

*Percentage of Energy Value Derived From Certain Nutrients*

| | | | | | | | | | |
| --- | --- | --- | --- | --- | --- | --- | --- | --- | --- |
| Protein | 12·5 | 11·8 | 11·9 | 11·6 | 11·4 | 11·6 | 11·3 | 11·2 | 11·6 |
| Fat | 43·7 | 42·1 | 42·5 | 40·4 | 39·4 | 38·9 | 39·7 | 40·5 | 40·3 |
| Carbohydrate | 43·7 | 46·0 | 45·5 | 47·9 | 49·0 | 49·3 | 48·8 | 48·2 | 48·0 |

*Percentage of Protein Derived from Animal Protein*

| | | | | | | | | | |
| --- | --- | --- | --- | --- | --- | --- | --- | --- | --- |
| Animal Protein | 67·5 | 63·7 | 64·6 | 60·5 | 57·8 | 57·4 | 59·7 | 60·7 | 60·1 |

*Source: Domestic Food Consumption and Expenditure Survey, 1964, London, HMSO, 1966.*

The reports of the National Food Survey and the Report of the Committee on Nutrition of the British Medical Association express their findings in statistical terms. They deal with average households, average families and average allowances. Those who are concerned with the standard of nutrition for the whole community will not be satisfied merely because average people are adequately fed, but will wish to ensure that, provided a surplus does no harm, the average intake will be so much greater than the average requirements that even the individuals whose intakes are most below average still receive enough.[6]

Doubts also exist regarding the accuracy of the estimates of vitamins and other nutrients available from various foods. For example, the National Food Survey indicates that potatoes provide one-third of the Vitamin C in our diet. However, recent studies have shown that the Vitamin C content of potatoes fluctuates very substantially between samples. Storage may also reduce vitamin value considerably and cooking is always a source of great uncertainty.[7] Thus the quantity of water used in the cooking of vegetables and the length of time they are allowed to cook will have a substantial influence. In the event a potato nine months old will only have a content of Vitamin C a quarter that of a new potato and much of the Vitamin C that remains may be lost in cooking. The National Food Survey figure for the Vitamin C content of potatoes cannot therefore hope to be very precise.

Not only the estimate of intake may be difficult to ascertain accurately. Estimates of requirements vary according to sex, age, degree of activity and other factors (Table 4). Some account can be taken of these influences in estimating average requirements for the family. However, since the recommended intake of calories, protein, niacin, thiamine and riboflavin can change by several hundred per cent according to degree of activity the question of assessing leisure activity arises. Clearly, the keen athlete's requirements will differ from the man whose most active leisure time pursuit is to change the channel of the TV set he is watching, but the problem is how to record this in a national study. Moreover, there is no way of assessing whether the food consumed and therefore the nutrients available for absorption are distributed in a correspondingly correct manner within the family.

Even given the same stature and activity, individual requirements will differ considerably. A number of studies have demonstrated that given a number of individuals the levels at which apparently adequate nutrition can be maintained varies very substantially. The FAO Committee on Protein Requirements defined average

6. *Report of the Panel on Composition and Nutritive Value of Flour*, London, HMSO, 1965.
7. *Vitamin Contents of Modern Dietaries: Losses due to Various Procedures*, Basle, Roche, 1967.

## TABLE 4

*Summary of daily allowances as recommended by the Nutrition Committee of the British Medical Association (1950)*

| Sex/Age | Heaviness of Work | Calories | Protein | Calcium | Iron | Vitamin A and Carotene | Vitamin D | Thiamine | Niacin | Riboflavin | Ascorbic Acid | Iodine |
|---|---|---|---|---|---|---|---|---|---|---|---|---|
| | | | g. | g. | mg. | i.u. | i.u. | mg. | mg. | mg. | mg. | ug. |
| *Both Sexes* | | | | | | | | | | | | |
| 0–1 year | — | 1,000 | 37 | 1·0 | 6·5 | 3,000 | 800 | 0·4 | 4 | 0·6 | 10 | — |
| 2–6 years | — | 1,500 | 56 | 1·0 | 7·5 | 3,000 | 400 | 0·6 | 6 | 0·9 | 15 | 150 |
| 7–10 years | — | 2,000 | 74 | 1·0 | 10·5 | 3,000 | 400 | 0·8 | 8 | 1·2 | 20 | 150 |
| 11–14 years | — | 2,750 | 102 | 1·3 | 13·5 | 3,000 | 400 | 1·1 | 11 | 1·6 | 30 | 150 |
| *Males* | | | | | | | | | | | | |
| 15–19 years | — | 3,500 | 130 | 1·4 | 15·0 | 5,000 | 400 | 1·4 | 14 | 2·1 | 30 | 150 |
| 20 years and over | No work, lying in bed | 1,750 | 51 | 0·8 | 12·0 | 5,000 | — | 0·7 | 7 | 1·0 | 20 | 100 |
| | Sedentary work | 2,250 | 66 | 0·8 | 12·0 | 5,000 | — | 0·9 | 9 | 1·4 | 20 | 100 |
| | Light work | 2,750 | 80 | 0·8 | 12·0 | 5,000 | — | 1·1 | 11 | 1·6 | 20 | 100 |
| | Medium work | 3,000 | 87 | 0·8 | 12·0 | 5,000 | — | 1·2 | 12 | 1·8 | 20 | 100 |
| | Heavy work | 3,500 | 102 | 0·8 | 12·0 | 5,000 | — | 1·4 | 14 | 2·1 | 20 | 100 |
| | Very heavy work | 4,250 | 124 | 0·8 | 12·0 | 5,000 | — | 1·7 | 17 | 2·6 | 20 | 100 |
| | Extremely heavy work | 5,000 | 146 | 0·8 | 12·0 | 5,000 | — | 2·0 | 20 | 3·0 | 20 | 100 |
| *Females* | | | | | | | | | | | | |
| 15–19 years | — | 2,500 | 93 | 1·1 | 15·0 | 5,000 | 400 | 1·0 | 10 | 1·5 | 30 | 150 |
| 20 years and over | No work, lying in bed | 1,500 | 44 | 0·8 | 12·0 | 5,000 | — | 0·6 | 6 | 0·9 | 20 | 100 |
| | Sedentary work | 2,000 | 58 | 0·8 | 12·0 | 5,000 | — | 0·8 | 8 | 1·2 | 20 | 100 |
| | Light work | 2,250 | 66 | 0·8 | 12·0 | 5,000 | — | 0·9 | 9 | 1·4 | 20 | 100 |
| | Medium work | 2,500 | 73 | 0·8 | 12·0 | 5,000 | — | 1·0 | 10 | 1·5 | 20 | 100 |
| | Heavy work | 3,000 | 87 | 0·8 | 12·0 | 5,000 | — | 1·2 | 12 | 1·8 | 20 | 100 |
| | Very heavy work | 3,750 | 109 | 0·8 | 12·0 | 5,000 | — | 1·5 | 15 | 2·2 | 20 | 100 |
| *Pregnancy* | | | | | | | | | | | | |
| First half | — | 2,500 | 93 | 0·8 | 12·0 | 6,000 | 400 | 1·0 | 10 | 1·5 | 40 | 150 |
| Second half | — | 2,750 | 102 | 1·5 | 15·0 | 6,000 | 600 | 1·1 | 11 | 1·6 | 40 | 150 |
| Lactation | — | 3,000 | 111 | 2·0 | 15·0 | 8,000 | 800 | 1·4 | 14 | 2·1 | 50 | 150 |

minimum requirements as 'the smallest amount of protein which will maintain nitrogen balance when the diet is adequate in other respects'.[8] However, as long ago as 1920 Sherman reviewing 109 balance experiments showed that the mean intake required was 44·4g. per 70kg. body weight, but that individual requirements varied between 21 and 65g.[9] A study just reported by Garrow and Pike has suggested that the child whose genetic make-up is such that he would grow very rapidly if well fed, will suffer more on a restricted diet than one with more modest demands. This could explain both the fact that in a given family on a restricted diet some children suffer much less harm than others, and also the tendency of the child who has been successfully treated for malnutrition to outgrow his siblings.[10]

In the light of such opinions, it is not surprising that there is no consensus of opinion even at official levels as to the quantity of nutrients various individuals require. Thus the United States National Research Council (1964) recommended allowance of Vitamin C for adults is 70 milligrams per day whilst the British Medical Association (1950) recommends 20 milligrams per day.[11] This is by far the greatest variation between recommendations, but there are many smaller variations between other items on these two lists. There are also variations on lists produced in other countries. In each case they occur not only for the normal adult, but also for special groups at risk such as the pregnant women or lactating mothers[12] (Table 5). Clearly, there are differences in definition. Thus the US allowances are 'those which will maintain good nutrition in essentially all healthy persons under current conditions of living'. The BMA figures 'are believed to be sufficient to establish and maintain a good nutritional state in representative individuals in the groups concerned. It is recognized that in every group there must be cases where the need for one or other nutrients is greater than that of the average'. In part the variations may also reflect differences in views as to requirements.

Any assessment of the nutritional adequacy of a diet will depend

8. *Protein Requirements: Report of the F.A.O. Committee*, Food and Agriculture Organization, 1957.
9. Sherman, H. C., *Journal of Biological Chemistry*, 41, 1920, pp. 97–109.
10. Garrow, J. S., and Pike, M. C., *The Lancet*, 1, 1967, pp. 1–4.
11. National Research Council, Food and Nutrition Board, *Recommended Dietary Allowances*, National Academy of Sciences, USA, 1964.
12. Marks, J., *The Vitamins in Health and Disease*, London, Churchills, 1967.

TABLE 5

*Variations in recommended daily dietary allowances for certain nutrients during pregnancy and lactation for different countries*

| Nutrient | | USA | GB | W. Germany | USSR |
|---|---|---|---|---|---|
| Vitamin A (i.u.) | normal | 5,000 | 5,000 | 5,000 | 4,500 |
| | pregnancy | 6,000 | 6,000 | 6,000 | 6,600 |
| | lactation | 8,000 | 8,000 | 8,000 | 6,600 |
| Thiamine (mg.) | normal* | 0·8 | 1·1 | 1·7 | 3·0 |
| | pregnancy | 1·0 | 1·1 | 2·1 | 2·5 |
| | lactation | 1·2 | 1·4 | 2·3 | 3·0 |
| Riboflavin (mg.) | normal* | 1·3 | 1·4 | 1·8 | 3·0 |
| | pregnancy | 1·6 | 1·6 | 2·0 | 3·0 |
| | lactation | 1·9 | 2·1 | 2·5 | 3·0 |
| Vitamin C (mg.) | normal | 70 | 20 | 75 | 100 |
| | pregnancy | 100 | 40 | 100 | 100 |
| | lactation | 100 | 50 | 120 | 120 |

* GB rates are those for women occupied in light work.

*Source:* Marks, J., *The Vitamins in Health and Disease*, London, Churchills, 1967.

upon the series of recommendations against which it is rated. Thus if Vitamin C intake in the United Kingdom is expressed as a percentage of US standards it would indicate that the average for all households was 27 per cent *below* recommended allowances instead of 136 per cent *above* when rated against the BMA figures.

All of this means that only a limited and general impression can be obtained from figures of average dietary intake. Such a view has long been held by nutritionists.[13]

If the results of a dietary survey show that the diet has a very low calorie content, the conclusion that the group in question is suffering from under-nutrition is perhaps a legitimate one. But the fact that intake of certain nutrients falls below some recommended allowance does not justify the conclusion that a proportion of any group surveyed is suffering from malnutrition. In such circumstances the possible presence of malnutrition may be inferred, but the dietary survey *per se* provides no evidence of its existence.[14]

13. Hollingsworth, D. F., *Federation Proceedings*, 20, 1961.
14. Norris, T., *F.A.O. Nutritional Studies No. 4*, 1949.

For this and other reasons the members of the National Food Survey Committee have also always stressed the limitations of the Survey as an assessment of nutritional status.

Since the Survey is concerned primarily with food purchases by family units it cannot at the same time provide detailed information on diet and nutrition of individuals. Moreover, with the derationing of food, emphasis has shifted from the nutritional to the economic aspects of the Survey. Thus the results are used for the analysis of demand for food and for making demand projections for administrative purposes. On the nutritional side less interest attaches to the relatively minor changes in the estimates that occur from year to year, than to the study of long term trends. The results are of importance in enabling, for example, calculations to be made of the probable consequences of a change in Government policy concerning the fortification of foods with certain nutrients. With regard to the assessment of nutritional status the Survey has always been recognized as an imprecise instrument, *but it is nevertheless of value in indicating sections of the community which might merit closer investigation by more appropriate methods* (my italics).[15]

## Clinical and Biochemical Evidence

Each year there are references in the medical literature to cases of vitamin and other nutrient deficiencies in the United Kingdom. Such reports are usually limited to fairly clear-cut groups. These are the elderly, often incapacitated or living alone without the means or incentive to provide a diet of any real value, and the poverty-stricken large families. Both groups find it very difficult not only to make ends meet but also to make the maximum use in a nutritional sense of available income; the latter group may even fail to collect subsidized supplements. In a different way, the immigrant who is short of money but has set food habits based on his indigenous diet which is both expensive and relatively difficult to provide for in this country may also be vulnerable. Nutritional deficiencies may also emerge as a secondary response to serious illness, either physical or psychological, which diminish the individual's appetite. In such circumstances the need for certain vitamins may also be increasing.

Nevertheless, it seems that general practitioners believe that nutrient supplements are required by a much greater section of the population than those just mentioned. A study of the morbidity

15. Private communication from the Secretariat of the National Food Survey Committee.

statistics from general practice for 1955/6 indicated that just under one person per thousand was being diagnosed by doctors as suffering from avitaminosis of one type or another. The figure is highest for the young and the old. 5·7 persons per thousand were diagnosed as suffering from iron deficiency anaemia and as might be expected the figure was much greater for women than men, reaching nearly 13 per thousand for women between 15 and 45.[16]

Estimates of prescriptions indicate that 16¾m. prescriptions were issued in the United Kingdom in 1965 for vitamins and other nutrients including iron. Over half of the 16m. is for iron preparations with another 4m. going on tonics which include nutrient supplements and another million going both to multivitamin and B Vitamin tablets. Again the pattern indicates a substantially large number of prescriptions going to women especially of child-bearing age. In both sexes a relatively high percentage goes to the over 65s.[17] Some of these prescriptions may have been used as little more than placebos. But this number compares with only 3m. prescriptions for anti-obesity preparations.

As is indicated by the morbidity statistics perhaps the most widespread deficiency state in this country is iron deficiency anaemia and this may in part be due to malabsorption of nutrients rather than to inadequate intake. In this case the figures indicate very clearly the limitation of the current statistics on consumption. According to the National Food Survey every group of the population is receiving an adequate intake of iron. Yet malabsorption or excessive loss, especially in menstruation, appears to have led to many individuals having anaemia.[18] Indeed, where deficiencies do occur, they may be due just as frequently to the phenomena of malabsorption as to inadequate intake. Certainly the whole issue of malabsorption places a limit on the value of relating nutrient requirements to intake and from this making some pronouncement about nutritional status.

Another problem is to assess how far clinical reports of nutritional deficiencies in the literature represent the only cases within the country. If this is so, they indicate that the problem is very small. On the other hand, many other doctors may not write up reports

16. Logan, W. P. D., and Cushion, A. A., *Morbidity Statistics from General Practice*, London, HMSO, 1958.
17. Private communication from Intercontinental Medical Statistics.
18. It is interesting that the BMA recommend the same allowance for both men and women.

of similar cases. It is possible that the published reports represent only a small minority of the cases.

Many studies are based simply upon biochemical tests. Andrews, Brook and Allen examined 136 subjects aged 59 to 98 years living either at home or in different types of residential care. They showed that there was a significant fall in the leucocyte Vitamin C content of these subjects during the winter and that the majority of the subjects were likely to be receiving less than 30m.g. a day of Vitamin C in their diets. Vitamin C status was significantly inferior in those resident in two hospitals and a large welfare home.[19] In March 1966 Griffiths, Brocklehurst, MacLean and Fry reported on an investigation of ascorbic acid and thiamine blood levels in the elderly. They showed that in Farnborough in Kent 41 per cent of elderly people were deficient in ascorbic acid and 59 per cent deficient in thiamine on admission to hospital. Of people living at home and not ill, or not sufficiently ill for admission to hospital 27 per cent were deficient in ascorbic acid and 22 per cent in thiamine.[20] This particular study is now being extended to assess the impact upon health of improving these nutritional levels.

Studies of this sort have been used to imply directly that many individuals are suffering from malnutrition and consequently facing ill health. This may not be the case. Biochemical tests are important in that they give a clear-cut scientific measurement for use as a yardstick. But the significance of borderline deficiencies as indicated by such tests needs to be established. Thus women with evidence of marginal iron anaemia present no clinical symptoms and are not demonstrably fitter when their haemoglobin levels are improved. Similarly in the diagnosis of diabetes there are many people with a borderline elevation of blood sugar who occupy an intermediate position in terms of pathology between the normal person and the grossly diabetic.

At this stage much research is needed to assess whether or not a biochemical test indicating a low nutrient level is of itself sufficient to justify the term malnutrition; whether such non-specific symptoms as loss of appetite, general malaise, insomnia, increased irritability can be and on occasions are the result of nutritional problems; whether 'sub-optimum' nutrition leads to lowered resistance to infectious disease or to a health problem at a later period of one's

19. Logan, W. P. D., and Cushion, A. A., *op. cit.*
20. Griffiths, L. L., Brocklehurst, J. C., MacLean, R., and Fry, J., *British Medical Journal*, I, 1966, p. 739.

life. For example, it is now agreed that 'the nutritional status of a pregnant woman depends more upon her life experience of diet than upon the nature of the diet she happens to take during pregnancy'.[21]

One of the remarkable things about nutrition is that in the area between chronic deficiency and optimum health, more is known about animals than about man. Thus in animal nutrition a clear distinction is drawn between minimum requirements for health, under which no specific symptoms of deficiency occur, and 'optimum-nutrition' where maximum growth occurs. No study designed to examine whether a similar concept is valid for humans has been undertaken. Indeed it is difficult to assess whether such a study would be realistic because one of the major difficulties is to decide what we mean by 'optimum' health for humans. Does it mean maximum growth, maximum resistance to disease, long life, or what? For animals the issue is usually more clear cut—they are fed for maximum growth, maximum milk yield, or some other specific criterion.

The issue may also be sufficiently imprecise to defy quantification. 'It is relatively simple to establish minimum levels just sufficient to prevent the development of specific overt signs of deficiency, exceedingly difficult to ascertain at what point additional supplies cease to confer additional advantage.'[22] Thus the recent Ministry of Health report on protein requirements commented, 'We have attempted to delineate as closely as possible a gap in our knowledge concerning protein requirements. This gap is bounded at the lower level by what can be derived (albeit with much uncertainty) from the result of balance studies and similar information, and at the upper level by information about the average dietary intake of protein in Britain. Somewhere between these limits which themselves are not precise, lie physiological requirements'.[23] In fact, it may not have been correct in accepting that the present average intake exceeds the optimum physiological level.

To some extent the problem also involves the subjective nature of clinical assessment:

The state of nutrition of the population of this country is such that it is rare to see people with classical signs and symptoms of deficiency

21. Thomson, A. M., *Proceedings of the Nutrition Society*, 16, 1957.
22. Greaves, J. P., *Nutrition Reviews*, 23, 1965.
23. *Requirements of Man for Protein*, London, HMSO, 1964.

diseases. . . . The clinical examination therefore raises not only the problems of the comparability of assessments by different observers and the consistency of assessment by the same observer, but also doubts of the ability of clinicians to detect relatively small changes in the state of nutrition which would not be reflected in specific diagnostic features, but in unspecific elusive and subtle changes.[24]

However, there is no doubt that anthropometric evidence of optimum growth and fitness does demonstrate that health is related to social factors. Health and physique is directly related to social class.[25] As health and physique deteriorates, the percentage of still births and neo-natal death rate increases[26] (Table 6). There is also a good deal of evidence to show that in large families the height of children is less than that for the average, or for 'only children'[27] (Table 7).

## TABLE 6

*Incidence of obstetric abnormalities in Aberdeen primigravidae by maternal health and physique, as assessed at the first antenatal examination (Twin pregnancies have been excluded)*

|  | Health and Physique | | | |
|  | Very Good | Good | Fair | Poor; Very Poor |
| --- | --- | --- | --- | --- |
| Prematurity* (%) | 5·1 | 6·4 | 10·4 | 12·1 |
| Caesarean section (%) | 2·7 | 3·5 | 4·2 | 5·4 |
| Perinatal deaths per 1,000 births | 26·9 | 29·2 | 44·8 | 62·8 |

\* Birth weight of baby 2,500g or less.

*Source:* Thomson and Billewicz (1963).

24. British Medical Association, *Nutrition Committee Report, op. cit.*
25. *Annual Report of the Ministry of Health for the year 1965*, London, HMSO, 1966.
26. Thomson, A. M., and Billewicz, W. Z., *Proceedings of the Nutrition Society*, 22, 1963.
27. Berry, W. T. C., and Hollingsworth, D. J., *Proceedings of the Nutrition Society*, 22, 1963.

## TABLE 7

*Mean height in inches of boys of school or pre-school age in England with no siblings or with three or more*

| Mean Age | Place | No Siblings | Three or more Siblings |
|---|---|---|---|
| 5 years 6·1 months | Croydon | 43·8 | 43·1 |
| | Salford | 43·9 | 42·1 |
| | Exeter | 43·6 | 42·3 |
| | York | 43·4 | 42·7 |
| | Sheffield | 43·8 | 42·1 |
| | Southampton | 43·7 | 42·6 |
| | Lancashire | 44·4 | 42·7 |
| | Nottinghamshire | 44·3 | 43·6 |
| | Northumberland | 43·6 | 43·4 |
| | Gloucester | 44·0 | 43·3 |
| 14 years 6·0 months | Croydon | 64·9 | 63·5 |
| | Salford | 62·8 | 59·8 |
| | Exeter | 65·4 | 62·7 |
| | York | 64·3 | 62·7 |
| | Sheffield | 64·1 | 61·7 |
| | Southampton | 63·9 | 62·1 |
| | Lancashire | 65·0 | 63·0 |
| | Nottinghamshire | 64·1 | 62·9 |
| | Northumberland | 65·1 | 62·8 |
| | Gloucester | 64·5 | 63·9 |
| | Cumberland | 63·6 | 61·2 |

*Source:* Berry and Hollingsworth, 1963.

## Lack of Data

In 1950 the British Medical Association's Report on Nutrition ended in the following way:

> The final assessments of the states of nutrition of the various groups of the population came from a synthesis of the mortality and morbidity, clinical, anthropometric and biochemical data which the committee has considered. Perhaps the first feature of importance which emerges from that synthesis is the patchy nature of the data available, especially in regard to certain population groups, so that it is difficult to speak with certainty concerning them. But this is not surprising since the methods of assessing nutrition in the main are new and still relatively undeveloped; they deserve to be the subject of more investigation and research.

Such a summary would still be a fair one seventeen years later in 1967.

The evidence deduced both from a critical study of the National Food Survey and from the clinical material shows how insufficient is the evidence available on which to assess the nutritional status of the community. There is need to consider whether the National Food Survey should be developed in order to assess more realistically individual intake of nutrients. There is also need to examine the position of individuals such as students in hostels, those in prison and others who are not living in households. If this is not possible within the existing framework then further dietary studies as well as detailed morbidity surveys should be undertaken. Only then will we be able to isolate the percentage of the community suffering from symptoms of deficiency. Above all, there is a need for substantial research into the level of nutrient intake required for the maintenance of health and an assessment of how far this differs from the level required for optimum well-being. Until such work is done, uncertainty as to the precise nature of the position will remain and with it not only the inability adequately to isolate and deal with potentially vulnerable groups but also perhaps an over-readiness to discount any suggestion of malnutrition.

## *Freedom to Choose: The Problem and the Illusion*

It has been demonstrated that even in a country such as the United Kingdom which is relatively proud of the quantity of information it collects about the population, there are visible gaps which need to be filled as well as areas in which considerably more research is needed. However, even if more information is made available and the position becomes much more clear cut, other problems of significance will confront the sociologist attempting to assess the impact of poverty on nutritional status. Even if there is evidence of malnutrition he will need to decide whether this is directly the result of poverty: is a bad diet in nutritional terms due to the individual's financial inability to obtain a better one or simply to his unwillingness to consume a different sort of diet or to give food a higher priority on his list of purchases? Certainly we know that it is possible to survive on a diet costing a shilling a day.[28] Nobody would ask any section of the community to subsist in this way, but whether

28. Miller, D. S., and Mumford, P., *Getting the Most out of Food*, London, 1966.

in fact the individual should be expected to adjust his food choice so as to achieve an adequate nutritional intake within the limits imposed by his financial means is a different issue and one which I would hope will be discussed at this Conference.

It has been indicated earlier that in reality man consumes food whilst his body absorbs nutrients.[29] Yet of course the individual is not equally concerned with both these issues. He is primarily interested in getting a diet that he likes rather than one that is necessarily good for him. The foods he wants are by no means certain to be the ones he needs. Thus it might be argued that a person is at the poverty level irrespective of his nutritional status if his income is so limited that he is unable to have a reasonable opportunity of selecting the foods which he would ideally like.

Some indication of the variety obtained by different groups and the degree to which they are able to choose their 'ideal' diet may be obtained from an examination of:

(a)  Total expenditure on food
(b)  The quantity of particular foods selected and their cost
(c)  The types of food which people want to eat

## Variety of Food Choice in the United Kingdom

It is usually asserted that the proportion of expenditure going on food declines as income rises. This is to some extent supported by an analysis of data from the Family Expenditure Survey (Table 8). However, the 'drop off' is slower than might have been imagined and does not hold true for the lower income groups where the percentage of expenditure attributed to food actually rises as income rises. In money terms, however, such an analysis masks the vast variation in expenditure by different groups. Thus on average a family with an income of under £5 per week spends only £1. 16s. 0d. on food and a family with an income between £5 and £10 only £2. 16s. 0d. This compares with £7. 17s. 0d. for a family earning between £35 and £40 and £8. 16s. 0d. for families whose total income is £40 or more. Perhaps most important of all, the average household expenditure on food is £6. 12s. 0d. Therefore the lowest income group spends only just over a quarter of the average amount on food.

29. Yudkin, J., and McKenzie, J. C., *Changing Food Habits*, London, MacGibbon and Kee, 1964.

## TABLE 8

*Percentage of Average Weekly Expenditure Spent on Food*

| Household Expenditure | Under £5 | £5 but under £10 | £10 but under £15 | £15 but under £20 | £20 but under £25 | £25 but under £30 | £30 but under £35 | £35 but under £40 | £40 or more | All House-holds |
|---|---|---|---|---|---|---|---|---|---|---|
| Percentage spent on food | 33 | 33 | 34 | 34 | 30 | 29 | 28 | 27 | 22 | 28 |

*Source: Report of the Family Expenditure Survey for 1964, London, HMSO, 1965.*

There are also major variations between groups regarding the type of food consumed. Comparing those families where the head of the household earns more than £24 with those where he earns between £9. 10s. 0d. and £15, consumption of milk, eggs, and in particular fruit, is greater for the higher income group. Whereas bread and potato consumption is a good deal higher amongst the lower income groups. Similar variations occur for different sized families[30] (Tables 9 and 10).

## TABLE 9

*Consumption of Various Foods Related to Income*

| | Income of head of household | | | |
|---|---|---|---|---|
| | More than £24 | £9 10s. to £15 | Under £9 10s. | OAP |
| Liquid milk (pints) | 5·6 | 4·5 | 4·3 | 4·9 |
| Meat (ozs) | 40·1 | 36·2 | 38·0 | 36·0 |
| Fruit (ozs) | 43·6 | 25·1 | 22·3 | 24·3 |
| Bread (ozs) | 34·3 | 45·9 | 48·9 | 41·2 |
| Potatoes (ozs) | 47·1 | 60·3 | 60·6 | 42·0 |

*Source: See Table 8*

30. *Malnutrition in the 1960s, op. cit.*, p. 8

TABLE 10

*Consumption of Various Foods Related to Size of Family*

| | Man and Woman with: | | |
| --- | --- | --- | --- |
| | No children | 2 children | 4 or more children |
| Liquid milk (pints) | 5·2 | 5·1 | 4·3 |
| Meat (ozs) | 46·6 | 30·3 | 23·5 |
| Fruit (ozs) | 36·2 | 30·0 | 17·6 |
| Bread (ozs) | 43·2 | 35·6 | 40·9 |
| Potatoes (ozs) | 50·9 | 51·2 | 55·8 |

*Source: See Table 8*

These variations do not necessarily demonstrate unreasonable restriction on selection for those who are less wealthy or with larger families since it is possible that they may select differently on the basis of choice rather than necessity. However, other studies would seem to refute any suggestion of preference for a different diet. In a recent survey I asked housewives to indicate foods they would buy more of if they had a little more money to spend on food. The results were illuminating. The foods most frequently mentioned included milk, meat, eggs and fruit; the very foods where variations exist between different groups (Table 11). A similar picture emerged when the question was reversed and housewives were asked which foods they would hate to do without for a month or so, although here the picture is complicated by the fact that nobody wants to be completely without the major staples (Table 12). Thus even a cursory glance at food choice suggests that there are severe restrictions upon those who have a small income or a number of children.

Some might argue that any major restriction in choice is 'self imposed' by a desire to give other products a higher priority within a limited budget, rather than due to 'real poverty'. When a higher percentage than average of total income is being spent on food and a substantially smaller percentage than average being spent on the so-called luxuries of life, such as alcohol, tobacco, cars, to say nothing of clothing and durable household goods, then such a thesis becomes little more than an illusion[31] (Table 13).

31. *Report of the Family Expenditure Survey for 1964*, London, HMSO, 1965.

TABLE 11

*Foods People would Buy More of if they had More Money*

| Item | Total % | Social Class | | | Children | | Area | |
|---|---|---|---|---|---|---|---|---|
| | | AB % | C₁ % | C₂DE % | With children 15 and under % | Without children under 16 % | South % | North % |
| Meat | 51 | 46 | 48 | 53 | 61 | 42 | 49 | 54 |
| Chicken | 40 | 27 | 38 | 43 | 43 | 39 | 34 | 52 |
| Apples | 28 | 17 | 26 | 30 | 34 | 23 | 28 | 29 |
| Oranges | 28 | 20 | 24 | 30 | 34 | 22 | 27 | 29 |
| Butter | 21 | 12 | 15 | 24 | 20 | 21 | 16 | 30 |
| Fish | 19 | 19 | 16 | 20 | 18 | 20 | 18 | 21 |
| Milk | 14 | 6 | 12 | 16 | 14 | 14 | 12 | 17 |
| Eggs | 14 | 7 | 13 | 15 | 13 | 14 | 12 | 17 |

*Source: See Table 8*

TABLE 12

*Foods People Hate to do Without for a Month or Two*

| Item | Total % | Social Class | | | With children 16 and under % | Without children under 16 % |
|---|---|---|---|---|---|---|
| | | AB % | C₁ % | C₂DE % | | |
| Butter | 58 | 64 | 62 | 56 | 57 | 59 |
| Milk | 58 | 59 | 61 | 56 | 57 | 58 |
| Tea | 54 | 45 | 52 | 55 | 49 | 57 |
| Meat | 50 | 58 | 55 | 47 | 56 | 44 |
| Eggs | 47 | 53 | 53 | 44 | 51 | 43 |
| Sugar | 29 | 27 | 25 | 30 | 33 | 26 |
| Bread | 28 | 23 | 28 | 29 | 29 | 28 |
| Cheese | 27 | 30 | 29 | 26 | 26 | 27 |
| Potatoes | 17 | 14 | 16 | 17 | 20 | 13 |
| Apples | 16 | 21 | 22 | 14 | 16 | 16 |
| Fish | 16 | 22 | 18 | 14 | 14 | 17 |
| Coffee | 15 | 26 | 19 | 12 | 18 | 13 |
| Oranges | 14 | 19 | 17 | 12 | 14 | 14 |

*Source: See Table 8*

TABLE 13

*Percentage of Total Expenditure Spent on Different Items by Households with Different Incomes*

| | Household Income | | |
| --- | --- | --- | --- |
| | Under £5 % | £5 but under £10 % | All households % |
| Housing | 19 | 18 | 11 |
| Fuel, light and power | 14 | 13 | 6 |
| Food | 33 | 33 | 28 |
| Alcoholic drink | 3 | 2 | 4 |
| Tobacco | 3 | 5 | 6 |
| Clothing and footwear | 6 | 6 | 9 |
| Durable household goods | 3 | 4 | 6 |
| Other goods | 6 | 7 | 7 |
| Transport and vehicles | 3 | 4 | 11 |
| Services | 9 | 8 | 11 |

*Source: See Table 8*

Thus poverty can be demonstrably shown to be curtailing food choice; curtailing choice in an area in which man is particularly vulnerable for we are all intensely involved emotionally with food. This is partly because it is so vital to our very existence. We are very aware that if we do not eat and drink we are not going to stay alive for very long. Food is also one of the very first means by which we demonstrate our mood and individuality; thus a baby demands food and then perhaps rejects it; it asserts its personality by demanding particular foods and rejecting others. As we grow older, simply because we eat three meals every day, we come to regard ourselves as experts on the subject. In the same way, food asserts itself as an integral part of our culture and many social events in our lives take place round the meal table.[32]

It would be unfortunate if today one per cent of the population of the United Kingdom face very real poverty every time they turn to the meal table or open their larder door. Yet evidence such as that indicated above suggests that at least 10 per cent may be affected in this way.

3. McKenzie, J. C., *Proceedings of the Nutrition Society*, 26, 1967.

## Conclusion

The tools required for measuring poverty specifically in terms of food consumption are clear and in the case of the United Kingdom are readily available. The assessment of malnutrition is complicated not only by lack of data but also by the limitations of current nutritional knowledge and the lack of precise methods of assessment. Further research and the collection of information is a matter of top priority.

The evidence at present available concerning the United Kingdom indicates that there is a major restriction on food choice of those with low incomes or with large families. The fact that the evidence is too imprecise to indicate whether or not malnutrition still exists should not lead us too readily to assume by inference that because of this the case for no malnutrition has been conclusively proven.

# 4. The Problem of Establishing Equivalent Standards of Living for Families of Different Composition

## Brian Abel-Smith and Christopher Bagley

What criteria should be used to decide whether two households of different composition are at the same standard of living? Given a poverty line for a household consisting of husband and wife, how much extra is needed for children of different ages to provide the same standard of living? The question arises whatever method is used for establishing the original poverty line.

A solution to this problem is needed not only to make possible measures of poverty but also to operate programmes which attempt to combat poverty with cash grants. In both research and policy, much more attention has tended to be devoted to establishing the poverty level than to securing equity between different types of household. For example, the early crude calculations of the numbers of the poor in the USA virtually ignored the problem altogether. Though many countries do not have the elimination of poverty as the sole or necessarily the principal aim of their social security policy, the lack of equity in the treatment of households of different composition is a remarkable feature of most income maintenance programmes.

### Equity in Social Security Policy

Bagley[1] has demonstrated the anomalous provisions for children within existing British provisions for social security. There are three sets of provisions for children. The first—national assistance (now supplementary benefit)—is subject to a test of means. The second is benefit as of right which comes in two parts—family allowances for all second and subsequent children and national insurance benefits available only for children of the sick, unemployed etc. The third

1. Bagley, C., *The Cost of a Child*, London, Institute of Psychiatry, 1969.

consists of allowances for children in the income tax. The first and third but not the second provide allowances which differ according to the age of the child. The second (and in certain circumstances the third) vary the allowances according to the number of children in the family.

From 1948 onwards the National Assistance Board (now the Supplementary Benefits Commission) has employed a uniform national basic scale for calculating the needs of household members. This scale represents the minimum level of living which is normally provided to those who apply for help and have no other resources. The subsistence scale has been revised periodically to take account of changes in prices and on occasions changes in the national income. The scale excludes rent for which separate provision is made. The highest and lowest ratios established within the scale for different household members between 1948 and 1965 are shown in Table 1 as a percentage of the allowance for a married couple.

The National Assistance Board increased the benefits for a married couple (excluding rent) by 18–19 per cent for a child under 5, 22–3 per cent for a child aged 5–10, 26–8 per cent for a child aged 11–15. The same percentages are used irrespective of the number of persons in the household. The variations between the highest and lowest percentages for each age group cannot be explained by price changes or by the desire to round each allowance figure to the nearest 6d. The Board has never explained precisely how it calculates its allowances.

TABLE 1

*Highest and Lowest National Assistance Ratios*
*1948–1965*

(Percentages of rate for married couple)

| | Highest | | Lowest | |
|---|---|---|---|---|
| | Year | Percentage | Year | Percentage |
| Married Couple | | 100 | | |
| Single Person | 1963 | 60·8 | 1959 | 58·8 |
| Other household member: | | | | |
| Aged 21 or over | 1961 | 55·0 | 1948 | 50·0 |
| 18–20 | 1952 | 44·1 | 1965 | 41·0 |
| 16–17 | 1948 | 37·5 | 1958 | 34·2 |
| 11–15 | 1950 | 27·6 | 1948 | 26·2 |
| 5–10 | 1956 | 23·1 | 1965 | 21·5 |
| − 5 | 1956 | 19·4 | 1965 | 17·9 |

The benefits as of right (national insurance plus family allowances) provided in 1965 allowances for children at the following percentages of the married couple allowance: first and second child 17 per cent, third and subsequent children 19 per cent. These ratios have also varied widely over the years. The first child rate was as high as 24 per cent in 1951. The rate for six children has varied between 77 per cent in 1948 and 122·5 per cent in 1958. In some years certain rates for national insurance have been above those for national assistance: more often the rates for national assistance have been above those for national insurance. In 1965, six children (aged 2, 3, 5, 7, 11 and 15) would have led to a supplement to national assistance benefits of 132·3 per cent of the married couple benefit and to national insurance benefits of 110 per cent of the married couple benefit. The difference is logical as national insurance embodies an allowance for rent while national assistance treats rent separately. But it has the result that there is a greater need for a large family to apply for national assistance than a small family.

Allowances for wives and children are also provided in the income tax. These allowances are larger than those either in national assistance or in benefit as of right. A single person in 1965 received an allowance at the rate of 60 per cent of the married couple rate. A child up to 11 had an allowance of 21·5 per cent of the married couple; a child 12–15 at the rate of 26·7 per cent, and a child of 16 or over at the rate of 41 per cent. Thus a family of six children of the ages specified above would earn allowances in the income tax of 218 per cent of the rate for a married couple compared to 132 per cent in national assistance and 110 per cent in benefit as of right.

In the United States, the additions for children under the assistance programme vary in the different states. In New York, only 10 per cent of the main benefit is added for each dependant. The Swedish system of social assistance also provides lower proportionate benefits for children than are found in Britain. While a single person receives 61 per cent of the married couple allowance, the first child receives 18 per cent, the second and third child 14 per cent and the fourth and fifth child 12 per cent. Rent is handled separately as in Britain. In Western Germany allowances for children are higher than in the other countries we have mentioned. A child aged 0–6 earns an allowance of 23·8 per cent of the married couple's allowance according to geographical area of residence; the allowance for a child aged 7–13 varies from 39 per cent to 41 per cent of the married couple's allowance; the allowance for a child aged 14–17 varies between 46 per cent and 50 per cent of the married couple's allowance.

The Germans have recognized that different price relativities justify different allowances for children in different parts of the country. It is likely that different rates should exist in different countries for similar reasons. But the rates actually found in the various countries cannot be explained in this way. How have the various scales been constructed? How much should allowances differ between children and married couples? How much should allowances vary according to the age of a child? How much should allowances be adjusted according to the number of children in the family?

## The Subjective Approach

Peter Townsend has discussed the subjective method of evolving poverty scales which has been traditionally used in Britain and in many other countries. Poverty is seen as insufficient income to purchase a particular basket of goods regarded as 'necessary'. Minimum needs are determined by subjective judgement supported in the case of nutrition by professional knowledge. From this approach to poverty measurement, answers to the problem of equity for different households emerge fairly easily. Thus the extra food costs of each household member can be calculated on the basis of assumed nutritional requirements, taking account of the customary diets which meet these requirements. An allowance can be added for the clothing of each additional household member and a variety of means can be used to calculate the value of this allowance. Thus the number of necessary clothing purchases per annum can be worked out and the schedule priced either at the minimum prices for new articles or at current secondhand prices. To the resultant figure an addition can be made for repairs—particularly boot or shoe repairs. Alternatively, the lowest quartile of clothing expenditure found in household expenditure surveys can be used. Other specific items can be included or a general individual or household allowance can be added to cover other needs, inefficient spending etc.

Even as a crude measure of what individuals or households need for minimum physical subsistence, such calculations involve a considerable element of subjectivity. The nutritional data lack scientific precision. The acceptance of customary diets and clothing fashions introduces further imprecision and lack of objectivity and the additional allowances are almost wholly arbitrary. Moreover, the whole concept of physical efficiency tends to be used without consideration of the effects of psychological deprivation on work efficiency.

It would seem likely that it is easier to make subjective judgements about need in a poorer than in a more affluent society. What were the ratios for the needs of different household members which were derived from such studies? Rather than go right back to the earliest studies at the turn of the century, let us look at the standards evolved in the late 1930s. The standard which Rowntree used in 1936 for his second survey of York[2] was more 'humane' than his 1901 standard: there was a more generous allowance for household sundries. He gave single persons an allowance of 81 per cent of that for married couples—much higher than that which was later to be used in social security benefits. His allowances for children were, however, very low. The first child was given 19 per cent of the married couple rate, the second child 10 per cent, the third 7 per cent and the fourth 17 per cent. In the study Rowntree conducted in 1950,[3] the rates were very different. A single person was given 67 per cent, first and second children 26 per cent and other children 25 per cent of the married couple scale. From the explanations given by Rowntree it is not possible to explain why these allowances for children were so much higher—particularly as the food standard was only slightly altered between the two yaers.

Similar in method were the calculations made by Beveridge in his report of 1942. He calculated the cost in 1938 prices of minimally nutritious diets adequate for health using League of Nations data. He added allowances for expenditure on clothing, fuel, light and sundries, plus a marginal allowance. In producing the scale a study was made of the 1937–8 Ministry of Labour survey of the expenditure of working class families. Taking no account of rent, he calculated that a single man needed 57 per cent of the married couple allowance. His allowances for children varied according to age. A child aged 0–4 warranted an allowance of 24 per cent of the married couple's allowance; a child aged 5–9, 32 per cent; a child aged 10–13, 37 per cent; a child aged 14–15, 41 per cent. These allowances for children are much larger than those used by Rowntree or those actually introduced within the Social Security scheme.

2. Rowntree, B. S., *Poverty and Progress*, London, Longmans Green, 1941.
3. Rowntree, B. S., *Poverty and the Welfare State*, London, Longmans Green, 1951.

While in theory it would seem likely that there would have been a wide measure of agreement on the relative needs of different household members in the less affluent period immediately before and after the second world war, there were in fact wide variations. One would expect there to be even wider variations in attempts to establish relative needs in a more affluent society. A brave attempt to produce a minimum budget in an affluent society is the US Bureau of Labor Statistics' 'modest but adequate' City Workers' Family Budget. The budget provides 'the goods and services necessary to a healthful, self-respecting mode of living,' allowing normal participation in the life of the community in accordance with current American standards. Social and conventional as well as physiological needs are taken into account.[4] The budget is derived from an analysis of consumer expenditure. 'The quantities of various items purchased at successive income levels are examined to determine the income level at which the rate of increase in quantities purchased begins to decline in relation to the rate of change in income, i.e. the point of maximum elasticity'.[5] The rates of allowance for children derived by this method as a percentage of the married couple rate were first child (aged 6–16) 31·8 per cent varying in different cities and suburbs; second child 19·7 per cent; third child 30·3 per cent.[6]

## Attempts to Find Objective Criteria

The use of income elasticities in the 'modest but adequate' budget represents one attempt to introduce an objective element into the selection of allowances for different household members. A number of different approaches to this question have been made in Britain.

In 1949, Nicholson published the results of an analysis of data collected in the 1937–8 survey of 704 working class budgets conducted by the Ministry of Labour. He attempted to study how much expenditure on particular goods varied in families of different composition. He calculated regression coefficients between expenditure on particular items, and total income, and investigated how differences in family size affected the various regression lines. He pointed out that the methods he used were experimental, and that the data

4. Orshansky, M., 'Budgets for an Elderly Couple', *Social Security Bulletin*, No. 12, December, 1960, pp. 20–27.
5. *Ibid.*, p. 34.
6. Haber, A., 'Poverty Budgets: How Much is Enough', *Poverty and Human Resources Abstracts*, 1966, 1, pp. 5–22.

on which he worked were deficient in that the number of large families was too small for reliable estimates to be made about their expenditure patterns.

He concluded that:

> When the figures for any given set of families, containing 0, 1 or 2 children were examined, it was found that the relations between E and Y [expenditure on a good and total expenditure] could not, in general, be represented by simple linear equations . . . there is definite evidence, in some cases (e.g. food) of a curvilinear relationship; while in other cases (e.g. rent) the points are rather widely dispersed, and it is probably not possible to say definitely that the relationship is non-linear.

Nicholson compared expenditure by families with differing numbers of children on various goods, at three income levels—50s., 72s. 8d. and 100s. a week. At 50s. a week, as the number of children increased, more was spent on food. The amount on dairy products went up, but in fact the amount spent on meat actually declined as the families in this income group had more children.

At 72s. 8d. a week, the amount spent on food showed a substantial rise with family size; expenditure on fuel and light showed little change; that on clothing a slight increase, and that on sundries a marked decline. With the food expenditure, the amount spent on dairy products increased with family size, the amount of fruit and vegetables stayed the same, while the amount on meat only rose when the number of children increased to three. The pattern when income was 100s. a week was similar, except that expenditure on dairy products showed a particularly marked increase as family size went up.

Nicholson then categorized 'necessities' as products on which the proportion of income expended on them declined as income rose, and 'luxuries' as products on which expenditure rose, as income rose. By this definition rent, fuel and light, and dairy products were necessities, and meat, fruit and vegetables, tobacco and drink were luxuries. Meat was less of a 'luxury' than fruit and vegetables. The categorization of these last two products as 'luxuries' underlines the fact that these figures were derived from what working class families actually spent, and not from any nutritional standards for basic health.

Having established a series of regression lines between expenditure on various goods, and total income, for families of different income,

Nicholson then attempted to calculate the additional budget outlay caused by an additional child. In order to make this calculation Nicholson had to assume that some expenditure was entirely for adults only, and did not vary as the number of children in the family varied—as the author admitted, this was not a very realistic assumption. However, '. . . without a much more thorough knowledge of family spending habits than we have at present, it is impossible to make any allowances for differences of this kind'.

Nicholson considered three different but overlapping kinds of adult expenditure: on men's and women's clothes, tobacco, drink and sundries; on men's and women's clothes—with the additional expenditure made when a child, or children were added to the family, at different income levels. He concluded that at the average standard of living, the amount spent on a married couple alone was 63s.; on a couple plus one child 79s.; on a couple plus two children 89s. These calculations showed that the first child added another 16 per cent. Nicholson stressed that these figures were estimates only, based on averages, and made no allowance for the sex or age of the child.

In pointing to the difficulties of making such a study, Nicholson commented that in the family expenditure data on which he was working:

. . . Some items, of course, are consumed jointly by adults and children (e.g. most meals), and in such cases it would clearly be difficult, if not impossible, to find out exactly how much is consumed by each person. But a family budget enquiry in which householders were carefully instructed to keep separate accounts (so far as possible) for adults and children, and to give full details of all meals consumed by each member of the family, should enable a reasonably good estimate to be made of expenditure which is due to the child. Until such a special enquiry is organized, it will not be possible to obtain any really accurate information on this problem.

Nicholson's comment was made in 1949, but it still remains relevant for the present day. No family expenditure survey has provided data suitable for the calculation of accurate, comprehensive equivalence ratios.

Further attempts have been made by Nicholson to calculate equivalence ratios from budget expenditure data. He calculated an equivalent adult scale, by the simple method of comparing the levels of income in 1961 at which different types of family spend the same proportion of net household income on food. The results showed a single person requiring 54 per cent of the income of a married couple. The rates for children were: first child 31 per cent, second child 24 per cent, third child 20 per cent and fourth child 18·5 per cent.

A variant of this last method is used by Orshansky for relating families of three or more persons in the United States.[7] However, her calculation was based not on actual food expenditure but on the 'economy food plan' prepared by the Department of Agriculture for 'temporary or emergency use when funds are low'. The food allowances in this plan are adjusted for the age and sex of household members and some adjustment is included for economies of scale. For households of *three or more* members Orshansky sets the poverty line as an income of three times the cost of the economy food plan for that household. The multiplicator of three was used because there was reported in a survey in 1955 'for all families of *two or more* . . . an expenditure for food approximating one-third of money income after taxes'. For families with two members the ratio of 27 per cent was used as was found in the 1955 survey among non-farm households. The ratio for one-person families was taken as 72 per cent of the allowance for couples 'following BLS recent practice'. It is of interest to observe that lower proportions of food expenditure were allowed for one and two person families than the standard proportion allowed for families of three or more persons.

The Orshansky method of measuring poverty is a combination of subjective and objective elements. The food standard from which she works is low. It is for temporary or emergency use; it is 75–80 per cent of the Department of Agriculture's low-cost plan: 'Meals eaten by family members at school or on the job, whether purchased or carried from home, must still come out of the same household food allowance.' While the plan, 'if strictly followed, can provide an acceptable and adequate diet', the low-cost plan involves 'restricted kinds and qualities of food' and 'skill in marketing and food preparation'. It is implicitly assumed that men generate more need for non-food spending than women and that this need amounts to three times the cost of the additional food they are entitled to in the low-cost food plan. It is implicitly assumed that in families of three or more persons economies of scale in non-food expenditure are proportional to economies in scale in food expenditure.

The method used for determining levels of public assistance in

7. Orshansky, M., 'Counting the Poor: Another Look at the Poverty Profile', *Social Security Bulletin*, XXVIII, No. 1, January, 1965.

Japan is essentially the same as the Orshansky method of measuring poverty in the United States. The method was introduced in Japan in 1961. 'Estimates are first made of the cost of food requirements and then an Engels coefficient is applied to calculate the total consumption of a standard household. This method recognizes the freedom of consumer choice as to the pattern of consumption within a given income. It also implies that the diversity of goods and services consumed, even at the public assistance standard of living, has increased so much that item-by-item enumerations cannot adequately cover the whole consumption pattern.'[8]

A number of general comments can be made about attempts to calculate adult equivalence scales from budget data. As Nicholson has stressed, calculations of this kind can only be as reliable as the data on which they are based. The procedures for collecting survey data in Britain involve the keeping of a diary for two to three weeks. This in itself reduces the response rate and introduces a particular selective element in the respondents. The Ministry of Labour has consistently achieved response rates of around 80 per cent but among non-respondents the aged, infirm and chronic sick are disproportionately represented. One suspects also that those with more limited budgetary and recording skills are also likely to be under-represented. Secondly, there is a wide divergence between the income and expenditure of households with low levels of living.[9] Thus while the data where aggregated may conform with other data of expenditure on the main items of goods and services, the distribution of expenditure between particular types of household may be distorted.

Secondly, attempts to calculate adult equivalence based on expenditure incurred by adults on themselves run up against further problems of data accuracy. Expenditure on tobacco and alcohol inevitably play an important role in such calculations. Such items are notoriously difficult to ascertain correctly in expenditure surveys: only about half the actual expenditure on alcohol and about three-quarters of the expenditure on tobacco is generally recorded.

Thirdly, there are difficulties in comparing like with like if comparisons are made between married couples with children and

8. Taira, K., *Country Reports: Japan*, International Trade Union Seminar on Low Income Groups and Methods of Dealing with their Problems, OECD, 1965.
9. See Abel-Smith, B., and Townsend, P., *The Poor and the Poorest*, London, Bell, 1965, pp. 75–78.

all married couples without children in the population. The bulk of married couples without children are middle-aged and elderly. In most cases their expenditure on themselves is affected by the long period during which they have had the care of dependent children. For example, they may be out of the habit of going out much in the evening. Their expenditure patterns are also influenced by their less affluent youth. Thus it seems more appropriate to look at married couples of roughly the same age span. But once again the group is heterogeneous: it includes couples who have married late or postponed the start of child-rearing to a later age than average: it includes also couples who have decided not to raise a family or have been unable to do so. Whichever group of childless married couples one chooses to regard as comparable for an adult equivalent scale, the whole process involves major value assumptions which need to be brought out into the open and examined.

The care of children, and particularly young children, involves parents in a major change in their way of life. The obligations of family life reduce the time which can be devoted to hobbies and reduce the extent to which parents can purchase meals away from home and pay for entertainment outside the home. Thus one would expect parents with children to be able to spend less on 'entertainment', to 'need' a less varied or fashionable wardrobe and to find day trips and holidays more difficult to arrange. Normally, parents can be said to have chosen to start a family and therefore, in a sense, to regard themselves as compensated to some extent for the resultant obligations and restrictions. The concept of equivalent adult expenditure implies that children are exclusively an economic burden and that parents have the same need, desire and ability to spend on themselves as married couples without children.

What is really meant by the same standard of living for couples with children and couples without? Carried to its logical conclusion it could mean that parents must spend on themselves precisely the same amount as couples without children. How is expenditure on a baby sitter to be classified? Such household aids as dishwashers and clothes washers become more 'needed' as household size grows, how are such 'indivisibles' to be allocated? Joint outings which include the children may replace outings of married couples only. Are such expenditures to be disregarded in calculating adult equivalences? The addition of children to a household changes its whole way of life. Before and after comparisons do not seem very meaningful.

If expenditure equivalence were used to try and relate men without wives to men with wives, similar and perhaps stronger objections of the same kind could be made. If young married men were compared with unmarried men of the same age, it would be found that a considerable proportion of the latter's expenditure was devoted to expenditures associated with courting. Such costs are not incurred on the same scale once a marital partner has been found.

Similar objections can be raised to the use of the percentage of household expenditure devoted to food as a means of establishing that households are at the same level of living. It is probable, however, that such data will be subject to fewer data errors. Food expenditure seems to be more likely to be reported correctly than expenditure incurred exclusively on adults. However, it seems particularly dangerous to compare the average of *all* households without children with households which include children for making this calculation, as the former will include a disproportionate number of elderly persons. The latter may need less food and more fuel. On the other hand, they may spend less on entertainment outside the home than younger couples.

The underlying assumption is that the needs of adults for non-food expenditure are proportionately the same as for children. Why should this be so? It is likely that there are economies of scale in both the food and non-food sectors of household management. There is probably less food waste in a large family than in a small one. Larger packs of food can be bought. The same amount of fuel and light can be used for a large family as for a small one. Clothes can be handed on within the family. Accommodation with extra rooms may be obtained without a proportionate increase in expenditure. Why should the economies of scale be the same in the food and non-food sectors?

It would seem valuable to see what actually happens in practice. Would it be possible to divide household expenditure into four categories:

A. Value of adult food consumption.
B. Adult non-food expenditure including household overhead expenditures which would need to be incurred if there were no children.
C. Value of child food consumption.
D. Child non-food expenditure including any addition to household overheads which they have generated.

If such a division could be made would we find that $\frac{B}{A} = \frac{D}{C}$? If these ratios were equal the percentage of expenditure on food would be an acceptable way of relating the level of living of households of different composition. It would however be extraordinarily difficult to identify the variables A and B in a survey. While this might be an acceptable tool for determining relativities among households with children, it seems more questionable for determining relationships with households without children.

As a method of establishing equivalent standards of living for households of different composition, the percentage of expenditure on food has a number of obvious advantages. Whatever the underlying assumptions, at least it is based on the actual behaviour of consumers rather than on their assumed behaviour. Secondly, it can be relatively easily re-calculated as new data on consumer expenditure patterns become available. In this sense it is a dynamic rather than a static criterion which adjusts to changing behaviour. Thirdly, it is theoretically capable of great refinements, though large expenditure surveys would be needed to produce them. As we have seen the old subjective scales for children incorporated adjustments for family size or for age of child but not for both. It is possible to produce calculations for both variables from food expenditure/total expenditure data.

Nicholson's data for Britain in 1961 showed that the additional expenditure which a married couple needed to incur for a first child was 31 per cent, for a second child 24 per cent, for a third child 20 per cent. Under the British social insurance scheme, including family allowances, a married couple received a supplement in 1965 of 17 per cent for the first or second child and 19 per cent for a subsequent child. Nicholson's data suggest that these allowances are too low to preserve equity between different households in receipt of benefits. In other words, a household living on benefit which includes children will spend a substantially higher proportion of its income on food than a household without children. If the level of assistance provided *to a married couple* is accepted as the 'official' poverty line, the application of assistance scales to households with children results in a serious under-estimation of the number of children in poverty. In other words, the generally accepted figure of half a million children in poverty in Britain in 1966 is by this criterion considerably too low.

In conclusion, the percentage of expenditure on food appears to be the most promising tool for equating families of different composition. Work is therefore needed to refine this tool so that comparisons are made between households where the adults are in the same group and to examine the expenditure patterns on non-food items in households judged by this criterion to be at the same level of living.

# 5. Measures of Income and Expenditure as Criteria of Poverty *

## Peter Townsend

---

Statements about the extent of poverty in a society usually depend on obtaining information about living standards from a sample of households in that society. First, this information is difficult to collect, particularly (though for different reasons) from the poorest and from the richest households. Second, the living standards of a disturbingly large number of households seem to be understated or overstated, whichever criteria are adopted. Again, this seems to be true more often of the richest and of the poorest households than of those households around the median of wealth. Third, different criteria of living standards tend to lead to different results. Some households that would be classed in poverty on the basis of their expenditure would not be classed in poverty on the basis of their income, and vice versa. Finally, the financial resources of households fluctuate and at any single time there will be some whose resources are unusually low and others whose resources are unusually high. On what grounds, and after what period, would it be justifiable to categorize some of these households as temporarily in poverty, and others as temporarily out of poverty?

I shall try to illustrate and discuss these various problems with the aim of making specific recommendations for a future survey of living standards. In doing so I shall describe some of the results of income and expenditure surveys in the United Kingdom.

## The Family Expenditure Surveys

The Family Expenditure Survey (as it is called) is a continuing annual inquiry into the expenditure of private households in the United Kingdom which was started in 1957. The first national survey of this kind to be undertaken after the war was carried out

* Based on a draft paper prepared for a meeting of the International Committee on Poverty Research, Paris, 30th September, 1965.

in 1953–4. The Ministry of Labour (now the Department of Employment and Productivity) is responsible for the inquiry, though the fieldwork is carried out by the Government Social Survey. Between 1957 and 1966 about 5,000 addresses were selected each year and eventually about 3,500 households provided information. In 1967 the sample was increased to about 11,000 addresses. Information is based upon interviews and budget records (for which each adult member of the household is paid £1). The objects of the survey are to help the task of compiling official estimates of national expenditure; to provide information to allow the weights of the Retail Price Index to be reviewed; to allow demand analyses to be carried out and (more recently) to allow the redistributive effects on income of taxation and social benefits to be studied. Further accounts of the methods are given elsewhere.[1]

## The Phenomenon of the Expenditure Surplus

Serious efforts are made in the Family Expenditure Survey to obtain accurate data on income. Care is taken, it is said, to cover all sources.

The first part of the income schedule asks for information about employment status, occupation and industry in which the member of the household is employed; the remainder is devoted to income and covers all sources. The 1953 survey used a relatively simple income schedule which, in the light of experience, has gradually been expanded to ensure that all sources are covered, including income from investments and benefits from the State. The part of this schedule now devoted to income takes up three pages. It includes questions about income tax so that income can be calculated both net and gross of tax, and also questions about income of any member of the household under 16 to ensure that the income of the whole household is covered. Windfall payments such as legacies or paid up insurance policies are excluded.[2]

Expenditure information is gained partly by interview (chiefly to cover annual or quarterly payments, such as rates and payments for gas and electricity bills) but also by each adult member of a

---

1. See the Reports of the Family Expenditure Survey published by HMSO. See also Kemsley, W. F. F., 'Expenditure Surveys: Descriptions of the Sample, Fieldwork Procedure and Response Rate', in the *Report of the Committee of Inquiry into the Impact of Rates on Households* (The Allen Report), Cmnd. 2582, London, HMSO, Appendix 2.
2. Kemsley, W. F. F., *op. cit.*, p. 151.

household completing a diary record book over a period of fourteen days.

Yet expenditure exceeds income for all income groups. Table 1 compares gross income with gross expenditure for 1967, the latest year for which data exist.[3] With the exception of the highest group, it will be seen that the excess of expenditure over income tends to be greatest for the lowest income groups.[4] For the income groups falling in the ranges of £20–£60 per week, nearly two-thirds of the households in the sample, the excess ranges from only 2 to 10 per cent.

TABLE 1

*Average Gross Income and Average Gross Expenditure of Different Household Income Groups in the U.K., 1967*

| Income per week | Average gross income in shillings | Average gross expenditure in shillings | Expenditure as % of income |
|---|---|---|---|
| Under £6 | 103·40 | 128·56 | 124 |
| £6 but under £8 | 137·09 | 198·77 | 145 |
| £8 but under £10 | 179·05 | 209·62 | 117 |
| £10 but under £15 | 250·75 | 283·29 | 113 |
| £15 but under £20 | 352·90 | 417·52 | 118 |
| £20 but under £25 | 450·19 | 494·61 | 110 |
| £25 but under £30 | 549·64 | 599·78 | 109 |
| £30 but under £35 | 647·03 | 686·97 | 106 |
| £35 but under £40 | 747·97 | 779·69 | 104 |
| £40 but under £50 | 887·42 | 950·77 | 107 |
| £50 but under £60 | 1,088·97 | 1,115·04 | 102 |
| £60 or more | 1,666·12 | 2,028·55 | 122 |

3. Department of Employment and Productivity, *Family Expenditure Survey Report for 1967*, London, HMSO, 1968, Table 2.
4. There are of course fluctuations in the pattern from year to year. Generally the excess is considerable for the lowest one or two income groups and is least for the highest income groups. For 1963, for example, there was an excess of expenditure over income of 67 per cent for the lowest income group, but an excess of income over expenditure of 3 per cent for the highest income group. Ministry of Labour, *Family Expenditure Survey, Report for 1963*, London, HMSO, 1965, Table 2.

TABLE 2

*Average Gross Income and Average Gross Expenditure of*
*Different Household Income Groups, Cambridgeshire, 1953–4*

| Income per annum | Average gross income £ | Average gross expenditure £ | Expenditure as % of income |
|---|---|---|---|
| Under £150 | 117 | 181 | 155 |
| £151–£260 | 208 | 275 | 132 |
| £261–£420 | 366 | 480 | 131 |
| £421–£620 | 518 | 633 | 122 |
| £621–£830 | 720 | 869 | 121 |
| £831–£1,040 | 941 | 1,061 | 113 |
| £1,041–£1,560 | 1,242 | 1,527 | 123 |
| £1,561 or more | 2,469 | 2,458 | 100 |

The phenomenon of a surplus of expenditure over income is neither new nor peculiar to the United Kingdom. It was observed in England by Sir Frederick Eden at the end of the eighteenth century,[5] and by Rowntree and others at the end of the nineteenth century.[6] It was discussed in an important paper by Cole and Utting, published in 1956, which also gave the results of a survey of a sample of over 3,000 households in Cambridgeshire which had established household expenditure, income and saving with particular care.[7] Table 2 gives an extract from their data. The total expenditure figures for the Cambridgeshire Survey, unlike those for the Family Expenditure Survey, were reduced to allow for dissaving. For the lowest income group dissaving represented about 12 per cent of total expenditure. Even so, expenditure for the lowest income group exceeded income by 55 per cent.

## Implications for Surveys of Poverty

In the late 1950s social scientists in the United Kingdom began to take greater interest in contemporary poverty. The possibility of re-analysing the data collected by the Ministry of Labour seemed to be an economical first step before a special survey needed to be

5. Eden, Sir F. M., *The State of the Poor*, abridged edition by Rodgers, London, Routledge, 1928.

6. Rowntree, B. S., *Poverty: A Study of Town Life*, London, Macmillan, 1901.

7. Cole, D., and Utting, J. E. G., 'Estimating Expenditure, Saving and Income from Household Budgets', *Journal of the Royal Statistical Society*, Series A, General, Vol. 119, Part IV, 1956, pp. 371–387.

commissioned. A special analysis of the data collected in 1953–4 and in 1960 was undertaken by Professor Abel-Smith and myself.[8] When a first draft of this secondary analysis was prepared and sent to readers some were inclined to dispute the cautious conclusion that poverty as defined by national assistance standards had increased between 1953–4 and 1960 in the United Kingdom.

We had been advised by the Ministry of Labour that the income data for 1953–4 were incomplete and unreliable and hence we depended primarily upon expenditure data for conclusions reached about the distribution of standards of living. But a similar procedure was difficult to apply to 1960. Total expenditure was extraordinarily difficult to compile. Total expenditure and sub-totals of expenditure were not given for each household in the Ministry records but only itemized expenditure for large aggregates of households. To compile individual household expenditure meant recording each item of expenditure by hand from special sheets. The individual household's serial number had to be traced from sheet to sheet. Not surprisingly we chose instead to analyse the income data for that year in order to reach conclusions about the distribution of standards of living. We believed that comparisons could be drawn between the results for the two years, although careful reservations had to be made.

Our critics, however, were not convinced that data for the two years could be compared with any confidence. As a consequence we carried out the laborious task of tracing tiny amounts of expenditure for a small sub-sample of households. The Ministry was able to provide information for all 60 households in the sample with an income of under £3. In addition we analysed data for 212 households drawn at random from the households included in relatively low income groups. The overall results were within the limits we had predicted but the individual distribution caused us to begin thinking seriously about some questions involving the measurement of household resources. This chapter arises from our belief that there needs to be a thorough-going review of the methods by which the financial resources of the poor are measured.

Table 3 shows how many persons in the United Kingdom were living below a 'national assistance' standard of living in 1960, on

8. Abel-Smith, B., and Townsend, P., *The Poor and Poorest*, London, Bell, 1965. See also preliminary reports: Townsend, P., 'The Meaning of Poverty', *British Journal of Sociology*, Vol. XIII, No. 3, September, 1962; Wedderburn, D., 'Poverty in Britain Today—The Evidence', *The Sociological Review*, Vol. X, No. 3, Autumn, 1962.

the basis of the data in the Ministry of Labour survey about income. The national assistance standard may be regarded as the government's definition of a 'poverty line'. Its use for research into poverty is discussed elsewhere.[9]

Table 4 shows, for a sub-sample of households investigated in that year, how many had an expenditure, and how many an income, which was below the national assistance standard. Comparable definitions were used. It is evident that if an expenditure rather than

TABLE 3

*Percentage of Households and of Persons with Low Income, 1960*

| Total income as percentage of national assistance scales plus housing cost | Households % | Persons % | Estimated nos. in the U.K. (thousands) |
|---|---|---|---|
| Under 100 | 4·7 | 3·8 | 1,990 |
| 100 but under 140 | 13·3 | 10·4 | 5,448 |
| 140 and over | 82·0 | 85·8 | 44,945 |
| Total | 100 | 100 | 52,383 |
| N= | 3,540 | 10,765 | — |

TABLE 4

*Number of Households in Different Income Groups with Low Income and Low Expenditure (Sub-sample, 1960)*

| Total income or expenditure as % of national assistance scales plus housing cost | Household income | | | | | | | | | | | |
|---|---|---|---|---|---|---|---|---|---|---|---|---|
| | Under £3 | | £3–£6 | | £6–£8 | | £8–£10 | | £10–£14 | | All under £14 | |
| | Total inc | exp | Total inc | exp | Total inc | exp | Total inc | exp | Total inc | exp | Total inc | exp |
| Under 100 | 6 | 10 | 7 | 9 | 6 | 6 | 3 | 2 | 0 | 2 | 22 | 29 |
| 100 but under 140 | 54 | 27* | 22 | 18 | 18 | 16 | 10 | 6 | 6 | 4 | 110 | 71 |
| 140 and over | 0 | 23* | 9 | 11 | 26 | 28 | 20 | 25 | 25 | 25 | 80 | 112 |
| Total | 60 | 60 | 38 | 38 | 50 | 50 | 33 | 33 | 31 | 31 | 212 | 212 |

* Estimated on basis of information supplied by the Ministry of Labour.

9. Abel-Smith, B., and Townsend, P., *op. cit.*

an income basis is used for measuring poverty, a smaller proportion of households and of persons will be found to be in poverty. Instead of 18 per cent of households, and 14·2 per cent of persons, living below or just above the national assistance standard in the United Kingdom (see Table 3) there would have been 15·9 per cent and 12·4 per cent respectively, if expenditure instead of income had been taken as the criterion. Instead of nearly 7½ million persons being in poverty or on the margins of poverty there would have been about 6½ millions.

How disturbing is it to find such a discrepancy in the numbers in poverty, if expenditure instead of income is used as the criterion? Is one more accurate than the other? Or is one more *appropriate* than the other for exploring the dimensions of poverty? I shall first describe the results for the special sub-sample in a little more detail and then discuss the relationship between income and expenditure.

## Income and Expenditure Distributions

We have already seen that 132 of the 212 households in the sub-sample (see Table 4) had an *income* and 100 an *expenditure* below the national assistance scales or less than 40 per cent above those scales. Much of the difference is in fact accounted for by those with an income of under £3 per week and Table 5 shows the results only for those in the £3–£14 income groups. In fact only 45 households had both income and expenditure below the scales, as Table 5 shows. Another 45 were below the scales according to *one* criterion.

TABLE 5

*Number of Households in Sub-Sample with Income and Expenditure Below National Assistance Scales, 1960*

| Relationship of income and expenditure to National Assistance Standard | £3–£6 | £6–£8 | £8–£10 | £10–£14 | All groups £3–£14 |
|---|---|---|---|---|---|
| Income only below national assistance standard | 7 | 10 | 9 | 1 | 27 |
| Expenditure only below standard | 5 | 8 | 4 | 1 | 18 |
| Income and expenditure below national assistance standard | 22 | 14 | 4 | 5 | 45 |
| Total | 34 | 32 | 17 | 7 | 90 |

Table 6 shows, for the sub-sample, the relationship between mean income and mean expenditure. Expenditure exceeded income for each of the income groups but the proportionate excess was considerably higher for the £6–8 and £8–10 income groups than the £3–6 and £10–14 income groups. However, the small numbers comprising the sub-sample should again be borne in mind.

TABLE 6

*Mean Income and Mean Expenditure (Sub-Sample, 1960)*

| Income per week | Mean income | Mean expenditure | Expenditure as % of income | Number in sub-sample |
|---|---|---|---|---|
| £3–£6 | £4  4  1 | £4  7  4 | 104 | 38 |
| £6–£8 | £6 15  2 | £8 17  6 | 131 | 50 |
| £8–£10 | £8 16  3 | £12 16  6 | 146 | 33 |
| £10–£14 | £11 15 11 | £12 15  9 | 108 | 31 |

Table 7 also presents rather disturbing information. It shows the number of households in the sub-sample, according to the percentage by which expenditure exceeds or falls short of income. There is rather less extreme variation in the £10–14 income group than in the lower income groups but expenditure still differs from income by more than 50 per cent for one household in six.

Tables 5, 6 and 7 deal with small numbers of households but have been included in this analysis because it is unusual for such information to be published. They raise important questions for expenditure and income surveys in general and for poverty surveys in particular.

## Explanations of the Phenomenon of Expenditure Surplus

Cole and Utting concluded that expenditure tends to be overstated and income understated. In the Cambridgeshire inquiry they estimated that expenditure was too high by about 5 per cent and income too low by about 10 per cent. Houthakker also concluded that expenditure figures tend to be overstated.[10] The most common reasons for overstatement of expenditure are as follows. Individuals keeping records or reporting information tend to try to impress

10. Houthakker, H. S., 'The Econometrics of Family Budgets', *Journal of the Royal Statistical Society*, A, Part 1, 1952, Vol. CXV, pp. 1–26.

## TABLE 7

*Number of Households in Sub-Sample, According to the Percentage by which their Expenditure Exceeds their Income (Sub-Sample, 1960)*

| Expenditure exceeds income by | £3–£6 | £6–£8 | £8–£10 | £10–£14 | All groups £3–£14 |
|---|---|---|---|---|---|
| 100 per cent or more | 1 | 6 | 3 | 1 | 11 |
| 50–99 per cent | 4 | 6 | 5 | 3 | 18 |
| 40–49 | 1 | 3 | 2 | 0 | 6 |
| 30–39 | 3 } 20 | 4 } 32 | 4 } 19 | 1 } 18 | 12 } 89 |
| 20–29 | 2 | 2 | 1 | 2 | 7 |
| 10–19 | 3 | 6 | 0 | 2 | 11 |
| 0– 9 | 6 | 5 | 4 | 9 | 24 |
| – 0– 9 | 10 | 5 | 7 | 6 | 28 |
| – 10–19 | 1 | 5 | 3 | 2 | 11 |
| – 20–29 | 5 | 5 | 3 | 4 | 17 |
| – 30–39 | 2 } 18 | 1 } 18 | 1 } 14 | 0 } 13 | 4 } 63 |
| – 40–49 | 0 | 1 | 0 | 0 | 1 |
| – 50–99 | 0 | 1 | 0 | 1 | 2 |
| – 100 or more | 0 | 0 | 0 | 0 | 0 |
| Total | 38 | 50 | 33 | 31 | 152 |

and provide as many positive answers as possible. They also tele-
scope time and attribute expenditure to the more recent past than
the facts justify. If records are kept for at least two weeks, expenditure in the first week is always higher, on average, than in the
second, third or fourth weeks. This is called 'the end-period effect'.[11]
There appears to be some exaggeration of expenditure on 'necessities' and under-reporting of expenditure on 'luxuries'—especially
drink, but also cigarettes and tobacco, meals out, ice cream, choc-
olates and sweets. (There is some reason for supposing that expenditure incurred by children is not always reported.) There may also
be some unwitting double counting of expenditure by husband and
wife (each of whom separately keep records for the Ministry of

11. Kemsley found that expenditure in the first week was about 7 per cent
higher than in the second and third weeks. Kemsley, W. F. F., 'The Household Expenditure Enquiry of the Ministry of Labour: Variability in the
1953–4 Enquiry', *Applied Statistics*, Vol. X, 1961, pp. 117–135. See also
Kemsley, W. F. F., 'Interviewer Variability in Expenditure Surveys', *Journal
of the Royal Statistical Society*, Series A, General, Vol. 128, Part 1, 1965, p. 136.

Labour) which cannot always be picked up during clerical checks. There is the further possibility that behaviour changes while records are kept. Finally, estimates of some expenditure incurred irregularly over the year may be inflated by extrapolation from the last payment (e.g. a quarterly fuel bill). When wages and prices are changing rapidly it is difficult to put together information referring to different periods over a year.[12]

Income tends to be understated for a variety of reasons. First of all, it is difficult to trace certain sources of income—particularly windfalls. Money given to children and adults by their relatives, income from goods sold, occasional earnings in evenings or at weekends, lump sums paid on certain insurance policies, return of money on overpaid bills and rebates from slot meter payments for gas and electricity are a few examples. Possible sources of income are so various that it is difficult in an interview to cover them all. Small sources of income can easily be overlooked. Second, the definition of income may be relatively narrow and details of some types of income may not be collected. In the annual surveys carried out by the Ministry of Labour income does not include withdrawals from past savings, proceeds from the sale of houses, cars, furniture or other capital assets, or receipts from legacies, maturing insurance policies or other windfalls.[13] Third, certain kinds of income appear to be considerably understated, particularly by the highest income groups. Income from rent, dividends and interest and from self-employment are examples. However, although part of the problem may be due to the same kind of deliberate under-reporting that might be encountered by the tax authorities some of it seems to be due to the difficulty of establishing accurate figures without elaborate inquiry. Finally, income information usually relates to periods further in the past than expenditure information. For example, professional income and the weekly equivalents of weekly bonuses paid to employees are based on the previous twelve months. Since expenditure information mainly relates to the previous 14 days it is

12. There may be other reasons for error. For example, interviewers collecting information in the Ministry of Labour's surveys are instructed not to allow records of expenditure to be kept until all members of a household are present. Holidays at the expense of relatives or friends (with a saving of expenditure during certain days or weeks of the year) are not allowed for. Yet, this kind of hospitality is common.

13. Ministry of Labour, *Family Expenditure Survey, Report for 1963*, London, HMSO, 1965. See also Department of Employment and Productivity, *Family Expenditure Survey, Report for 1967, op. cit.*, Appendix 2.

evident that in a period of rising prices the income given for a particular household may appear to fall short of its expenditure.

I have given only a brief summary of the factors involved in relating income to expenditure. It would be useful if a comparative analysis of the results of surveys in different countries could be made to find whether the phenomenon reported here is of the same kind and magnitude outside the United Kingdom.

## Special Problems Affecting the Poor

The poor tend to be under-represented in income and expenditure surveys.[14] They have difficulties in keeping records. Their educational level may be low, their homes and their days may be crowded with children, or they may be old or sick.

There is the further problem of deciding whether 'current' or 'normal' income or expenditure is the best criterion of their living standards. A man who is unemployed may have a low income but his expenditure may still nearly reflect the wage he was receiving, say, five weeks previously. His weekly wage may have been spread out over the first two or three weeks of unemployment. He may have received an income tax rebate and payments from a trade union, and he may have relied on various forms of temporary 'credit' or loans. Yet he is also using up the financial and psychological 'reserves' which most other people in society retain, and in certain important senses is much worse off. It is now customary in the Ministry of Labour surveys not to treat income in unemployment or sickness as 'normal' unless it has been received for at least 13 weeks. In a survey of poverty it is necessary to distinguish between temporary and long-term poverty, but it seems important not to assume that high income can be averaged with low income over certain periods for purposes of calculation unless families not only have the powers (whether formal or informal) to redistribute fluctuating income in this way but also reasonable fore-knowledge that income is in fact going to fluctuate.

## Conclusions

This paper is destructive rather than constructive. It produces evidence to show that in household income and expenditure surveys

14. In the survey carried out in 1953–4 by the Ministry of Labour the aged were under-represented by 20 per cent and the sick by about 40 per cent. Abel-Smith, B., and Townsend, P., *op. cit.*, p. 20.

a big discrepancy between total income and total expenditure is found for (i) all income groups except, sometimes, the highest groups, and (ii) a high proportion of individual households. The discrepancies are sufficiently serious to justify a review of the general technical direction of such surveys but also the special problems that are involved in carrying out future surveys of poverty. In particular we need to reconsider the nature and size of the financial resources that are to be measured.

Until further pilot research is undertaken the conclusions that can be reached must be highly provisional. First, it seems desirable to concentrate on improving income information rather than expenditure information. There is reluctance among some sections of the public to provide this information, but for most households it is a less complex matter to obtain, though new techniques must be developed if it is to be reliable. If an accurate representation of levels of living is to be reached, expenditure information cannot be confined to limited periods of the recent past. For some items the time period must be fairly extensive.[15] This means that accuracy is almost as difficult, if not as difficult, to ensure for expenditure as for income.

Second, the widest possible definition of income must be used. 'No concept of income can be really equitable that stops short of the comprehensive definition which embraces all receipts which increase an individual's command over the use of society's scarce resources—in other words, his "net accretion of economic power between two points of time".'[16] For low-income households special efforts will have to be made to trace fluctuations in income during the previous year (carefully noting the changes in sources and size of income during sickness, unemployment and so on).

Third, supporting measures of other resources such as assets, private gifts and income in kind from the social services, will need to be worked out.

At this stage research on small groups of households is likely to be of greater value than large-scale surveys. In particular, studies with follow-up interviews which seek to 'explain' discrepancies between expenditure and income or which otherwise seek to check

15. For example, see the exchange between Durant and Cole and Utting in the *Journal of the Royal Statistical Society*, Vol. 120, Part 1, 1957, pp. 86–87.
16. Memorandum of dissent by a minority of the Royal Commission on Taxation, *Report of the Royal Commission on Taxation*, Cmnd. 9474, 1955, p. 8.

measures of household resources are strongly recommended.[17] Until such work is completed it will be difficult to use family expenditure survey data to define the scope and nature of poverty or low levels of living in modern society with any confidence.

17. Some research on these lines is at present being carried out at the University of Essex and the London School of Economics under the auspices of the Joseph Rowntree Memorial Trust.

# 6. Housing Policy and Poverty

## Alvin L. Schorr

It must be possible to develop a conception of fundamental human need that is more related to the body's need than to society's wealth. One knows intuitively—not to say, scientifically—that the body's intake of nutrients affects its functioning and, at some level, determines illness or health. It may not be possible to define biological need for shelter quite as sharply; nevertheless, it is worth discussing this primordial relationship between man and shelter. It is this relationship—in which people remake their surroundings and are themselves literally remade—that is most discussed in the literature of poverty, and most misunderstood. We shall then discuss separately the manner in which society determines housing need, and touch on the measurements that have been used as standards.

### Primordial Standard

The following conclusion about the effect of poor housing on its residents is based on a review in 1964 of all the relevant studies that could be found:

> The following effects may spring from poor housing: a perception of one's self that leads to pessimism and passivity, stress to which the individual cannot adapt, poor health, and a state of dissatisfaction; pleasure in company but not in solitude, cynicism about people and organizations, a high degree of sexual stimulation without legitimate outlet, and difficulty in household management and child rearing; and relationships that tend to spread out in the neighborhood rather than deeply into the family.[1]

The sequence from poor housing to poor health is readily visualized; the links from cause to effect in terms of low self-valuation or child-rearing may seem more obscure. People see themselves in their surroundings and tend to value themselves accordingly. The Princess sleeps on twenty down featherbeds. A pea bothers her not

1. Schorr, A. L., *Slums and Social Insecurity*, London, Nelson, 1964, pp. 20–21.

113

because she has royal blood but because she is accustomed to a soft bed and to being indignant about small discomforts. By contrast, if surveys ask a man in a miserable hovel what he needs, he will not speak of an inside toilet . . . or running water . . . or electricity. He *may* ask for a new paraffin lamp. Usually, it does not occur to a man who is accustomed to very little that he is worth more or can have more. Of late we have papered over this simple observation with pretentious labels, such as 'poorly motivated' and 'culture of poverty'.

Let us turn to the matter of child-rearing. It is common in the slum areas of our cities to observe how extensively family life is conducted out of doors. Depending on which slum one is considering, the pattern may be attributed to habit brought along from another country or a rural region of one's own country. On the other hand, in a historic Chicago settlement house, an observer once questioned the soundness of a daily program for teenagers. They were kept away from home every night until curfew at 10 p.m. It did not seem entirely a good thing. The settlement worker's response went as follows: These 13- and 14-year-olds live in flats so small that there is no room for them. When they have eaten, sitting on a couch and stools around the table, they drift outside. They will be either at the settlement house or on the streets, but not at home.

A study of poor families in the District of Columbia makes this point quite simply:

> In these so-called apartments [it says], there is no place for children. . . . The close quarters, the drabness, the lack of something to do drives these children into the street.[2]

Elsewhere, the same group of researchers observe that these children escape parental control at quite early ages, some as early as the age of six.[3] One can hardly overlook the connection between escaping control and the fact that the children cannot reasonably be kept inside.

Children are, of course, sometimes inside the house. They come home to sleep, for example. A study of working class Negroes at the close of World War II found that the majority slept less than five

2. Lewis, R., report quoted in *The Washington Post*, Washington, D.C., by Eve Edstrom, January 12, 1964.
3. Lewis, H., 'Child Rearing Among Low Income Families'. Presented to the Washington Center for Metropolitan Studies, Washington, D.C., June 8, 1961.

hours a night. The reason: there simply was not enough space for beds.[4] Lack of sleep affects children's growth and health. Implications spring to the mind, too, about sexual relations between adults and sexual stimulation of children. Nor can one expect the most patient and permissive child-rearing from a mother who has slept only three or four hours.

When children play inside the house they are, of course, underfoot. There do not appear to be studies of the tension that arises between parents and children in very crowded quarters, perhaps because researchers are unwilling to dwell upon the obvious, but there has been a study of families with two children living in flats with two bedrooms. *They* experience tension—because there is not adequate room for the activities of parents and children.[5] When children are older, interchange with their parents more directly concerns their careers. Dr Carter's study in Sheffield has looked into the question of how that interchange takes place. In crowded housing, even an attempt at parental advice leads to frustration. A youngster is having dinner, somebody is watching television, and a neighbor stops in to see the mother. Guidance takes place in passing and is conducted in shouts. 'You can't hang about this summer, boy! Not like last year!' And the boy's irritated answer is swallowed up in the neighbor's story or in a television gun battle.[6]

These are two illustrations of the chain from cause to effect— that is, from poor housing to poor self-valuation and to a particular kind of child-rearing. A chain can be described and, in some measure demonstrated, for all the effects that are named in the summary quoted above.

In turn, the effects that are ticked off lead to or help to maintain poverty. Poor health, pessimism and passivity, poor household management, and inability to handle stress readily lead to poverty. The child-rearing patterns described above—the child out of the home and out of control at an early age, poor communication between parents and children, overly strict demands alternating with no requirements at all—train a child for the poverty his parents have known. Attachment to a neighborhood rather than

4. Davis, A., 'Motivation of the Underprivileged Worker', in *Industry and Society*, Whyte, W. F. (ed), New York, McGraw-Hill, 1946.
5. Blood, R., *Developmental and Traditional Child-Rearing Philosophies and Their Family Situational Consequences*, Chapel Hill, University of North Carolina, doctoral dissertation, 1952.
6. Carter, M. P., *Home, School, and Work*, London, Pergamon, 1963.

to one's family interferes with physical and social mobility, tending to maintain poverty. Obviously, any of these handicaps can be overcome; one does not suggest a mechanical equation. But taken together, these effects of poor housing tend to maintain poverty. One who looks closely at the lives of poor men or poor families must be struck with the notion that poverty was not merely necessary but over-determined.

This is the primordial connection between poor housing and poverty: poor housing causes or maintains poverty. This conclusion may seem simple and self-evident or, on the other hand, startling. Rather few people in the United States, whether experts or laymen, subscribe to it; many believe that poor housing has little effect on poverty. It may be worth speculating on why they come to this conclusion.

In the first place, tracing a causal connection from housing to poverty presents an enormously difficult research task. When, infrequently, the task is attempted, conclusions may be frustrated by the singular perversity of human beings. There was, for example, the Baltimore study that planned to use a control group in slum housing for comparison with an experimental group that was offered improved housing. In the period of the study, most of the control group moved from one flat to another on their own initiative—carelessly improving *their* housing.[7] So much for that painstakingly devised study design! And there is the famous depression study that showed that improved housing led to a higher *death rate*.[8] It seems that families that moved to better housing found themselves paying higher rents when, catastrophically, everyone's income went down, and so they had less for food and medical care. Inconclusive studies such as these should leave all conclusions still open, but somehow we tend to read 'no evidence' as meaning there is no causal connection.

Second, the task of demonstrating a connection lies at the door of social scientists who are, on the whole, uninterested in the problem. In recent decades, they have been interested in institutions and interpersonal relationships; these are the stuff of which theories are built.

7. Wilner, D. M., Walkley, R. P., Pinkerton, T. C., and Tayback, M., *The Housing Environment and Family Life: A Longitudinal Study of the Effects of Housing on Morbidity and Mental Health*, Baltimore, The Johns Hopkins Press, 1962.

8. Ferguson, T., and Pettigrew, M. G., 'A Study of 718 Slum Families Rehoused for Upwards of Ten Years', *Glasgow Medical Journal*, Vol. 35, 1954, pp. 183–201.

Many social scientists take as an aspersion on their profession the suggestion that bricks and mortar shape the people they enclose, and therefore the suggestion is not treated seriously. Third, it is possible that, in the United States at any rate, people are in some deep sense anti-sensual. (This is not to deny that American literature runs heavily to Anglo-Saxon words and advertising to French pictures. The two observations are not inconsistent.) Americans see themselves as manipulators of the physical world rather than at one with it. The idea that poor people are a product of their housing might lead to the disturbing thought that we are all, after all, products of our environment.

Finally, it is widely believed that we have already conducted a grand trial and the verdict is negative—that is, no effect of improved housing on poverty. The US public housing program was begun with high hopes that cleanliness and decent housing would lead to godliness or, anyway, a somewhat more middle-class way of life. It has widely failed to do so; in fact, many housing projects have deteriorated rapidly under the battering of uneducated, disorganized tenants. That grand trial had at least two major defects. First, no one in fact knows the long-term effect of public housing on the families that lived in it. Children may well have grown up freer of disease and better educated than they otherwise would have; we do not know. We only know that the housing itself deteriorated. More important, improved housing was not the only change that was being tested. Quite often, in addition to improved housing the new situation meant segregation, unfamiliar surroundings and requirements, inadequate schools and police service, and rigid and unfriendly management. It is difficult to sum up in a sentence all the factors that have operated against public housing in the United States; the point here is simply that improved housing was not the only variable in this experiment.[9]

The experience with public housing has had an impact on public opinion; there is no doubt about that. There was once considerable enthusiasm for improving opportunities for poor people through improved housing. It is now the fashion to be cynical about improved housing. Not only ordinary citizens but sophisticated

9. For researcher's and tenant's views of the variables that public housing includes see, Porter, E., Miller, J., Rainwater, L., and Koestler, F. A., 'Pruitt-Igoe: Survival in a Concrete Ghetto. I. The View From Inside; II. Strategies For Survival', *Social Work*, New York, XII, No. 4, October, 1967.

researchers turn to this history for their view of the relationship of housing and poverty. So quick and dubious a conclusion must betray, more than anything else, a terrible impatience with poor people. If we do not get quick results, it seems that we shall not get any results.

## Relative Standard

We turn now to a different dimension of the relationship of housing and poverty—the relationship of one's view of decent housing to the needs and wealth of the surrounding society. Three observations should be made about this relationship. First, the argument made so far is entirely contained by the kind of society we know. On one hand, decent housing is implicitly defined by the demands of an urban, industrial society. For example, it seems quite possible that inside space is less desirable or is even undesirable when farm land or hunting range stretches all around. An expensive system of disposing of human wastes may be a needless luxury rather than a necessity.

On the other hand, the patterns of behavior that people develop would have other consequences in other societies. For example, poor housing tends to produce a pattern of attachment to one's group and neighborhood, as opposed to a pattern of intimate one-to-one relationships. Attachment to a group and to 'turf' may operate against self-advancement in a society where one must be willing to change location in order to seize opportunities, but it may be functional on a farm, or ranch, or feudal holding. In other words, poor housing in the cities we know prepares people for poverty in the cities we know. If a similar causal connection existed in other historic periods or exists in essentially agrarian societies, the content of the connection is certainly different.

Secondly, people's perception of their own housing is deeply colored by the view on the television screen or over the rooftop across the street. A squatter's shack is not such a self-indictment in Caracas as in Paris. Conversely, slum dwellings that would be regarded as palatial in South America are not cherished by the residents of Harlem or Watts. We are well aware that the general perception of the level that defines poverty bears a direct relationship to the perception of *average* living standards.[10] Therefore it is hardly surprising that minimally acceptable housing is defined in relation

10. See Schorr, A. L., *Poor Kids*, New York, Basic Books, 1966, pp. 88–90.

to the average housing that is available. Within a century, the rule-of-thumb for adequate space, in the United States and Britain, has gone from one-person-per-bed to one-person-per-room. Similarly, in both countries *official standards* for living space were suddenly reduced when building materials were short, and raised when materials became available.

The primordial standard that we dealt with earlier and the relative standard we deal with now carry different implications for behavior. People are largely unconscious of the effect on their behavior and attitudes of the inadequate housing in which they live. For example, people do not value privacy who have never known it. That they would have cherished privacy if they had known it is obviously not an idea that comes readily to mind. More than that, people are attached to their own patterns; habits are part of one's self-image. They may form new habits under new conditions, but it takes time. For example, families that are moved from crowded into uncrowded housing continue for a time to study and eat and converse together, all at once.[11] In short, people are not aware that they would have been different if their housing met a primordial standard, nor are they likely to want to be different. By contrast, a relative standard is defined precisely by the fact that people want more or less as much as others and recognize that they have not got it.

The damage that is done in failing to meet the primordial standard is the pain or want of the people who suffer it and the diffuse economic cost of their failure to contribute as much as they otherwise would. The damage that is done in failing to meet a relative standard is the pain or despair of the people who suffer it and whatever consequences flow from their feeling disadvantaged and left behind. The latter may have more serious consequences for civil order. It is possible to meet the primordial standard without meeting the relative standard, and vice versa. For example, the United States has probably done rather better with the first and Great Britain rather better with the second. Moreover, although we may think we are striving towards some fixed goal in housing standards and quantity, we have an exceedingly volatile relative standard—at least in the dynamic economy of the western world. Like Alice, we must run if we want merely to stand still. If we want to get somewhere, we shall have to run twice as fast as that.

11. Hole, V., 'Social Effects of Planned Rehousing', *The Town Planning Review*, 25, No. 2, July, 1959, pp. 161–173. See also Michel, A., *Famille, Industrialization, Logement,* Centre National de la Recherche Scientifique, Paris, 1959.

## Housing Standards

With the distinction between primordial and relative housing need in mind, we appreciate the difficulty in arriving at standards that will remain acceptable for long periods of time. In fact, with temporary fluctuations, standards of adequate housing have risen steadily over the long term. In the wealthy western countries, standards are agreed upon that are naturally beyond the requirements of primordial needs, although these standards are not universally met in any of the countries.

Standards are, in general, developed for two qualities: (i) internal space or, viewed conversely, crowding; and (ii) physical qualities variously referred to as fitness, adequacy, dilapidation, and so forth. Housing and neighborhoods are also sometimes referred to as slums. In general, slum seems to mean a state of crowding or unfitness so severe that it produces an emotional reaction in the resident or observer. Not infrequently, in using the term, observers are characterizing the residents without really knowing about their housing.

Crowding has been measured in a variety of ways. Both the American Public Health Association and the Central Housing Advisory Committee in Great Britain establish space requirements by number of square feet—400 square feet for one person, 750 for two, 1,000 for three, and so on.[12] Such a standard is useful in building, but presents difficulty in census-taking or research. An easier standard to use counts the number of people per room in a housing unit. One person or less per room is currently considered adequate. A more complicated standard may combine people, rooms, and total space into a mathematical formula. Thus, three people in two bedrooms require 554 square feet.[13] There has been some interest, finally, in developing definitions more descriptive of family functioning. 'Use crowding' describes the situation in which a room designated for one function (living room) is also used for a different function (bedroom).[14] Such a definition, if elaborated,

12. American Public Health Association, Committee on the Hygiene of Housing, *Planning the Home for Occupancy*, Public Administration Service, Chicago, Ill., 1950; and Ministry of Housing and Local Government, *Homes for Today and Tomorrow*, Central Housing Advisory Committee, London, HMSO, 1961.
13. International Union of Family Organizations, *Minimum Habitable Surfaces*, Cologne, Family Housing Commission, 1957.
14. Chapin, F. S., 'The Relationship of Housing to Mental Health', Working paper for the Expert Committee on the Public Health Aspects of Housing of the World Health Organization, June, 1961 (mimeographed).

would make it possible to take into account both space and family needs at the same time. Numerical measures, on the other hand, assume that all families carry on more or less the same activities in the same ways.

Fitness or adequacy are defined in terms of the physical state of the structure ('dilapidation' or 'deterioration' in the United States) and the presence of a variety of facilities. Facilities that now generally figure in a standard include an inside bath, attached water closet, hot and cold running water, a proper source of heat (central heat in the United States), and a stipulated source of power. Even when these standards vary considerably from country to country, it is well to have them specified in objective terms. For example, in 1955 the British Government appraised housing need by asking local authorities to estimate the number of unfit houses in their jurisdictions. The estimate that was made was plainly too low.[15] In retrospect, it appears that the estimates were influenced by local judgments of the size of a building program that might conceivably be undertaken.

With an international standard or with a variety of national standards that incorporate objective measures of internal space and fitness, building and improvement programs may be developed and progress charted. As has been indicated, the standards themselves may be expected to shift but that is also an indication of progress.

### Investment Standard

The relative standard discussed above is a personal one; it is the relationship between each particular family's housing and its perception of normality. Before closing, it is important to note a different relative standard, reflecting a relationship between a nation's income and its investment in housing. At some balance point, a country can be said to be investing an acceptable portion of its resources in housing. It is possible that housing need exerts more pressure on the world economy in this particular period than it ever has. Population increase and migration from rural areas to cities exert crushing pressure for housing in underdeveloped countries, and readily perceptible pressure in the developed countries. It has, in fact, been argued that mankind is now worse housed than at any time in history. '. . . By all relevant criteria— space, light, sanitary conditions, shelter against the elements,

15. Schorr, A. L., *Slums and Social Insecurity, op. cit.*, p. 116.

security of tenure, aesthetic satisfaction—the majority of the inhabitants of this world had better dwellings during the Neolithic Age. . . .'[16]

In this circumstance most, if not all, of the nations of the world determine their national investment in housing under the severest pressure. On one hand, need seems to exceed anything that is being done. On the other hand, even wealthy nations tremble for their economies if they were to do everything that is proposed to them. It is therefore possible to have a country that seems poor not solely or chiefly because people are generally poor but because no one but the very rich can afford housing.

Argentina, for example, has a low unemployment rate and an average level of nutrition that must rank fairly high. Although in economic difficulty, Argentina is wealthy in natural resources. Yet the housing *objective* in Argentina—one does not even speak of the achievement—is only 5 or 6 new units a year per thousand population. Because of an assortment of national policies, only the comparatively rich are able to secure housing. Hundreds of thousands of families who would not, by income or other tests, be regarded as poor, live in so-called 'towns of misery'. They are poor as a matter of national policy.

One looks, therefore, for a number to use as an investment standard for shelter. The United Nations has estimated that Africa, Asia, and Latin America need to produce 10 or 11 dwellings per thousand per year for the next decade.[17] The needs of underdeveloped areas of the world are well in excess of the needs of the wealthy western countries. Still, the western world faces pressure for housing and balances it against other domestic needs. As it turns out, western and northern Europe and Canada and the United States all produce housing at a rate that ranges from 5 or 6 units per thousand population (Belgium, Austria, Great Britain) to 10 units per thousand (Sweden, Germany, Switzerland).[18] Whatever magic resides in the figure, it appears that in this period in history, countries need to produce roughly 10 housing units a year per thousand population. Those that fall regularly below this figure will find themselves housing-poor, whether they are wealthy or poor in all other ways.

16. Taper, B., 'A Lover of Cities', *The New Yorker*, February 4, 1967, Vol. XLII, No. 50, p. 39. See also Abrams, C., *Man's Struggle for Shelter*, Cambridge, Mass., the M.I.T. Press, 1964.
17. United Nations, *World Housing Conditions and Estimated Requirements*, 1965.
18. United Nations, *Annual Bulletin of Housing and Building Statistics*, 1962–63.

## Conclusion

It should be noted that we have dealt only with explicit relationships between housing policies and poverty. We have not dealt with the policies that may prevent housing from being used as an instrument of segregation and the consequences for poverty. We have not dealt with the policies or lack of policies that separate people from their work and the consequences for poverty. And we have not dealt with the housing policies that would build a sense of community rather than a sense of division, and the consequences of such policies for poverty. These are not less important relationships; just less direct or less deliberate than the ones we have considered.

The relationships that have been considered can be summed up as follows:

First, in the city-culture that we know, housing that falls short of specified standards rears people for poverty. A longer statement would contain qualifications but there should be no doubt about the basic statement: housing can make a family poor—by the attitudes and behavior into which it leads them—and it can keep a family poor. If we want to do away with poverty, we shall provide sufficient housing of sufficient quality so that our young people may grow up competent to deal with the world that they will know.

Second, even housing that is adequate by a primordial standard will seem slum housing if it falls too far short of the standard that most people enjoy. This is a taxing observation and it will leave us no peace, especially in the wealthy countries. If we want to do away with poverty, we require mechanisms to see that housing regarded as minimum is upgraded at a faster rate than average housing. A faster rate at the bottom is necessary to keep the gap between those at the bottom and those in the middle from growing.

Third, housing is the most expensive component of a modest standard of living. It appears to be the component that countries postpone improving when they are under other pressures. It is impossible to offer a rule for balancing housing needs against other national needs that will apply to rich and poor countries, in peace and war, in crisis and in prosperity. It is nevertheless clear that countries that cut their investment in housing too deeply make their populations poor, whatever else they achieve.

# 7. Poverty: Changing Social Stratification

## S. M. Miller and Pamela Roby

Poverty can be viewed in many contexts. Generally neglected has been the context of social stratification. The limited results of poverty programs based upon subsistence standards are now forcing a realization that not pauperism but inequality is the main issue within high-income industrial societies. When we begin to discuss poverty in terms of relative deprivation and inequalities, we are posing questions about the over-all social stratification of a nation: What are considered 'acceptable' gaps between the poor and other groups? What are the relevant dimensions for viewing differences among groups within the society today?

This chapter's first objective is to recast approaches to poverty in terms of stratification.[1] A thorough poverty analysis questions the level of living of the non-poor as well as the poor. As the late Polish sociologist Stanislaw Ossowski wrote in his brilliant analysis of social stratification, '. . . a class (is) a member of a certain system of relations. This means that the definition of any class must take into account the relation of this group to other groups in this system.'[2] Not just the poor but the entire society is at issue. As yet, poverty programs have not been adequately seen as efforts to engineer changes in the stratification profiles of the United States.

A stratificational analysis requires not only viewing the poor as those who are lagging behind relative to others in society, but extending the concept of poverty beyond the narrow limits of income. When poverty is viewed within the stratificational framework, we see that Max Weber and Richard Titmuss have already made major contributions to its analysis. One of Weber's outstanding contributions to social science was to untwine three components of

1. This is one of a series of papers. For further discussion of what is gained by putting poverty into a stratification perspective see Miller, S. M., Rein, M., Roby, P., and Gross, B., 'Poverty, Inequality and Conflict', *The Annals, 373,* September, 1967, pp. 16–52.
2. Ossowski, S., *Class Structure in the Social Consciousness,* London, Routledge & Kegan Paul, 1963, p. 133.

stratification: class, status, and power.[3] The Marxian analysis centered on the economic (or class) dimensions of stratification, but Weber believed that the prestige (social honor) and political dimensions of stratification were sometimes independently important. These other dimensions could change without change in the economic or they could remain stable despite changes in the economic dimension of stratification. With his widely ranging erudition, Weber illustrated his thesis by showing that, for example, a high status group, such as the Prussian Junkers, could retain considerable political power despite its reduced economic importance. Conversely, a rising economic group, like the bourgeoisie, could have a long struggle to obtain prestige equivalent to their economic position. Weber sought not to overturn Marx's analysis but to go beyond it, to broaden its perspectives.[4]

In this century, Titmuss has further refined our tools of analysis by conceiving of income as the 'command over resources over time'.[5] He argues that wage-connected benefits (e.g. pensions) and fiscal benefits (e.g. tax deductions for children which benefit the better-off more than the low-income tax payer) as well as welfare (transfer) benefits must be included in any discussion of the command over *resources*.

Recently we have suggested that governments in any society with significant inequalities should at least provide for rising minimum levels not only of incomes, assets, and basic services, but also of self-respect and opportunities for social mobility and participation in many forms of decision making.[6] To gain a better understanding of the objectives of various poverty programs and the relationships between these goals, we can look at efforts to reduce poverty in terms of (i) what aspect of poverty is the program aimed at, e.g. the economic, political, educational and social mobility, or status dimensions of stratification; and (ii) who is the program aimed at, e.g. is the program aimed at improving the social conditions of those who are poor (i.e. jobs, income, housing, health, self-respect) *or* at moving some of those who are poor out of poverty into other

3. Weber, M., 'Class, Status, Party', in *From Max Weber*, edited and translated by Gerth, H., and Mills, C. W., London, Routledge & Kegan Paul, 1958.
4. See 'Introduction' to Miller, S. M. (ed), *Max Weber: Readings*, New York, Thomas Y. Crowell, 1964.
5. Titmuss, R. M., *Income Distribution and Social Change*, London, Allen & Unwin, 1962; and *Essays on 'The Welfare State'*, New Haven, Yale University Press, 1958.
6. Miller, S. M., *et al*, *op. cit.*, p. 17.

niches in society (i.e. via educational programs). The following diagram may help the reader to think through these various objectives with us.

*Governmental and Private Property Reduction Reports*

| Program Objectives | Stratificational Dimensions | | | |
| | Economic Incomes, Basic Services, Assets | Political Participation in Decision Making | Education and Social Mobility | Status |
|---|---|---|---|---|
| Improving social conditions | Guaranteed Annual Income | 'Maximum Feasible Participation' | Consumer Education | Open Housing |
| | Medicare—Medicaid | 'Black Power' | | |
| | Social Security | 'Parent Participation in school decision-making' | | |
| | Concentrated Employment Program | | | |
| | Housing | | | |
| | | | New Careers | |
| Promoting social mobility | Job Training | Negro Separatist Movements | Headstart | Income Guarantees without Stigma |
| | Manpower Programs | School Integration | Upward Bound | 'Black is Beautiful' |

This typology can aid social scientists in program *planning* by pointing out the diverse and frequently conflicting goals of programs and by highlighting the relatively neglected aspects of poverty. The typology may also assist in program *evaluation* by providing a framework for pinpointing the goals of programs in question and for showing the relationship among the goals of various programs—first steps in any critique.

The typology leads policy makers dealing with the poor to ask what kinds of responsibilities and burdens we wish our society to have. For example, to what extent do we wish to improve the conditions of today's youth? To a large extent these are not narrow technical issues, but value issues which may be expected to produce acrimonious debate.

The second purpose of this paper is to show that stratification theory can be refined and modernized through understanding of poverty action. The bearing which empirical research and theory have upon one another has long been emphasized by Robert Merton and others.[7] Applied social science should also be a 'two way street' both drawing from and contributing to social theory. The many recent 'applied' analyses of poverty need to be distilled and added to the general corpus of sociological theory.[8] Conceptually, the writings of Titmuss on the distribution of 'command over resources' need to be connected with those of Parsons and Marshall on the meaning of citizenship.[9]

The interpretation of any particular historical period may require expanding the number of stratificational dimensions or, at least, recognizing the peculiar and changing content of each dimension.[10] Which dimension is of most importance may also shift.[11] In this essay we will deal with the dimensions of economic class, status, and power, and then with a fourth dimension of education and social mobility. Weber's order will be changed to have the discussion of status, which in the long run is the basic and most difficult issue of poverty programs, follow that of 'education and social mobility'. We have added the 'education and social mobility' dimension because over the past fifty years educational attainment and social mobility of offspring have become factors differentiating members

7. Merton, R. K., *Social Theory and Social Structure* (revised edition), New York, The Free Press of Glencoe, 1957, pp. 85–117.

8. Cf. the first essay by Gouldner and the concluding article by Miller in Gouldner, A. W., and Miller, S. M. (eds), *Applied Sociology*, New York, The Free Press, 1965. Other essays by Miller that bear on the issues of this paper are 'Poverty' in *Proceedings*, Sixth World Congress of Sociology, 1967, and 'Social Change' and 'The Age of Psychiatry' (with Frank Riessman) in Miller, S. M., and Riessman, F., *Social Class and Social Policy*, New York, Basic Books, 1968.

9. Parsons, T., 'Full Citizenship for the Negro American? A Sociological Problem', *Daedalus*, 94, 4, Fall 1965; Marshall, T. H., 'Citizenship and Social Class', *Class, Citizenship, and Social Development*, New York, Anchor Books, 1965.

10. Cf. Weber, M., *op. cit.*, p. 185.

11. Many American sociologists have been misled into believing that today's society is characterized by consensus simply because conflicts centering around the workplace are considerably less violent today than in the 1880s or 1930s. Rather than disappearing, conflicts have shifted from the workplace to ghetto streets where rebellions are aimed at societal and governmental injustices.

of the working and depressed classes. Today, not only class, status, and power but educational attainment and social mobility of offspring determine persons', particularly the poor's, future standard of living. Therefore, we believe that education and social mobility have become independent stratificational dimensions and should be treated as such.

We hope that other social scientists will also attempt to relate 'applied' and 'theoretical' social science. We believe that doing so will enrich American social science by forcing consideration of generally neglected facts, by pressing for reconsideration of misleading or incorrect theories, by clarifying vague concepts, and by generating new theories or conceptual schemes. We are persuaded with Dahrendorf that if we as social scientists 'regain the problem-consciousness which has been lost in the last decades, we cannot fail to recover the critical engagement in the realities of our social world which we need to do our job well.[12] We believe that refinement of stratification theory through analysis of applied sociology will in turn strengthen social scientists' efforts to reduce poverty.

## Class

Weber's discussion of the class or economic dimension of stratification built on Marx, but as elsewhere Weber attempted to broaden the Marxian perspective. Marx's analysis was based on the material and social relationships to the production process. Weber shifted from the sphere of production to that of the market or exchange and defined class as 'a number of people who have in common a specific causal component of their life chances in so far as this component is represented exclusively by economic interest in the possession of goods and opportunities for income, and is represented under the conditions of commodity or labor markets'.[13] The economic dimension of stratification, in Weber's conceptualization, included a great variety of explicit and implicit market relationships. As we shall discuss later, the major development today in many societies is the beginning of an important break between the market and well-being.[14]

12. Dahrendorf, R., 'Out of Utopia: Toward a Reorientation of Sociological Analysis', *American Journal of Sociology*, 64, pp. 115–127.
13. Weber, M., *op. cit.*
14. Many sociologists have observed portions of this development. For example, Parsons has noted that public control of private business contributed to the inclusion of Negroes and other groups and that government control over the value of the dollar shapes the distribution of wealth. Parsons, T., 'Full

The post-World War II era saw a proliferation of studies in which the central explanatory or classificatory variable was occupation.[15] The current concern with poverty is, by contrast, focusing on income. There are several reasons for the growth of interest in income as the definer of class position:

1. The links between occupation and income are becoming fuzzier. The range of income of incumbents of particular occupational positions appears to be getting wider.[16] The result is that a description of occupation poorly predicts income.

---

Citizenship for the Negro American? A Sociological Problem', *Daedalus*, 94, 4, Fall, 1965.

15. Lipset and Zetterberg maintain that historically, occupation has been the most common indicator of stratification. Lipset, S. M., and Zetterberg, H., 'A Theory of Social Mobility', in Reinhard Bendix and S. M. Lipset (eds), *Class, Status, and Power* (second edition), New York, The Free Press, 1966, p. 155. Great attention has been paid to the consistency with which prestige is accorded to occupations among different nations. However, international comparative studies pose many methodological problems. These frequently appear to result in a spuriously high degree of inter-country similarity. Following the most recent comparative study of occupational prestige, Hodge *et al* wrote, 'It is quite possible that much genuine diversity in occupational-prestige systems not captured by our analysis is reflected in the relative placement of occupations that are not comparable across societies, or even across subsectors of any given society. In Tiryakian's study of the Philippines, only a small number of occupations could be found about which it was sensible to ask both peasants in remote villages and the residents of Manila. . . . Invoking even so gross a distinction as the manual-nonmanual dichotomy reveals divergences between national prestige structures which are concealed by the total correlation over all occupations. The evidence mustered not only points to dissimilarities from country to country in occupational prestige structures, but also suggests that this variation is intertwined with economic development in a way which is not fully captured by a simple "structuralist" or simple "culturalist" expectation of prestige differences.' Hodge, R., Treiman, D., and Rossi, P., 'A Comparative Study of Occupational Prestige', in Bendix and Lipset, *ibid*, pp. 318, 321. Lenski contends that 'the great importance of the occupational class system is . . . indicated by the fact that one of the chief rewards distributed by most other class systems is access to favored occupations'. Lenski, G., *Power and Privilege*, New York, McGraw-Hill, 1966, p. 347. We believe, however, that the importance of the occupational class system is declining as the role of government expands.

16. For instance, in only two years, the *interquartile* range of *weekly* earnings of accounting clerks increased by $2.50, of material handlers by $8.00, of maintenance electricians by $2.00 in the New York S.M.S.A. US Department of Labor, Bureau of Labor Statistics, *Area Wage Survey*, Bulletin No. 1530–83, April 1967: US Dept. of Labor, Bureau of Labor Statistics, *Occupational Wage Survey*, Bulletin No. 1430–80, April, 1965.

2. The poor are a congeries of groups who share low income in common but frequently not many other things. While some of the poor are definable by their low-paying jobs, many other poor are outside the labor force and dependent upon transfer income of various kinds.[17]

3. Government policy, growing in importance, defines groups mainly by income levels whether for purposes of income taxes or welfare assistance.

In turn, income is an adequate indicator of economic level. Within the 'welfare state', the resources that are available to individuals are a mosaic of the income derived from market activities, from the 'fringe benefits' attached to various occupations and organizations, from the operation of the tax system, from various public and private transfer and pension systems, from assets whether protected or pseudo as in the case of many capital gains, and from the availability, utilization, and quality of public goods.

Weber's notion of class must be widened beyond that of property and the market. In particular, in the 'welfare state' many important elements of the command over resources become available as public services. The distribution and quality of these public services affect the absolute and relative well-being of individuals.[18] Considerable inconsistency *may* exist between the income and basic services of persons or groups. While the two are fairly closely linked in the United States, poor basic services are *not* associated with low income in Sweden.[19]

17. Cf. Hamilton, R., 'The Income Question', Department of Sociology, University of Wisconsin (manuscript).

18. Brian Abel-Smith has contested some prevailing views of the distribution of benefits in his trenchant 'Whose Welfare State?' in MacKenzie, N., (ed) *Conviction*, London, MacGibbon and Kee, 1958.

19. In his critique of Davis and Moore's proposition that 'social stratification, the uneven distribution of material rewards and prestige, is functionally necessary', Wesolowski maintains that in Poland and Norway the range of income has been distinctly narrowed but education and other services have been expanded. In these countries, he contends, not 'material rewards' but authority (which gives one the opportunity to express one's own personality) and education are viewed as 'end values'. In support of his thesis that occupational prestige is not an important motivational force under the Polish value system, Wesolowski cites Dr. Adam Sarapata's finding that 50 per cent of the respondents in a survey of Lodz 'replied, "No" when asked if some of the occupations were more important than others'. Wlodzimierz Wesolowski, 'Some Notes On The Functional Theory of Stratification', in Bendix and Lipset, *op. cit.*

A larger issue is also involved. As Marshall has argued, the welfare state approach is to break the link between the market and well-being.[20] The role of government is tremendously increased.[21] To a growing extent, the command over resources of the individual depends on his relation to government, whether in terms of income tax, subsidies, licensing, or public services.[22] The concept of 'property' has therefore to be enlarged and altered to include the perspectives of time in pension accumulations and of rights to governmental largesse and services, especially education. Property in the more conventional sense still remains important, but other forms of rights of determination are beginning to possess similar importance.

This broadened view of the command over resources has important political implications.[23] If government plays a major role in

20. Marshall, T. H., *Class, Citizenship and Social Development*, New York, Doubleday and Company, Inc., 1964.

21. Ossowski has noted, for instance, '. . . the experiences of recent years incline us to formulate the Marxian conception of social class in the form of a law which establishes a functional dependence: the more closely the social system approximates to the ideal type of a free and competitive capitalist society, the more are the classes determined by their relation to the means of production, and the more are human relationships determined by ownership of the means of production . . . the majority of American citizens are becoming accustomed to large-scale activities planned by the central authorities. . . . Hence comes the talk about the crisis facing political economics, whose laws were formerly rooted in the basic and inevitable tendencies of human behavior, but which today faces a dilemma caused by the growing influence of the government as a factor which consciously directs the country's economic life.' Ossowski, *op. cit.*, p. 185.

22. The importance of government subsidy and licensing has led Charles Reich to speak of 'largesse' in his seminal essay, 'The New Property', *Yale Law Review*, 93, 1964.

23. A new and neglected aspect of income is its stability. Just as the assurance of future income through pensions is an increasingly important component of well-being, the security and predictability of income within and over the years is becoming more significant. One of the most important differences today between factory workers and lower-level white collar workers in the United States and perhaps some other countries is not the level of income. Frequently, factory workers receive more income than do white collar employees. The more important difference in many ways is that the latter have a stability of income which as yet is not available to factory workers. This is true both within a year where factory workers may suffer layoffs and among years where white collar workers can have more confidence about the drift and certainty of their incomes. As a consequence, collective bargaining negotiations in the United States in the next years are likely to center to a large extent on the obtaining of greater employment surety and income guarantees for factory workers. Obviously, the stability of income can be

affecting the command over resources, then organized action will be increasingly centered on the governmental arena. When Marx wrote, the arena of action was more narrowly the workplace, the setting of production. In the United States, low-income persons have been organizing to affect their rights to welfare and to other forms of government services rather than to affect the economic market. As we shall see in our discussion of power, the relationships to government bureaucracy have become important not only for the poor but for all segments of American society.[24]

The primary point, then, in the effort to modernize the discussion of class is to become aware of the different and new elements in the command over resources over time and of the new role of the government as a direct distributor of resources. The issues of class and economics are intimately politicized as the market-place and property are affected by governmental action and political formations.

## Power

Not only is the government becoming a direct dispenser or withholder of resources but it is also regulating, controlling and directing

---

even more important for the poor who suffer from insecurity and unpredictable as well as inadequate income. The poor are unsure because of bureaucratic arbitrariness as well as because of unemployment and underemployment. Indeed, the war on poverty programs, it could be argued, have increased some income uncertainties among the poor by their sudden starting up and then emergency curtailing or ending because of budgeting or political difficulties. In 1963, the unemployment rate for unskilled laborers except farm and mine was 12·1 per cent as compared to the national average of 5·7 per cent, the 4·8 per cent rate for craftsmen, foremen and kindred workers and 1·6 per cent for managers, officials and proprietors except farm. In November 1967, in the midst of the Viet Nam involvement, the unemployment rate for unskilled laborers (7·3 per cent) remained over three times that of craftsmen, foremen and kindred workers (2·2 per cent) and over eight times that of managers, officials and proprietors except farm (0·9 per cent). US Department of Labor, *Manpower Report of the President and a Report on Manpower Requirements, Resources, Utilization and Training*, Transmitted to the Congress, March, 1964, p. 25; US Dept. of Labor, *Employment and Earnings*, December, 1967.

24. Dahrendorf links class and politics even more closely when he writes, '. . . class is about power and power is about politics'. Dahrendorf, R., 'Recent Changes in the Class Structure of European Societies', *Daedalus*, 93, Winter, 1964. While class and power are closely related, we also believe that for conceptual purposes they have to be independently analysed.

the economy, even in non-socialist societies. Efforts to spur economic growth and to prevent recessions inevitably involve questions of who is to benefit, who is to pay the costs of trying to keep prices from rising rapidly, who is to be disadvantaged by economic changes. The expanding role of government means that presumed notions of market automatically succumb to political decisions about who gains and loses.[25] These decisions are supposedly made on immutable technical grounds alone.[26] But, with greater sophistication, these decisions are found to be based upon a political struggle among groups and individuals possessing different values.[27]

Consequently, political position becomes increasingly important in affecting the command over resources. The political dimension of stratification grows in significance. Political organizations are based not only on relations to the private market but to the developing 'public market' in which key decisions are made.

The political dimension has its roots in the right to vote.[28] As voting becomes a widespread legal right in many societies like the United States with large differences in inter-group voting rates, the issue becomes how to get all groups to use their vote and how to get important issues before the electorate. This means dealing with the

25. Dahrendorf has observed, 'Just as in a modern shoe factory, it is hard to answer the question, "Who makes the shoes?", it is hard to tell who, in the bureaucratic administration of a modern enterprise, church, or state, holds the power'. Dahrendorf, R., *ibid*, p. 236.
26. Cf. Rein, M., and Miller, S. M., 'Poverty Programs and Policy Priorities', *Trans-action*, 4, 9, September, 1967.
27. For a strong attack on the 'assertion that the old sources of tensions and class conflict are being progressively eliminated or rendered irrelevant . . .', see Westergaard, J. H., 'Capitalism Without Classes?', *New Left Review*, No. 26, Summer, 1964, pp. 10–32. Also pertinent to these issues is John H. Goldthorpe's essay, 'Social Stratification in Industrial Society', in Bendix, R. and Lipset, S. M. (eds), *op. cit.*, pp. 648–659.
28. See the important discussion of citizenship in Marshall, T. H., *op. cit.* When describing nineteenth and twentieth century European changes in citizenship, Dahrendorf has stated, 'The slogan (political participation) points to a symptom of the development of equality of citizenship rights rather than to its entire substance. Citizenship is the social institution of the notion that all men are born equal. Its establishment requires changes in virtually every sphere of social structure. Apart from universal suffrage, equality before the law is as much a part of this process as is universal education, protection from unemployment, injury and sickness, and care for the old. Representative government, the rule of law, and the welfare state are in fact the three conditions of what I should describe as the social miracle of the emergence of the many to the light of full social and political participation.' Dahrendorf, R., 'Recent Changes in the Class Structure of European Societies', *op. cit.*, p. 239.

overt and covert barriers to voting.[29] Another level, connected with the interest in voting, is the degree, kind and effectiveness of organization of various interest positions. Currently, low-income groups are beginning to develop organizations (whether in the form of activist clubs for the aged, or political associations of slum residents) which push more effectively for programs dealing with their problems.

Today the social stratification theorist must devote attention to political issues that go beyond voting.[30] The emergence of many institutions dispensing services and resources has meant that the well-being of individuals depends to a large extent on bureaucratic decisions in an immediate sense rather than political decisions in the broad sense. The bureaucracies of the welfare state have considerable discretion in the way they disperse their funds and services. Bureaucratic decisions having deep impact upon the well-being of both the poor and the nonpoor have been somewhat removed from accessible political processes. As a consequence, there is a growing attack on 'welfare bureaucracy' as infringing rights of individuals, capriciously making decisions, 'professionalizing' and technicizing decisions which should be political decisions.

The concern in the United States with 'participatory democracy',

29. Janowitz and Segal note that in Great Britain, Germany and the United States 'there is a tendency for persons in the lower working classes to have a higher degree of non-party affiliation than in the other strata of society'. However, he notes that the source of ineffective political participation lies not in income and education *per se* but 'as a series of life experiences which produces persons . . . without adequate institutional links to the political system'. Furthermore, '. . . such disruption can occur at various points in the social structure, for example among elderly men and women living outside family units'. Janowitz, M., and Segal, D. R., 'Social Cleavage and Party Affiliation: Germany, Great Britain and the United States', *American Journal of Sociology*, 72, 6, May, 1967.

30. Parsons has pointed out that inclusion ('the process by which previously excluded groups attain full citizenship or membership in the societal community') requires not a 'mere statement that it is necessary for justice but that the group has the capacity to *contribute* to the larger society', . . . and as long as the group doesn't have that capacity, 'the larger society needs to develop it'. Because inclusion of an excluded group requires the mobilization of the entire society, Parsons suggests that it is useful to conceive of political power more broadly than usual. 'Essential as government is, it does not stand alone in implementing major political changes.' For example, 'the political problems of integration involve all fields of organizational decision-making, especially for business firms to accept Negroes in employment, for colleges and universities to admit them for study, for trade unions to avoid discrimination'. Parsons, T., 'Full Citizenship for the Negro American?', *op. cit.*

'maximum feasible participation' in the poverty programs, and 'community representation', are manifestations of the effort to deal with the growing impact of welfare state bureaucracies and the more obvious social control agencies like the police on the lives of most.[31] The ability to be relatively insulated against bureaucratic mishandling and injustice is differentially distributed in society— the better-off and better-educated manage more effectively than the low-income and the low-educated.[32]

At one level within the economic dimension, the issue is to what extent are individuals protected *against* control by bureaucratic agencies? At another level, the issue is becoming to what extent are political processes being transformed so that recipients of government benefits become consumers and citizens with a decision-making role rather than dependents without choice or any degree of sovereignty? Both levels require the extension of traditional stratificational analysis of power to the new instruments of government, administration and resource-distribution.

## Education and Social Mobility

In today's credential society which places heavy emphasis on educational attainment for entrance into higher-level occupations, education becomes a crucial dimension in social stratification.[33] The importance of education is illustrated by Wilensky's and

31. Marshall's categorization of 'four degrees of cooperation' is useful in the consideration of many forms of political participation as well as of the relationships between employers and employees for which it was originally intended: (i) 'information: . . . men though informed of decisions, have no share at all in the making of them'; (ii) 'consultation': persons 'are not only informed before a decision is taken, but have an opportunity to express their views on points that concern them. These views may or may not be taken into account when the decision is made; there is no transfer of authority'; (iii) 'delegation': persons 'have been informed and consulted and their views have been taken into account in formulating a plan, then . . . small groups of them may be asked to work out the details for executing part of the plan'; (iv) 'joint control' exists in cases such as those where 'workers are represented in the management'. Marshall, T. H., *op. cit.*, pp. 244–245.
32. After a four year court battle, Alameda County (California) awarded $23,000 in back pay to a social welfare worker who was fired for refusing to participate in the welfare department's 'operation bedcheck'. It is less likely that the female welfare recipients whose homes were invaded by welfare workers without search warrants will be recompensed. *Berkeley Barb*, 5, August 24, 1967, p. 7.
33. Cf. Miller, S. M., 'Breaking the Credentials Barrier', New York: The Ford

Duncan's findings that it is the only variable which consistently ranks all the white collar strata above each of the manual and farm strata.[34] In addition to its economic role, educational experience affects the way individuals are treated by other people and by organizations and bureaucracies of one kind or another. An individual with inadequate education is an outsider, less able to take advantage of the opportunities which exist, and is treated less well than those with the same income but a higher education. American Negroes' great interest in education, for example, is partially due to the protection which education provides against nasty treatment.

Educational attainment of children is only a partial function of the income of parents. Below the highest I.Q. levels, the education of parents is more important than their income in affecting the educational experience of children. Economic position is thus not a fully adequate indicator of the educational prospects of children.

Many governmental policies are aimed at reducing the correlation between the economic position of the child and that of his parent. The aim is *inter*generational social mobility rather than improving the conditions of the poor today. For example, the emphasis in the war on poverty, on job training programs (e.g. Job Corps, Manpower Development), and on education (e.g. Headstart, Elementary and Secondary Education Act) are essentially programs in social mobility. The programs aimed at the young, like Headstart, obviously aim for intergenerational mobility while those designed for older persons, like many of the Manpower Development and Training Act programs, seek *intra*generational mobility.

What is the value of casting these poverty and manpower programs in the language of mobility? In some cases, the mobility

Foundation, 1968. Lenski has written, 'Of all the changes linked with industrialization, none has been more important than the revolution in knowledge. . . . From the standpoint of the occupational class system, this development has been highly significant. To begin with, it has been responsible for the considerable growth in size, importance, and affluence of the professional class. Second, it has caused education to become a much more valuable resource, and made educational institutions far more important in the distribution of power and privilege, than ever before in history.' Lenski, G., *Power and Privilege*, New York, McGraw-Hill, 1967, p. 364.

34. Duncan, O. D., 'Methodological Issues in the Analysis of Social Mobility', in Smelser, N., and Lipset, S. M. (eds), *Social Structure and Mobility in Economic Development*, Chicago, Aldine Publishing Co., 1966; Wilensky, H., 'Class, Class Consciousness and American Workers', in Haber, W. (ed), *American Labor in a Changing World*, 1966.

perspective points out that program goals are too low. In some job training programs, for example, 'success' is recorded if the individual secures a job, even if the job pays no more or is no less of a dead end than his previous job. Similarly, low wage full-time employment may not be a substantial mobility step over unemployment or irregular employment.

The mobility approach may also indicate the possible importance of stratum or group mobility.[35] Important gains may be achieved not only by moving individuals out of particular low-wage occupations but by securing a substantial improvement in the occupation's relative position in terms of wages, status, and conditions. The large percentage of families living in poverty headed by males working full-time suggests that change. The returns for certain kinds of work may be crucial if poverty is to be rapidly reduced.

The stratificational approach also encourages studying the factors which impede or promote mobility. Lack of education may be a less important barrier than current common sense suggests while discrimination may continue to be significant.

As societies become increasingly future-oriented, a crucial dimension of stratification is what happens to the children of different strata. Current position of families only partially denotes future positions. Blau and Duncan found for instance that 'nearly ten per cent of manual sons achieve élite status in the United States, a higher proportion than in any other country'. Commenting on their findings, they wrote, 'the high level of popular education in the United States, perhaps reinforced by the lesser emphasis on form distinctions of social status, has provided the disadvantaged lower strata with outstanding opportunities for long-distance upward mobility'.[36] Hopefully, public policies will make sharper the break between the present of the family and the future of the child. Consequently, social mobility, an important part of Weber's concept of 'life chances', should receive attention as an independent vector of stratification.

Obviously, there are important questions concerning the significant economic-political-social boundaries of high and low position. Social stratification analysts have been slow to refine the manual/nonmanual divide. Our conclusion is that the increasingly important social divide is not between the manual and non-manual groups but

35. See Miller, S. M., 'Comparative Social Mobility', *Current Sociology*, 9, 1960.
36. Blau, P. M., and Duncan, O. D., *The American Occupational Structure*, New York, John Wiley and Sons, 1967, p. 435.

between those with and without a college diploma—between those in professional and managerial occupations and the rest of the society. As Kolko has remarked, 'economic mobility in a technology and society enormously—and increasingly—dependent on the formally trained expert ultimately reflects the extent of equality in education'.[37] Important differences obviously exist below the professional-managerial level, but the expanding 'diploma élite' is becoming distinctly advantaged in society.[38] Their advantage is not only economic but social and political as well. The diploma élite manages to achieve deference and decent treatment from governmental organizations and at the same time—perhaps because of this—is able to organize effectively as a political voice. As the complexity of life in the United States increases, we may expect the importance of education to grow.

## Status

Weber's discussion of the status dimension of stratification has frequently been compressed into an analysis of family or occupational prestige rankings. This reduction is an inadequate rendering of what was obviously intended to embrace the socio-psychological dimensions of stratificational systems.

Three dimensions are worth distinguishing here: 'social honor', styles of life, and self-respect. In Weber's usage, 'social honor' referred to the social evaluation by others of a class or political group. As we have noted earlier, a high economic class may or may not have high social prestige at any particular moment in time. This can be seen through patterns of interaction such as intermarriage among groups and classes.

Social honor is *externally* awarded on a variety of bases: income, occupation, education, family history. In the past, American sociologists probably overstressed the significance of prestige and understressed the importance of class, but prestige is again growing in importance as a dimension of stratification.[39] Because social honor significantly affects government policy, its importance

37. Kolko, G., *Wealth and Power in America: An analysis of social class and income distribution*, New York, Praeger, 1962, p. 113.
38. Cf. Miller, S. M., 'Comparative Social Mobility', *op. cit.*
39. In a seminal paper Richard Hamilton has contended that sociologists have overstressed the blurring of status or prestige lines. He believes this has occurred because (1) although sociologists talk much about status seeking activity,

increases with the increasing importance of government action affecting persons' well-being and command over resources. For example, a group which is regarded as an 'undeserving poor' is much less likely than a 'deserving poor' to be aided. Prestige, then, is intimately tied to access to resources. It also, as we shall discuss later, affects self-respect.

The issues of desegregation, especially in housing, in the United States also point up the significance of prestige. Undoubtedly, much of the slowness in making it possible for Negroes to have effective free choice in housing locations is due to class feelings—disturbance about 'lower class' Negro families. Nonetheless, a considerable part of the resistance against Negro mobility is directed against Negroes as a status group regardless of class levels.

The development of national states accentuated the problems of ethnic minorities. These problems will probably increase again with the tide of foreign, low-level workers in many European nations. Ethnic and class factors will intertwine to make the prestige of a grouping an important factor in the way that it is treated. Alwine de Vos van Steenwijk and Père Joseph of Aide à Toute Détresse tell us that in France the way that poverty is viewed largely depends on whether the poor are thought to be of French or foreign background. In the United States, attitudes toward dealing with poverty combine with the stress on the importance of Negroes as a poor group and the shifting compound of feelings about Negroes.

The increased significance of government as the conveyor of the command over resources also complicates the traditional relationships between source of income and 'social honor'. The conclusions of yesterday were simple: earned income is more prestigious than unearned income (unless it is very high unearned income); legitimate income is better than 'illegitimate' income. Today the evaluations of the different bases of income are cloudy. Income given to public assistance clients leads to low prestige; but financial assistance to farmers in the form of money subsidies or to entrepreneurs in the form of tariffs do not.[40] Payments to the retired which purportedly

---

they have inadequately researched the matter and (2) they consequently turn to income trends which they inaccurately assume to be becoming more equal and then assert that status and consumption patterns are also becoming equalized. Hamilton, R., *op. cit.*, p. 1.

40. Assistant Secretary of the Treasury Stanley S. Surrey has suggested that tax savings that accrue to individuals and groups from preferences or loopholes in the tax law should be reported as Federal 'expenditures'. If this were

have a relationship to their contributions to a fund during their lifetime are not stigmatized income, even if the relationship of contribution and payment is indeed remote. Payments to youth who go to school are not regarded as habit-forming or character-debilitating. When made to poor families, they are often so regarded.

Thus, it is not government payments and contributions *per se* but their basis which is unprestigious. If the payments are connected to the operation of the production system (tariffs, agricultural subsidies) or to the future productivity of workers (education) or to previous work status, then stigma does not attach to the support.

By styles of life, the second dimension of status, we refer to the norms and values of particular groups.[41] If social honor is the way the group is regarded from without, styles of life refer to the way the group behaves. Obviously, styles of life and their interpretation affect the bestowal of social honor.[42]

The determination of styles is no easy matter; it is difficult to have a summation of a style that is not judgmental and even more difficult to have a style description that does not fall afoul of competing efforts to utilize that description in the struggle for policy choices. The significance of style of life underscores the importance of status considerations in government decisions as well as the importance of government decisions.

Because of the importance of styles of life in affecting social honor and public policy, social science becomes particularly political. Its mode of interpretation has strong reverberations. Yet, the knowledge base from which descriptions and interpretations are made is

---

done, the Commerce Department would show $1-billion for aiding business in the form of special deductions. *New York Times*, November 12, 1967. 55 per cent of total 1963 government payments to farmers went to the top 11 per cent of all farmers, those with farm sales of $20,000 and over. Schultz, T., 'Public Approaches to Minimize Poverty', in Fishman, L. (ed), *Poverty Amid Affluence*, New Haven, Yale University Press, 1966. Cf. Stern, P. M., *The Great Treasury Raid*, New York, Random House, 1964.

41. As elsewhere in this paper, we assume that we are dealing with a group defined economically in class terms and that we are pursuing the political and social behavior components of this class group. Frequently, there is little convergence among the groups defined in class, political, or social terms.

42. The link between styles of life and their interpretation is not perfect, for as Lockwood has pointed out with regard to affluent manual employees whom he terms the 'new working class', to display the life styles of those 'above' and to be accepted by those 'above' are two quite different things. Lockwood, D., 'The New Working Class', *European Journal of Sociology*, 1, 2, 1960.

limited and controversial. In an important sense, however, this has always been true; the interpretation of the social stratification of a nation is always a most sensitive political issue. What is striking in the present is the particular importance of styles of life. The greater controversiality may be due not only to the fact of greater stakes (government is more likely to do something now than in the nineteenth century) but to the production of a larger number of fairly independent social scientists and to the politicalization of issues which provide once-neglected groups with spokesmen.

Current research on the poor is leading to the rejection of the notion of *the* one style of life among this group.[43] It is always difficult to make a historical statement, since much of the past is sentimentalized in the telling, but it does appear that life style heterogeneity within a grouping is indeed increasing. One reason for this is the greater variety of cross-pressures today in societies which are increasingly national and where more styles are visible through travel, the mass media, and more public life. A second reason underlines the mode of stratificational analysis proposed by Weber: change in one dimension of life does not automatically produce change in other realms. Discontinuities often result from a rapid pace of change in which spurts and lags are pronounced.

The heterogeneity of styles is important in two ways. One has been referred to already: the receptivity to aiding particular groups, and especially the poor, depends to a large extent on their 'social honor'. In turn, their social honor depends largely on what purports to be their life style. Those low-income groups with more appealing life styles are much more likely to be given some aid. The second way that heterogeneity affects policy is that any given policy is likely to fit more easily into the style and condition of one section of the poor than another. The result frequently is, whether intended or not, the process of 'creaming', working with the best off or most adaptable of the poor. It usually takes some time to discover that the policy left behind groups with other life styles or other class positions.

The process leads to the question of whether groups need to change their life styles in order to be able to take advantage of new oppor-

43. Other strata are also likely to be viewed as heterogeneous groupings. Cf. Miller, S. M., 'The American Lower Class: A Typological Approach', of *Social Research*, Spring, 1964; and Wilensky, H., 'Mass Society and Mass Culture', in Berelson, B., and Janowitz, M. (eds), *Reader in Public Opinion and Communication*, New York, The Free Press, 1966.

tunities in the private market or in governmental policies. Here, style of life becomes a problematic of the efficacy of change rather than a moral gatekeeper of whether or not a particular group should be helped.

Frequently, in the United States life styles are discussed in terms of relatively impenetrable barriers which the culture or sub-culture of poverty place in the way of advance. An alternative formulation, which Riessman and Miller have attempted to develop, emphasizes those aspects of low income life styles which must be considered in order to make public policies more effective.[44] The stress is on reducing strains, obstacles and difficulties of policy rather than on castigating the poor or ignoring their particular outlook.

In a sense, what is important about the styles of life of groups, especially those most needful of governmental aid, is largely determined by the political culture of a nation. Whether the bases of life styles are ethnic or marginal economic circumstances, what is crucial about them is the way they interact with political values concerning who should be helped, how they should be helped, and how the behaviors of those helped should change. The style of life variable has become more highly charged than it was for Malthus.

Self-respect, the third dimension of status, points to the way the grouping regards itself. It is a complex admixture of economic and political conditions, social honor, and styles of life. In it, feelings of relative deprivation generally represent only a rough approximation to actual inequalities existing within a society.[45] The discussion of poverty, at least in the United States, should make us aware that only the narrowest view of poverty would make it a problem of income alone. In the spongy openness of the affluent society, poverty becomes not only a shorthand expression for inequality but a truncated phrase for the many ways in which the poor are different in society.

One does not have to accept all the nostrums of change that are offered in the United States to concur in the importance of a feeling of dignity, of inclusion and participation in the society which goes

44. Miller, S. M., and Riessman, F., *Social Class and Social Policy*, New York, Basic Books, 1968.

45. Following his study of relative deprivation in England, Runciman concluded that for each stratification dimension, 'the only generalization which can be confidently advanced is that the relationship between inequality and grievance only intermittently corresponds with either the extent or the degree of actual inequality'. Runciman, W. G., *Relative Deprivation and Social Justice*, Berkeley, University of California Press, 1966.

beyond the attaining of an income above a minimum level. Obviously, rising income alone may not wipe out external stigma and internal group-hatred and deprecation. On the other hand, gains in group respect are unlikely if the group falls behind the rising standards of society. Between these two boundaries, many kinds of permutations are possible.

One can interpret Negroes' interest in 'maximum feasible participation' in the local decision-making of the war on poverty in many ways, but an important way for stratification theory is that it represents the politicalization of the issue of self-respect. One does not have to believe that the poor are the ultimate repository of all wisdom about what poverty means and what should be done about it to recognize that this politicalization recasts the search for self-respect in new ways, making a political issue out of what has appeared to be a personal struggle. Access to self-respect, despite its curious formulation, becomes one of the important dimensions of social stratification. The alienated nonpoor have had an opportunity to make a choice; not so with the poor.

## Conclusions

Casting the issues of poverty in terms of stratification leads to re-garding poverty as an issue of inequality. In this approach, we move away from efforts to measure poverty lines with pseudo-scientific accuracy. Instead, we look at the nature and size of the differences between the bottom 20 or 10 per cent and the rest of society. Our concern becomes one of narrowing the differences between those at the bottom and the better-off in each stratification dimension.

In casting many of the issues of poverty in terms of stratification, we do not wish to imply that the poor are a fixed, homogeneous group that shares a common outlook. Rather, we see the poor as those who lag behind the rest of society in terms of one or more dimensions of life. There may be considerable turnover in these bottom groups. Although we lack data showing what proportion of persons in the bottom groups move in and out of poverty, we do know that a life cycle pattern is of some importance for the risk of being at the bottom is much greater for the older individuals.[46]

46. Since the aged have different needs and consumption patterns than younger persons, it may make more sense to think in terms of stratification within the aged. Incidentally, there is a greater concentration of income among those above 65 than among any other age group.

There is undoubtedly greater turnover in the bottom 20 per cent of the population than is commonly believed by those who stress the inheritance and culture of poverty. Even with a high turnover, however, questions concerning what size and kind of disparities are acceptable between those who fall behind and others in society remain important.

We hope that our effort to place some poverty action issues in the context of social stratification is not merely a translation from one language of discourse to another. Therefore, we must ask what would be done differently if poverty problems were seen as issues in stratification.

First, we believe that poverty programs would aim for higher targets. Reforming the social structure so that the differences among individuals are reduced usually requires higher goals than bringing individuals up to a rather low economic standard.

Second, a stratificational approach requires constant adjustment of the targets, for as the better-off groups advance, new levels and kinds of concerns for the bottom-most should emerge. A fixed level of well-being is no longer the aim.

Third, a stratificational approach implies that economic goals are not the only important objectives. Frequently, the economic goal of raising incomes to a \$3,000 level has been treated as though it were the only significant objective. The multi-dimensional concerns of stratification force attention to the non-economic aspects of inequality.

Fourth, we see that changes and shifts in one dimension do not automatically produce changes in other dimensions. Economic gain does not insure automatic attainment of other goals. Indeed, much of contemporary stratificational analysis is about this problem —and much of the difficulty with appraisal of poverty strategies is that little is known about the multiplier effect of each strategy.[47]

Fifth, a stratificational approach suggests that style of life variables may be important in the construction and conduct of programs. This statement does not suggest a 'culture of poverty', but an effort to make policies and programs relevant and appropriate to the life styles of their intended consumers.

Finally, we see that many programs aimed at moving youth out of poverty have neglected vital dimensions of the youths' lives.

47. See Rein, M., and Miller, S. M., 'Poverty, Policy, and Purpose: The Dilemmas of Choice', in Goodman, L. H. (ed), *Economic Progress and Social Welfare*, New York, Columbia University Press, 1966.

Many social mobility programs have aimed at enhancing the prospects of youth without improving the conditions of their families. Other programs have sought to improve the education of children without improving the schools which they attend. Headstart and Job Corps, for example, have attempted to create a parallel educational system rather than change educational institutions. In these instances, the social setting of behavior has been neglected.

Conventional poverty discussions are thin because they are cast in terms of nineteenth-century concerns about pauperism and subsistence rather than in twentieth-century terms of redistribution. We are not clear about the goals of poverty-reduction and inequality-reduction because we have not forthrightly discussed our objectives. When poverty is viewed in the stratificational perspective we see that the goal of bringing all families up to a certain income level cloaks disagreements about the relative importance of differing, often conflicting, objectives. For example, at the level of objectives of efforts to change the stratificational system, are we seeking a classless society with only minor differences among individuals; or is the goal a meritocracy in which individuals have in actuality equal access to high-level jobs which are highly rewarded; or do we seek to connect an 'underclass', which does not improve its conditions as much as the rest of the society does, into the processes which will begin to make it less distinctive; or do we seek to reduce the gaps in some vital dimensions between the nonpoor and the poor? Each of these views implies a belief concerning what is important about stratificational systems, how permeable these systems are, and how other goals should be balanced against the concern with the underclasses.

The stratification perspective leads us to see that in dealing with poverty we are dealing with the *quality of life* of individuals and not just their economic positions. This means that not only individuals' relationship to government but the *quality of relationships among people* in society are important. Although governmental and organizational action is needed to diminish the economic and political inequalities separating people, we as individuals must assume responsibility for changing the quality of relationships among ourselves and others. Ultimately, change in the distribution of 'social honor', and self-respect, the most fundamental aspects of stratification, can only be accomplished by each of us, members of society, caring about the excluded and breaking down the walls of social and psychological exclusion. If poverty is about stratification, we cannot escape one another.

# 8. Poverty and Culture: Some Basic Questions about Methods of Studying Life-Styles of the Poor *

## Herbert J. Gans

The methods to be used by any study are determined by the purposes of that study, and this chapter addresses itself to what I consider the basic question about method: why, for what purposes, study the life-styles or the culture of poor people? By the purposes of a study, I mean more than its formal subject or its hypotheses, but also its intellectual aims, and especially its political aims and policy implications.

All studies have political aims and implications, whether these are consciously formulated or not, for as Louis Wirth once wrote, 'every assertion of a "fact" about the social world touches the interests of some individual or group.'[1] The study of culture as we know it derives largely from nineteenth- and twentieth-century ethnologists who wanted to describe pre-industrial cultures, sometimes to preserve them (at least in books), sometimes to show their own industrialized countries the virtues of pre-industrial ways of life. Today, anthropologists more often study reactions to modernization, although with a similar political agenda; they now argue that the values of pre-industrial cultures ought to be taken into account in the processes of urbanization and industrialization. Many anthropologists are still seeking to preserve at least parts of these older

---

* This paper draws in part on an earlier unpublished paper, 'Some Unanswered Questions in the Study of the Lower Class', written in 1963 after a Conference on Low Income Culture in New York City. Both papers are indebted to the work of Hylan Lewis, particularly his *Culture, Class and Poverty*, Washington, Cross-Tell, 1967. For a later version of this paper see 'Culture and Class in the Study of Poverty: An Approach to Anti-Poverty Research', in Gans, H. J., *People and Plans*, New York, Basic Books, 1968.

1. In the preface to his translation of Karl Mannheim's *Ideology and Utopia*, quoted by Lewis, H., *Culture, Class and Poverty*, Washington, Cross-Tell, February, 1967.

cultures in order to build humane and vital elements into a sometimes inhumane and bureaucratic process of modernization.

The study of poverty has followed a somewhat different political
path. The early studies of the ways of the poor were simple and
moralistic, in the nineteenth century cataloguing their moral lapses;
in the twentieth century, their pathologies. Some of the first students
of American poverty understood that immorality and pathology
resulted from economic deprivation, but many explained the life-
styles of the poor by what one would today call culture, particularly
the non-Puritan cultures of the Eastern and Southern European
immigrants.[2] Indeed, these observers, mostly people of high status
who were struggling to maintain their cultural and political power
in a rapidly urbanizing society, proposed that poverty could be
abolished by ending the European immigration—thus excluding the
masses of potential American citizens who were threatening the
dominance of the Protestant middle and upper classes. By the
twentieth century, American social scientists no longer held to such
a simple view; even so, the studies of the Chicago school of sociology
are, at one level, detailed statistical descriptions of lower class
pathology and deviance. The causes of the pathology and deviance
were ascribed largely to the peculiar social and economic environment of the city, and some of the researchers seemed to imply that
the solution to these ills lay in a non-urban society. But most were
debating sociological and theoretical issues, and paid little attention
to the political implications.

Current sociological research among the working and lower
classes has developed in reaction to this tradition. A legion of
researchers has exposed the myth of total social disorganization and
pathology among the poor. For example, Whyte emphasized the
complexity of working class social organization; Young and Willmott,
and others, showed the persistence of kinship and traditional
kinship forms; Walter Miller stressed that what the middle class
called pathology was a viable and independent culture; Oscar Lewis
demonstrated how much vitality and joy existed alongside the
deprivation and pathology; and Hylan Lewis called attention to the
diversity, pragmatism and strength he found among low income
people.[3]

2. For a useful review of these writings, see Bremner, R. H., *From the Depths*,
   New York University Press, 1956.
3. Whyte, W. F., *Street Corner Society*, University of Chicago Press, 1943; Young,
   M., and Willmott, P., *Family and Kinship in East London*, London, Routledge

These studies did not begin with overt political agendas; they sought only to describe and understand. Even so, in isolating the positive elements of the working and lower class life-styles, they argued that whatever the causes of poverty and whatever the policy for ending it, the ways of the poor were worthy of respect, and should not be rejected by middle class social workers or legislators.

The idea that the social sciences can be value-free is no longer accepted, but little attention has been paid so far to the policy implications of research addressed to conceptual and theoretical questions in the social sciences, or, for that matter, to developing social science research on the basis of overt policy considerations. But poverty is a highly charged political issue, and its elimination very likely requires considerable redistribution of economic and social privileges. Consequently, when middle class people study and write about poverty, they must be aware of the political assumptions and the policy implications of their work. For example, if the main purpose of a study is to describe the life-styles of the poor, does this purpose—or the study—include an overt or covert suggestion that the poor are culturally distinctive, and their culture is to be saved or protected, in part or in whole? Or is there an implicit assumption that the culture of poor people is so desirable that nothing should be done about their economic deprivation? Conversely, is the research aim to isolate the pathological elements in the life-styles of the poor, and if so, to suggest that the poor need help? Then one must ask what kind of help is being considered? Does the researcher want to show pathology in order to demand more social work counselling, or economic change? And what political strategies are proposed or implied? Does the study stress pathology to document the injustices of poverty, and thus arouse the guilt of middle class readers in order to induce them to change the economic system? Or does the analysis seek to show the strength of social organization among the poor, perhaps to support arguments that they can be organized politically, and that *they* can and ought to change or overturn the system?

These—and yet other—political assumptions, policy implications and political strategies which are embedded in various kinds of poverty research ought to be identified, but better still, researchers should put an end to formulating studies with overt theoretical

and Kegan Paul, 1957; Miller, W., 'Lower Class Culture as a Generating Milieu of Gang Delinquency', *Journal of Social Issues*, Vol. 14, 1958, pp. 5–19; Lewis, O., *The Children of Sanchez*, New York, Random House, 1961, and *La Vida*, New York, Random House, 1966; Lewis, H., *op. cit.*

schemes but covert political agendas. Instead, both ought to be overt, and political and policy considerations should have priority over theoretical ones. If the social scientist's aim is to contribute to the abolition of poverty—and I would consider this my personal aim —then research should begin by asking what kind of studies are necessary to help achieve this aim. Putting the question this way brings the need of social policy to the fore, and if the research is done properly, the findings can be used to formulate policy, and in the process, to develop new theoretical insights as well.

## II

If the prime purpose of research is the elimination of poverty, studies of the poor are not the first order of business at all; data on the extent of poverty, the kinds of poverty and of the life-styles of the poor are much less important than studies of the economy which relegates many people to underemployment and unemployment, and of the society which leaves teenagers and old people without viable economic and social functions. Research on the economy and on the ways of creating jobs and raising incomes is based on the hypothesis that if poor people can be provided with good jobs and satisfactory incomes, they will cease to suffer from the non-economic deprivations of poverty, and will not pass these deprivations on to their children.

This is a vitally important hypothesis, and one I share, by and large. I would argue that many if not most of the problems of most poor people can be solved by providing incomes and jobs. I believe this hypothesis applies not only to the short-term or intermittently poor, but also to the long-term or permanently poor, the people who have been immersed in poverty for a generation or more. Unfortunately, there are almost no data to test the hypothesis, and there is a crying need for studies of people who have moved out of underemployment, unemployment and poverty, to determine the impact of the change in economic status on the life styles and social-emotional problems associated with poverty, and particularly with long-term poverty.

Those who argue that jobs and income are the major policy measures for the elimination of poverty are not much interested in culture, but they do make a cultural assumption: that the culture of the poor will not interfere in their adapting to economic opportunity.

They take a *situational* view of social change; they suggest that people respond to the situations—and opportunities—available to them, and change their behavior accordingly. But there is an opposite conception, or set of conceptions, the *cultural* view of social change, which suggests that guaranteeing jobs and income are necessary but not sufficient to eliminate poverty. This point of view argues that poverty and the lowly position of the poor leads to a separate and independent lower class culture, in Walter Miller's terms, or to a culture of poverty, in Oscar Lewis' terms, which intervenes in the response to opportunities, sometimes making it impossible for poor people to develop the behavior and value patterns needed, say, to take a job.

Anthropologists studying developing countries have shown that some urban newcomers of tribal origin are sometimes unable or unwilling to adapt to the industrial economy of the time-clock; they work only until they have enough money and then spend it with and for their tribal peers. (Similar findings have sometimes been reported, anecdotally, among European immigrants and even Southern Negroes in America.) Here the 'obstacle' to accepting economic opportunity stems from the social and other time priorities of the culture. On the other hand, a number of observers, including most recently, Walter Miller and Daniel P. Moynihan, have suggested that the female-based family of lower class American Negroes creates behavioral and value patterns that make it difficult for children and adults to partake of economic opportunities.[4] Many other cultural characteristics of the lower class have been identified as impeding movement into the affluent society, ranging from deviant styles of dress to weak ego structure. In short, the cultural view of social change suggests that persisting cultural and personality elements prevent the poor from adapting to economic opportunities even when these are available. Sometimes analysts point to only a few such elements; but others, particularly anthropologists, accustomed to studying the interrelationships of individual behavior patterns, describe a holistic culture or subculture, a set of behavior patterns that hang together logically or psychologically, and as a whole impede the adaptation to opportunities.

Since academic society is as competitive as the larger society of which it is a part, the situational and the cultural views of social change have frequently been described as polar opposites, and

4. Miller, W., *op. cit.*, p. 9; US Dept. of Labor, *The Negro Family: The Case for National Action*, Washington, 1964.

theoretical battles have been fought over the data to find support for one pole or the other. Clearly, the truth lies somewhere in between, but right now, neither the data nor the conceptual framework to find that truth are as yet at hand.

The situational view is obviously too simple; people are not automatons who respond instantaneously and similarly to the same stimulus. But the cultural view is deficient on at least two grounds. *First*, the defenders of cultural variables take what I would call an overly behavioral view of culture, which ignores the role of conflicting *aspirations*. Some of them, although not all, determine cultural norms from people's behavior; they do not ignore values, but tend to deduce them from behavior patterns. Thus, Walter Miller sees values as focal concerns which stem from behavior.[5]

This conception of culture harks back to anthropological tradition. The fieldworker, studying a strange culture, began by gathering artifacts. As anthropology matured, he also collected behavior patterns, for these were most easily seen, and seemed most worthy of preservation. Typically, he isolated a behavior pattern, deduced the values underlying it, or inferred the functions this behavior pattern had for the survival of the group. How people judged this behavior pattern did not interest him unduly; he noted that infanticide was functional for the survival of a hunting tribe, but he did not devote much attention to how people felt about the desirability of infanticide, or about less deadly patterns of culture.

This approach may have been valid for the study of preliterate groups, and of cultures which had developed around a specific economy and ecology. Such cultures gave their people little if any choice; they bred fatalists who did not know that alternative forms of behavior and aspirations were possible, because usually they were not. But such an approach is not valid to the study of the contemporary poor. Many poor people are also fatalistic, not because they are unable to conceive of alternative conditions or behaviors, but because they have been frustrated in the realization of alternatives. Unlike preliterate people—or at least the classic version of the ideal type preliterate—they are unhappy with their state; they have values and aspirations which diverge from the norms underlying their behavior. Of course they can justify, to themselves and others, the behavioral choices they make, but they are also well aware of alternatives they would prefer.

The divergence between the behavioral norms and the aspira-

5. Miller, W., *op. cit.*, p. 7.

tions of the poor has been noted by observers and researchers for over a century, but empirical study is just beginning. For generations, many social workers have argued that basically, the poor want to be middle class; that they share the same aspirations even if their behavior differs, or, at least, they ought to. Many sociologists accept a more sophisticated form of this argument, suggesting that society is based on a common value system, which unites poor and rich. Others, however, argue that, as Rodman puts it, society is based on a 'class-differentiated value system',[6] and Walter Miller has taken perhaps the most extreme position. He suggests that when lower class people express middle class values, they are mainly giving lip-service to what they are expected to say, but their real aspirations reflect lower class culture. More recently, sociologists and anthropologists have openly considered the existence of a divergence between behavioral norms and aspirations, particularly in the debate over whether Caribbean lower class couples in 'living' relationships prefer to be married. Rodman sees the divergence as a value stretch, which enables people to have more than one aspiration; Rainwater, reviewing his data on lower class American Negro families, argues that poor people tend to share the aspirations of the society, but knowing they cannot live up to them, make up other norms which fit the situations to which they must bend.[7]

At present, not enough data are available to say more than that there is a divergence, and that more research is needed, particularly on areas of life other than marriage. Of course, behavior norms and aspirations always diverge somewhat in a modern society, but among the affluent, the gap is probably narrower than among poor people; the former can more often achieve what they want, and if not in one area of life, e.g., work, then at least in another, e.g., family life. The poor have fewer options; if they cannot make choices in work, they are equally restricted in other areas of life, and in a state of existence that S. M. Miller has called crisis-life, behavior and aspirations diverge almost across the board.

Consequently, research on the culture of the poor must encompass both behavioral norms and aspirations. The former must be analyzed because they tell us, after all, how people react to what

6. Rodman, H., 'The Lower Class Value Stretch', *Social Forces*, Vol. 42, December, 1963, pp. 205–215, at p. 205.

7. Rodman, H., *op. cit.*; Rainwater, L., 'The Problem of Lower Class Culture', Pruitt-Igoe Occasional Paper 8, Washington University, mimeographed, September, 1966.

they have now, but limiting the analysis to behavior can lead to the assumption that the behavior would remain the same under different conditions, when there is no evidence, pro or con, to justify such an assumption at this point. As Hylan Lewis puts it, 'it is important not to confuse basic life chances and actual behavior with basic cultural values and preferences'.[8] Therefore, cultural analysis must also look at aspirations, to see where they exist, how strongly they are held, and above all, whether they would be translated into behavior if economic conditions make it possible.

The second and more important deficiency in the concept of culture is its holistic quality and its emphasis on obstacles to change. When a behavior pattern is identified as part of a larger cultural system, and the causes of that pattern are ascribed to 'the culture', there is a tendency, first, to show that a behavior pattern is intrinsically interrelated with many others and hard to dislodge, particularly when it is functional for the survival of the whole society. Second, there is a tendency to see the behavior pattern as resistant to change, as persisting simply because it is culture, even though there is no real evidence for this view. To be sure, some behavior patterns are persistent, but others are not; they will change quite quickly when economic and other conditions change; and we do not yet know which are persistent and which are not. Indeed, I would argue that over the long run, all of the behavioral norms and aspirations by which people live are non-persistent; they are situational, developing as responses to situations which people face.[9]

Of course, not all behavior is a response to a present situation, and many of the behavioral norms people live by developed in past generations, and are learned from parents. Yet, the mere fact that these norms persist for a generation or more does not make them immutable. Going back into history, one can see how much culture is situational in origin; how changes in economic and social opportunities give rise to new behavioral solutions, which then become recurring patterns and are eventually complemented by norms which justify them.[10] Yet what parents teach their children is not entirely

8. Lewis, H., *op. cit.*, pp. 38–39.
9. For a persuasive illustration, see Mead, M., *New Lives for Old*, New York, Morrow, 1956.
10. For a more detailed analysis of the situational origin of culture, see Gans, H. J., *The Urban Villagers*, New York, The Free Press, 1962, Ch. 10. See also Kriesberg, L., 'The Relationship between Socio-Economic Rank and Behavior', *Social Problems*, Vol. 10, 1963, pp. 334–353.

or even predominantly from the past; it is a mixture of new and old, and both adults and children pick up yet other behavioral norms and aspirations from the constant stream of new circumstances to which they must adapt but for which tradition offers no solution, at least in modern society. People are also affected by aspirations current in the larger society; even those who live in a voluntary or involuntary ghetto are not isolated from external influences, and if people are unhappy about their lives, the aspirations which seep in from the outside are taken more seriously than if people are satisfied with their lot.

The total stock of behavioral norms and aspirations which people hold is thus a mixture of situational responses and learned patterns. Some parts of this stock are strictly *ad hoc* responses to a current situation; they exist because of that situation, and will disappear if it changes or disappears. Other parts of the stock are *internalized* and become an intrinsic part of the person and of the groups in which he moves, and are thus less subject to change with changes in situation. Even so, the intensity of internalization varies; at one extreme, there are values which are not much deeper than lip-service; at the other, there are behavioral norms which are built into the basic personality structure, and a generation or more of living in a new situation may not dislodge them. *They* become culture, and people may adhere to them even if they are no longer appropriate, paying all kinds of economic and emotional costs to maintain them.

This view of culture has important implications for studying the poor. Of course, if the researcher is merely interested in describing how the poor live now, and is not willing or able to confront the question of deliberate social change, it is enough to study present life styles. But if his research seeks to contribute to the abolition of poverty, then life-styles must be studied from a dynamic perspective of the kind I have proposed, comparing the divergence of behavior and aspirations, and relating both to situational origins, and to the degree of internalization and persistence. One must constantly ask: to what situation, to what set of opportunities and restraints do the present behavioral norms and aspirations respond, and how intensely are they held; how much are they internalized, if at all, and to what extent would they persist or change if the significant opportunities and restraints underwent change?

Moreover, supposing this change took place, and opportunities for decent jobs and incomes were made available, what behavioral norms, if any, are so deeply internalized that they interfere with taking hold of these opportunities, and if so, what can be done, either to change the norms, or preferably, to design the new opportunities in such a fashion that they can be accepted without requiring an immediate change in strongly persisting norms? Obviously, such norms are not easily changed, and it may be more effective to tailor the opportunities to fit the values, rather than the other way round. For example, *if* the inability to plan, often ascribed to the poor, is a real and persisting behavioral norm that will interfere in their being employable, it might be wrong to expect people to learn to plan at once, just because jobs are now available; the better solution would be to fit the jobs to this inability, and make sure that the adults, once having some degree of economic security, will learn to plan, or will be able to teach their children how to do so.

The prime issue in the area of culture and poverty, then, is to discover how soon poor people will change their behavior, given new opportunities, and what restraints or obstacles, good or bad, come from that reaction to past situations we call culture. To put it another way, the primary problem is to determine what opportunities have to be created to eliminate poverty, and how people can be encouraged to adapt to those opportunities that conflict with persistent cultural patterns.

I am using culture here in a special sense, as those norms (and aspirations) which are resistant to change, and by this definition, a culture of poverty would consist of those cultural patterns that keep people poor *when opportunity beckons*. This conception differs somewhat from that of Oscar Lewis, for in his view, the culture of poverty refers to the ways of life of people without opportunity but with aspirations for something better; it is as much a culture of deprivation and alienation as of poverty. Lewis' conception thus harbors within it a notion of value stretch; it is a culture of people who have other aspirations but cannot implement them because of situational factors. In the sense I use the term, I would exclude current situational factors and limit the culture of poverty to those *specifically cultural* patterns which keep poor people satisfied with, or at least resigned to their present situation when other opportunities are available. Whether or not the families who tell their life histories in Oscar Lewis' books fit my sense of the culture of poverty is hard to say. From the available data, it is impossible to tell how they might react under different circumstances, for example, if Puerto Rico and Mexico offered the men a steady supply of decent and dignified jobs. Almost all the members of the Sanchez and Rios families have aspirations for something better, and my hunch is that in a different economic situation, their lives would be quite different. As I use the term culture of poverty, then, it would apply more to people who lack such aspirations, and who do not know that change is possible: peasants and urbanites who have been left out of the revolution of rising expectations.

Moreover, if the culture of poverty is defined as those cultural elements which keep people poor, it would be necessary to include also the persisting cultural patterns among the affluent that combine to keep their fellow citizens poor. If one applies the concept of a culture of poverty only to the poor, the onus for change falls too much on the poor, when in reality, the prime obstacles to the elimination of poverty lie in an economic system that is dedicated to the maintenance and increase of wealth among the already affluent.

## III

The frame of reference for the cultural study of poverty I have outlined has specific methodological implications. The study of the life-styles of the poor should give up the notion of culture as largely behavioral with little concern about divergent aspirations, as holistic, and as something intrinsically persistent. Instead, insofar as poverty studies should focus on the poor at all, they should deal with behavior patterns and aspirations on an individual basis, relate them to their situational origin, and determine how much the behavioral norms related to poverty would persist under changing situations. Whether or not there is a persisting and holistic culture (or set of cultures) among the poor should be left as an empirical question.

In studying behavioral norms and aspirations among the poor, the following questions strike me as most important: Does a given behavioral pattern block a potential escape from poverty, and if so, how? Conversely, are there aspirations related to this behavioral pattern and do they diverge? If so, are they held to intensively enough to provide the motivation for an escape from poverty when economic opportunities are available?

In analyzing the behavior patterns that *do* block the escape from poverty, one must look for the social and cultural sources of that behavior. Is the behavior a situational response that would change readily with a change in situation, or is it internalized? If it is internalized, how does it become internalized (and at what age), what agents and institutions encourage the internalization, and how intensive is it? How long would a given behavioral norm persist when situations and opportunities change, and what are the forces that encourage its persistence?

Similar questions must be asked about aspirations: What are their sources, how are they internalized and by whom, and how intensely are they held? How responsive are they to changes in situation, and can they enable people to give up poverty-related behavior once economic opportunities are available. And, what kinds of non-economic helping agents and helping institutions are needed in addition to aid poor people to implement their aspirations?

Equally important questions must be addressed to the affluent members of society. First, many of the behavior patterns of poor people have nothing to do with poverty *per se*; they may be the result of poverty but they do not necessarily block the escape from poverty. They do, however, violate working class and middle class values, and thus irritate and even threaten working and middle class people. For example, the drinking bouts and extra-marital sexual adventures which Oscar Lewis and others have found among lower class people may be correlated with poverty, but they do not cause it, and probably do not block the escape from poverty.

They might persist if people had secure jobs and higher incomes, or they might not, or they might take place in more private surroundings, as they do in the middle class. But since they shock the middle class, one must also ask which behavior patterns must be given up or hidden as the price of being allowed to enter the affluent society. This question must be asked of the affluent people, but one would also have to determine the impact of changing or hiding the behavior on poor people. In short, one must ask: what changes are *really* required of the lower class, which ones are absolutely essential to the escape from poverty and the move into the larger society, and which are less important?

Second, assuming that the culture of poverty is less pervasive than has sometimes been assumed, and poor people are able and willing to change their behavior if economic opportunities come to them, what kinds of changes must take place in the economic system, the power structure, and in the behavior and aspirations of the affluent for them to permit the incorporation of the poor into the affluent

society. (As I have noted previously, such questions are more important for eliminating poverty than those to be asked of and about the
poor, but my emphasis in this paper is on the culture of the poor.)

These rather abstract questions can perhaps be made more
concrete by applying them to a specific case, the set of behavioral
norms around the female-based or broken family. The first question,
of course, is: Does this family structure block the escape from poverty?
Assuming that the answer *could be yes*, how does it happen? Is it
because a mother with several children and without a husband or
a permanently available man cannot work? Or is the female-based
family *per se* at fault? Does it create boys who do poorly in school
and on the job; and girls who perpetuate the family type when
they reach adulthood? If so, is the matriarchal dominance at fault
(perhaps by 'emasculating' boys) or is it the absence of a father?
Or just the absence of a male role-model? If so, could surrogate
models be provided through schools, settlement houses and other
institutions? Or are there deeper, dynamic forces at work which
require the presence of a stable father figure? Or is the failure of the
boys due to the mother's lack of income, that is, a result of her being
poor and lower class? Or does their failure stem from the feelings
of dependency and apathy associated with being on welfare? Or is
their failure a result of lack of education among the mothers, which
makes it difficult for them to implement their aspirations for raising
their children to a better life? (But lack of income and education
are not restricted to the female-based family.)

The next question, already suggested by some of the just mentioned
questions is: what are the social, economic, political—and cultural
—sources of the female-based family; and to what situations, past
and present, does it respond? Moreover, how persistent a pattern
is it, what behavioral norms perpetuate it, and what aspirations
exist that would alter or eliminate it if conditions changed? If the
female-based family is an adaptive response to frequent and
continuing male unemployment or underemployment, as I suspect
it is, one must then ask whether the family structure is a situational
response which would disappear once jobs were available. But if
the norms that underlie this family have been internalized, and
would persist even with full employment, one would then need to
ask: where, when and how are these norms internalized? Do the
men themselves begin to lose hope, and become so used to economic
insecurity that they are unable to hold a good job if it becomes
available? Do the women develop norms and aspirations for

independence, and, doubting that men can function as husbands and breadwinners, become unable to accept these men if they are employed? Are such attitudes transmitted to the children of female-based families, and if so, by whom, with what intensity, and at what age? Do the boys learn from their mothers that men are unreliable, or do they conclude this from the male adults they see around them? At what age does such learning take place, and how deeply is it internalized? If children learn it during the first six years of their life, would they have difficulty in shedding their beliefs under more favorable economic conditions? If they learn it when they are some-what older, perhaps 6 to 9, would they be less likely to internalize it? If they learn it from their mothers, is the norm more persistent than if they learn it later from their peers and the male adults they see on the street? And at what age does the boy begin to model himself on these male adults?

Such questions have not yet been asked systematically, and it may be that the entire set of norms underlying the female-based family are much less persistent than the questions in the previous paragraph assume. Whether or not they are persistent, however, one would have to go on to ask: under what conditions is it possible for people, adults and children, to give up the norms of the female-based family? Again, would it follow quickly after full employment, or would adults who have become accustomed to economic insecurity and female-based families pass on these norms to their children even if they achieved economic security at some time in their lives? If so, the female-based family might persist for another generation. Or are there helping institutions which could aid parents and children to give up irrelevant norms, and speed up the transition to the two-parent family? And, if it were impossible to help adults to change, how about 18-year-olds, or 13-year-olds, or 6-year-olds?

Moreover, what aspirations exist among the poor for a two-parent family? Do lower class Negro women really 'want' a two-parent family, and are their aspirations intense enough to overcome the behavioral norms that have developed to make them matriarchs? And more generally, what do poor people want, beyond higher incomes and secure jobs? Are their aspirations for the social and consumption styles of the stable working class, or do they want to be middle class? Are such aspirations strong enough to replace present behavioral norms, and is it possible for people to skip a class, and move directly from lower class to middle class ways of life?

Finally, one must also ask what functions the female-based family performs for the affluent members of society, and what obstacles the latter might put in the way of eliminating this family type. How quickly could they overcome their belief that Negro family life is often characterized by instability, illegitimacy and matriarchy? Would they permit public policies to eliminate male unemployment and to provide higher and more dignified income grants to those who cannot work? And most important, would they permit the changes in the structure of rewards and in the distribution of income, status and power that such policies entail?

If these kinds of questions were asked about every phase of life among the poor, it would be possible to begin to determine which of the life-styles of poor people are really associated with poverty, and which are not, but are shared with other groups in the population. I suspect that the answers to such questions would show that there is no pervasive culture of poverty. Undoubtedly there are many behavior patterns distinctive to the poor, but probably only a handful are in any sense cultural, that is, strongly internalized enough to persist regardless of economic conditions. Rather, I would argue, many poor people share the aspirations of the middle class, and yet more, those of the stable working class. If they could achieve the same economic security as middle and working class people, they would quickly give up most of the behavior patterns associated with poverty. I would agree with what Hylan Lewis concluded about the people he studied: 'The behaviors of the bulk of the low income families appear as pragmatic adjustments [*what I call situational responses. H. G.*] to external and internal stresses and deprivations experienced in the quest for essentially common values'.[11]

If poverty research paid somewhat less attention to the present behavior of the poor, and paid more attention to their aspirations— and to ways of achieving these, it might also be discovered that although the poor may be at the bottom of the socio-economic hierarchy, the number who are, culturally speaking, permanently and inevitably lower class is much smaller than sometimes imagined. Indeed, a different research focus should encourage the revision of current typologies of class. These typologies: of upper-lower and lower-lower classes, or working and lower classes, or the respectable and the rough, are in many ways only sociological terms for the old division between the deserving and the undeserving poor— even if their formulators had no such invidious distinction in mind.

11. Lewis, H., *op. cit.*, p. 38.

Moreover, such class labels are too formalistic; in essence, they only describe the social and economic distance between people on a hierarchical scale. In fact, they really refer to the economic and behavioral deviation of poor people from the middle class, for most current typologies of class are arranged by amount of deviation from middle class norms.

The questions I have asked would suggest a different typology, based on the criterion of whether people can adapt to changing conditions. Just as behavior patterns can be classified as situational or internalized responses, temporary or persistent, so people can perhaps be classified in relation to these behavior patterns as adaptable or non-adaptable; that is, whether or not they can respond positively to new economic opportunities. Obviously, there are some poor people who cannot adapt to any such opportunities. They include people who have so internalized the culture of poverty that they cannot escape, whom Jean Labbens calls the hereditary poor;[12] and people who have been ravaged so much by poverty that they are physically or emotionally too ill to escape, whom Hylan Lewis aptly describes as the clinical poor.

Conversely, there are many poor people who can adapt, and with different degrees of ease. But research may also show that people (poor or affluent) cannot be classified by ability to adapt, and that such classification is possible only with respect to *behavior patterns*. In other words, who adapts and who does not may vary with the specific behavior pattern under study. In that case, it would be impossible to use concepts such as lower class or culture of poverty.

## IV

The questions I have raised can be investigated through a combination of presently available research methods. One basic method is participant-observation; another is the mixture of ethnological description, participant-observation and life history collection used by Oscar Lewis. Both approaches allow the researcher to see behavior in its situational setting, to determine how much behavior is an *ad hoc* response to the situations people face, and to discover what

12. Labbens, J., 'Reflections on the Concept of a Culture of Poverty', Bureau de Recherches Sociales, Paris, mimeographed, 1967.

aspirations people hold, and how these converge with or diverge from behavior. But both methods also have some drawbacks; they can only be applied to small populations. Often it is difficult to study samples large enough to permit broad generalizations, and representative enough so that whatever generalizations are produced can be applied to a larger population.

These drawbacks can be reduced somewhat by other methods, intensive and extensive. Depth interviewing can develop more specific findings for somewhat larger populations, for the interviewer can build on data gathered through the first two methods, and can determine more systematically and in more detail the relationship between behavior and aspirations, and particularly the intensity with which behavioral norms and aspirations are held. A more extensive survey can then take the findings of depth interviewing, and explore at least some of these among a large population, so as to determine the numerical extent of the patterns unearthed by the other methods.

Yet none of these methods are able to get at the prime question about the culture of the poor: what behavioral norms will and will not persist under changed economic conditions. *This question can best be answered by altering the conditions, and then seeing how people respond.* Consequently, the most important method in poverty research is social experimentation which provides people an opportunity to live under improved and more secure conditions, and then measures their response: whether or not they change their behavior and implement their aspirations; and what effect the elimination of poverty has on family structure, consumer behavior, leisure, work and work performance, school attendance and school performance, participation in the larger society, and the like. Only experiments can discover how much the life styles of the poor are persistent cultural patterns, and how much they are *ad hoc* responses to the insecurity, instability, and lack of opportunity that mark the social situations in which they live.

A wide range of experiments is needed to determine (and compare) the response of different kinds of poor people to different changes in economic opportunity: the efficacy of secure and well paying jobs, a guaranteed income without employment, income derived from public welfare, the negative income tax or a family allowance, superior education for the children, better housing for families, and yet others. All of the alternative policies for eliminating poverty must be tested on the various kinds of poor people, with control groups established to determine how much the impact is a result of the specific policy or group of policies being tested.[13]

Most of these experiments would have to be set up *de novo*, but others are already available for research. Some can be studied historically; for example, it is possible to analyze the experience of the European immigrants in America as a field experiment, to measure, however imperfectly, the impact of stable jobs and decent incomes on the cultural patterns which they brought with them from Europe. More useful studies could be conducted among the Negroes and Puerto Ricans who have recently been able to move out of the slums of American cities, to determine what opportunities were available to them, how they took hold of these opportunities, and what changes in behavior followed. A comparison of an experimental group which escaped from a ghetto and a control group which did not might yield some useful preliminary answers to the questions raised in this paper.[14]

In addition, it is possible to study the various anti-poverty demonstration projects which are now being undertaken in the United States, analyzing them as experiments and determining how the participants reacted to the opportunities they were offered. Unfortunately, however, many of these experiments have not yet offered significant opportunities, and have not provided a viable chance to escape from poverty. Some call for job training but without providing jobs; others provide children with better education but cannot guarantee that the children will benefit occupationally afterwards. Rehabilitation experiments with narcotics addicts and with adolescent school dropouts often end by forcing their clients to go back to their old neighborhoods and their old milieus where they must adapt again to situations of poverty; and slum clearance schemes have offered poor people better housing, but not the jobs or the money to pay for the new housing or other necessities.

The need, in America, at least, is for social experiments that offer real economic opportunities to a significant sample of poor people, and intensive studies of how they react to these opportunities. Such

13. For a more detailed description of such experiments, see Gans, H. J., 'Planning for a National Income Maintenance Program: A Proposal for Systematic Experiments', Center for Urban Education, mimeographed, February, 1967. Excerpted in *Current*, No. 84, June, 1967, pp. 56–57.

14. Zahava Blum has suggested studies of American Indians who received large cash payments from the government for their reservations, to determine how they spent these funds, and what successes and failures they encountered in escaping from the poverty of reservation life.

experiments would provide important findings that can help to shape government anti-poverty policy in the future, for the successful experiments could be duplicated on a massive scale, and the failures could be studied to provide clues to improved anti-poverty programs. It goes without saying that such experiments would also be fruitful to social science, for they may answer more reliably than current research methods whether there is a culture of poverty and a lower class way of life.

# 9. Cultural Poverty of Working Class Youth

## Leopold Rosenmayr

### 1. *Some Theoretical Remarks on the Notion of 'Cultural Poverty'*

By cultural poverty we understand the total or partial lack of productivity of and/or receptiveness to symbols, norms and values in societies and their subsets, and in small groups and interpersonal relations.

We consider the constellations and systems of symbols as the 'core of culture' and the poverty in respect to symbolic culture as the central problem of cultural poverty. By symbols we understand the wide range of formalized means of information, learning, influence, and expression in the sciences, arts, literature, fact-representation and in legal, moral and religious codes. To an important degree norms and values depend on symbols for their formulation and transmission. On the other hand, values and norms—individual and socially stabilized ones—are reflected in symbolic representation and information; aside from this general relationship, symbolic culture, its products or the processes of its reception may be classified according to intellectual and/or scientific, esthetic, technological, economic criteria i.e., values or value systems.

It is the underlying yet unproved and still unspecified hypothesis of this chapter that the overcoming of poverty in symbolic culture is of great importance in the processes of the amelioration of physical, economic and social poverty. This hypothesis has several implications:

(a) Learning processes (formal schooling, occupational training etc.) *are part of and depend on* socialization processes in symbolic culture—although, of course, formal training in school systems inversely enhances at least certain aspects of the access to symbolic culture.

(b) If symbolic culture is produced or assimilated *consciously* it effects the perception of physical, economic and social poverty. (The 'interaction' of poverty variables and the 'intensifier phenomenon' need further research in order to

arrive at system- and cycle-models of poverty on the one hand
and of amelioration on the other.)

(c) Amelioration of physical, economic and social poverty is
based on certain elements of symbolic culture. The latter
are a necessary condition for amelioration. Socio-economic
welfare, however, is not a sufficient condition for the further
development of symbolic culture. (A study in the logical
relations of poverty elements is needed, and formal process
analyses for amelioration may be fruitful from a methodological and theoretical point of view.)

Our study is meant to furnish material for implications (a) and
(c), and should bridge the gap between classical poverty studies
on the one hand and educational sociology on the other. It
emphasizes the necessity for more rigid research on processes of
social development in youth, in depressed areas, etc. on the basis
of a strict control of variables and duration. On the other hand, it
attempts to generalize theoretically over different types of
development.

## 2. Empirical Evidence for Differences in Socialization of Adolescents: A Sociological Study in Austria

Here we describe briefly different models of socialization, related to
different types of social mediation of 'symbolic culture'.

For this purpose, we defined as 'cultural activities' of our respondents their (mainly receptive) participation in symbols. The
study is based on measuring and analyzing several areas of such
activities. For each of these areas—reading, movie-going, music,
theatre-going, etc.—we investigated some factors with which these
differences are associated. We also studied the interrelationships
between the different activities. We particularly attempted to
ascertain the respondents' position on the dimension of 'cultural
level' in terms of their attitudinal preference for, or factual participation in, sets of symbols of different quality represented by the various
works of literature, theatre, music, and art.

### (a) SCOPE AND METHODS

Our research was designed as a comparison between boys who
start work at the age of 15 and those who receive a full secondary
education. We therefore drew random samples among adolescent

males of 800 apprentices and 897 high school students[1] of equal age—15 and 17 years old. The samples covered the same geographical area: the city of Vienna and the province of Lower Austria. High school finishes with a diploma (Matura)—the entry requirement for Austrian universities—and therefore lies at the top end of the whole range of training and occupational possibilities open to male adolescents between the ages of 14 and 18 in Austria. Conversely, apprenticeship lies nearly at the bottom end of that range.[2] Apprentices constitute the largest group among boys aged 14 to 18. They work four days a week in a workshop or factory, receiving on-the-job training lasting for about three years, which is supplemented by attending a trade school ('Berufsschule') for one day per week.[3]

As was to be expected from research in other countries, apprentices and high school students differ in their education and social origin. As a matter of fact, there were so few high school students from working-class homes—only 7 per cent—that we had to define the three social classes used for main analyses throughout this study somewhat differently from Anglo-American practice. Classifying by parental occupation gave the following result.

The geographical spread of our samples permits regional comparisons by the size of the community in which the respondents live (city of Vienna, towns with more than 20,000 inhabitants, small towns and villages), and the distribution of the cases along the rural-to-urban dimension.

Our data were collected in 1959, 1960 and 1961 by written questionnaires that were filled in by the boys in their classrooms at school under the immediate supervision of our research staff, with no teachers being present. More recent studies on female youth with similar methods confirm the results.

(b) THE SOCIAL BACKGROUND
The great differences in the amount of education the parents have received offers an important clue to the educational careers of

1. We are using the term 'high school' as a translation for the Austrian 'Höhere Schule'. (Age groups from 11 to 18 at the time when the investigation was carried out.)
2. Except for the group receiving no formal training whatsoever after 14; this has become very small among boys of urban background.
3. Our sample consisted of engineering and woodworking apprentices because these may be considered, within the multiplicity of trades, as a medium group with regard to work prestige and intelligence, and because they are employed both in factories and in small workshops.

TABLE I

*Parents' Occupation and Training of Youth*

| Social origin of the respondents | Apprentices % | High school students % |
|---|---|---|
| Lower class (manual workers, low-grade sales and clerical workers) | 85 | 19 |
| Middle class (small business proprietors, medium administrative grades, semi-professions) | 15 | 39 |
| Upper middle and upper class (big business proprietors, top administrative grades, professions) | — | 42 |
| | 100% | 100% |
| | (681)[4] | (488/347)[5] |

their sons. 56 per cent of the fathers of high school students had themselves graduated from high school against only 6 per cent of the apprentices' fathers.

The parents' education was found to be closely linked to their occupational status and income, and it also strongly influenced their sons' educational choice. Put more specifically, a boy hardly ever seems to receive less education than his father. A similarly close link was found between the grandfather's social status and the father's schooling. The full data are reported in our study on symbolico-cultural activities.[6]

We found that the parents' ownership of both books and pianos varied very much with social class. A considerable part of this variation can be explained by parents' education but when this is held constant, family income also makes some difference. Thus, the better educated and the better off parents are, the more books they have and the sooner they own a piano. In contrast to this,

4. The difference between these totals and the figures quoted above is due to some deficiencies in the response and to the fact that the farmers' sons in our sample have not been included in this social stratification model.
5. Because the total number of high school students is very much lower in Lower Austria than in Vienna, different sampling fractions had to be used. Therefore the number of cases from which aggregated percentages have been calculated has to be quoted in two figures, e.g. N:488/347.
6. Rosenmayr, L., Köckeis, E., Kreutz, H., Kulturelle Interessen von Jugendlichen, Wien-München, 1966.

ownership of television sets (by no means ubiquitous in Austria at the time of the inquiry) has a positive correlation with income but a negative one with parents' education. This seems to show fairly clearly that both financial and cultural factors come into play when such goods are being bought.

The possession of a book-case was considerably more frequent both in manual workers' families and in those of the low clerical and sales grades when their sons went to high school than when they worked as apprentices. This was interpreted as indicating that an above-average cultural interest on the part of the parents seems to be one of the factors promoting high school attendance of lower class children. Also, it may illustrate the feed-back influence from peers on the family and "anticipatory" socialization.

The early separation of the school system—in Austria at the age of ten—has important consequences for peer relations: adolescent friendships and informal groups were found to be almost completely restricted to those having attended the same type of school.

The striking difference in educational achievement between apprentices and high school students was even evident from the way they had completed our questionnaire. Some measure indicating the respondents' verbal ability was obtained by a count of spelling and grammatical mistakes. The educational differential became clearly visible by an average of 1·8 spelling mistakes on a tested page for the apprentices as against 0·3 for the high school students. The number of errors made, varied according to the average of the students' marks (i.e. grades in American terminology) in German, mathematics and geography as well as with the respondents' self-assessment as 'good', 'average' or 'poor' students. Among the apprentices, spelling depended considerably on what type of school they had attended, but in addition there was also a connection with the internal social stratification of their parents.

Of particular interest were the correlations established between the standard of spelling and some leisure-time cultural activities. Spelling was particularly poor among those who had not read a book in the half-year prior to the investigation, among those who owned the smallest number of books, and among those who were particularly interested in comics.

(c) READING HABITS OF ADOLESCENTS

Apprentices read newspapers only a little less frequently than students, but there are considerable differences as to which sections of the daily paper they read. Local columns and the newspaper novel are favoured by the apprentices; domestic politics, foreign politics, and the cultural activities-pages are each read by about twice as high a percentage of students than of apprentices. Only the sports page ranges first with both groups.

A little insight into the process of how political, ideological and cultural values are perpetuated within a family was gained by comparing which newspaper the parents read with the one their son reads. In four-fifths of our cases, sons and parents read the same paper; among the readers of papers issued directly by political parties, this increases to 89 per cent. Probably this is mainly due to the fact that a youngster simply starts to read the paper he finds in his home, but the consequence is that direct value transmission from parents to child is thus considerably reinforced. Particularly in Austria, where several newspapers have a distinct ideological attitude, such an influence has to be reckoned with.

The analysis of the periodicals read by our respondents was even more interesting with regard to cultural habits in the narrower sense. Apprentices concentrate on movie-magazines with a definite teenager appeal, in addition they read the comic strips of 'Mickey Mouse' and illustrated weeklies. The high school students also partake in this fare, but to a much smaller extent. Frequently alongside with the magazines named above, they read other types of periodicals that are hardly or not at all mentioned by apprentices.

Youth magazines sponsored by organizations with pedagogical intentions do not seem to be able to compete successfully with the commercial periodicals (that are often German versions of American periodicals). Many members of youth organizations did not mention reading the paper published by the organization they belong to; the same happens with magazines distributed free of charge through the schools.

All the many different periodicals which our respondents had listed in response to an open question on their reading were grouped into three types by a cultural standard that parallels rather closely the frequently used American groupings of 'quality', 'slick' and 'pulp' periodicals. This brought out very clearly that the type of school attended, as well as social origin, influences the level of periodicals read, as is shown in Table 2.

Reading the 'quality'-type periodicals is also associated with a higher education of the father, and a greater number of books in the home. Residence outside the metropolitan area seems to shield

TABLE 2

*Social Class Background, Training of Youth and Reading 'Quality Type' Periodicals*

| Social origin | Respondents in Vienna, aged 15 | |
| --- | --- | --- |
| | Apprentices | High school students |
| Lower class | 6% (N: 156) | 29% (N: 45) |
| Middle class | 12% (N: 34) | 39% (N: 72) |
| Upper middle and upper class | — (N: 2) | 51% (N: 76) |

adolescents no longer from the products of mass culture: apprentices living in medium-size towns read even more movie-magazines and comics (as well as more books classified as unsuitable for adolescents) than those in the city. Strong religious ties, however, do appear to have such a 'protectional effect'. Among respondents regularly attending mass on Sunday there is a decrease in the percentage reading low-standard periodicals and books (but no increase in the percentage reading on the 'quality' level). Inversely, boys who are already going steady with a girl read more on the low level (especially movie-magazines) without, however, decreasing the amount read on the highest of the three levels we have distinguished.

(d) THE SOCIAL STRATIFICATION OF THE RECEPTIVENESS FOR SYMBOLIC CULTURE (BOOK READING)

Examining the adolescents' own supply of books we found that the average number of books owned by high school students turned out to be more than twice as high as among the apprentices (56:21). As with their parents' books, this figure varied also by social origin but even more along the regional dimension (e.g. apprentices in the city: 24, apprentices in small towns and villages: 16). The meagre supply of books in rural areas is apparently mainly obtained through book-clubs as the membership of book-clubs was higher there than in the city.

Owning books and borrowing from a library do not seem to constitute alternatives but rather occur cumulatively: the greater the number of books owned the larger the likelihood of membership in a lending library. Borrowing from friends and, especially among the high school students, also from parents are additional means of access to books.

Instead of asking respondents to state what type of book they prefer or like best (as most of the very numerous reading surveys in German-speaking countries had done) we required them to put down the title of the last book they had read. The several hundred titles thus obtained were then classified by (a) subject matter, (b) the age group they appeared suitable for, (c) literary (i.e. artistic and intellectual) standard, (d) whether the story had been turned into a film. (The quality criteria used by us were made explicit.)

The analysis by subject matter and by age-group-suitability proved particularly interesting in its developmental aspects. Our results tally with the general pattern evolved by psychologists, and first discovered by Charlotte Bühler.[7] During early puberty interest is focused on adventurous heroes, preferably far removed in time or space from one's own sphere of life. The second stage of puberty, however, is characterized by a return to realism, and a specific interest in learning what the adult world is really like.

We found, however, that the turning point between the first and the second stage occurs much earlier with high school boys than with apprentices. For instance, among those aged 15, 39 per cent of apprentices had read as their last book an adventure story as against only 23 per cent of students. By age 17, the percentage whose last-read book was on this subject had decreased to 24 per cent for apprentices and to 7 per cent for students. This led us to introduce a concept of 'literary age' to denote the stage an individual child or adolescent has reached in his reading interests.

The accelerated development of the high school students appears well confirmed by the results on age-group-suitability. The figures below show the percentages having last read a book of definitely adult character:

This is by no means meant to imply that boys staying on at school *generally* mature quicker than those who start to work early. We found other areas where the apprentices definitely behave more 'adult' than the students (e.g. money management, avoidance of direct parental control, evenings out, smoking, alcoholic drinks). Possibly, *adolescents receiving a full secondary education advance more quickly in respect of a kind of critical independence ('intellectual autonomy'), while the working-class adolescents seem more forward with regard to independence in practical matters of everyday life.*

7. Bühler, C., *Das Seelenleben des Jugendlichen* (5th edition), Jena, 1929.

### TABLE 3
*Age and Training of Youth and Content of Books Read*

|  | Apprentices 15 years | Apprentices 12 years | High school students 15 years | High school students 17 years |
|---|---|---|---|---|
| Low and middle standard fiction— |  |  |  |  |
| Adventure stories | 43 | 24 | 19 | 7 |
| War novels and stories | 16 | 23 | 7 | 9 |
| Historical novels | 7 | 13 | 20 | 15 |
| Detective stories | 11 | 9 | 13 | 10 |
| 'Fact'-books | 14 | 17 | 16 | 14 |
| Literary novels, poetry | 9 | 14 | 25 | 45 |
|  | 100% | 100% | 100% | 100% |
|  | (269) | (335) | (223/131) | (223/127) |

Very clear evidence of one effect of continued education was afforded by our variable 'literary standard of last book read' which we considered an indicator for the dimension we termed 'cultural level'. We believe cultural level to be distinct from, although not orthogonal to, the dimension represented by 'literary age'. Between the ages of 15 and 17, the percentage of students reading books of low literary standard decreased from 17 per cent to 9 per cent, and the percentage reading books of high standard increased from 23 per cent to 35 per cent. *Among the apprentices*, however, there is *no such development*; their standards do not rise at all.

The students' *development* towards a higher literary standard of the books read mainly depends on the influence of the school; yet *schooling* received only partially accounts for this influence. In the selection of books for private reading, peers are important, particularly via the exchange and borrowing of books among classmates. The fact that the majority of students comes from families with a high cultural level has probably thus—using Lazarsfeld's term—a strong 'group effect' on the book-reading choice of their peers from less cultured families.[8] The participation in other media—e.g. the frequency of visits to theatres, concerts, art exhibitions, and also the types of newspapers and periodicals read— seems to be much *more directly influenced by family habits*, and thus depends a good deal on social origin.

Our extensive comparisons with data on adolescent reading collected in the 1920s suggest that parallel to the well known acceleration in physical maturity, an *acceleration in 'literary age' also seems to have taken place during these last three decades*; i.e. certain types of books are being read by comparable groups at a somewhat lower demographic age now than thirty or forty years ago.

We observe that, as compared to apprentices,[9] students are controlled to a greater extent by their parents with regard to movie-going, dating, and dating partners. However, it seems to be the apprentices who are more liable to receive negative sanctions, especially all rough forms of punishment. As far as family relations go, discussion appears to be the dominating medium of control for the parents of students. In the working classes, socialization has a firmer footing in more supervisory forms of control. Aggression and its social presentation are shaped differently according to social stratification.

A comparison between students and apprentices shows that the former are relatively more interested in such topics as religion and politics.

(e) SOME STRATIFICATION DIFFERENCES IN FAMILY
    AND PEER RELATIONS

Several studies carried out by us have shown a detachment of apprentices from their parents in leisure behaviour, and the tendency for *shortening* puberty and the adoption of an adult status: relatively more apprentices drink alcoholic beverages, more of them smoke, more of them save their money for concrete purchases.[10]

8. Cf. the study by Kioshi Ikeda at Oberlin College that demonstrates well how the 'artistic band' of this college and the majority of its students created artistic interest and knowledge even among those students who had not initially been interested in the arts and did not attend any art courses. Ikeda, K., 'Extra-Classroom Factors and Formal Instruction in Art and Music: A Case Study', *The School Review*, Vol. 72–3, 1964, pp. 319–351.

9. Rosenmayr, L., *Familienbeziehungen und Freizeitgewohnheiten Jugendlicher Arbeiter*, Wien, 1963.

10. Cf. *Jugend in Wirtschaft und Gesellschaft* (Research Reports of the Social Science Research Center of Vienna University), ed. Österreichisches Institut

With regard to occupational expectations, *achievement* is connected with work more frequently by students than by the apprentices. The latter emphasize the profit of work and the *security of position* more strongly.[11] Furthermore, students understand achievement as something 'special' and 'difficult', while apprentices understand it as the fulfilment of concrete demands of their work.[12]

Students appear to be more sure about their choices in matters of leisure. They 'feel at home' in cultural systems of symbols extending into the fields of literature and art and thus they are less frequently induced to escape boredom by engaging in activities determined by the casual peer-group.[13]

Interactions and common activities with parents are more frequent with students; apprentices on the other hand go out more frequently. Two-fifths of the apprentices go out in the evenings four to seven times per week, while with students, this rate is only one-sixth.[14]

A comparison between the *most frequent leisure partners* of students and apprentices shows that more than half of them are friends and same-sex friend groups with both students and apprentices; the other, somewhat smaller half is made up of parents and girl friends, with parents predominating with the students in the ratio 3:1. With apprentices the ratio is 1:3.

Classmates play a leading role in friendships among high school students; the parents *know* these classmates or have at least better opportunities to come to know them as compared with parents of apprentices who are hardly able to inform themselves of their sons' social circle at their *working place*. In fact, serious, if not insurmountable limits are set to the co-operation between family and organizations and institutions working in the interest of apprentices.

As to the wishes for the *preferred* leisure partner about half of the answers in both groups indicated the friend and same-sex friend groups. This shows that for these leisure partners there is a certain balance between reality and desire. As to *preferred leisure partners*

für Jugendkunde, Vol. III: *Konsum, Besitzstücke und Spargewohnheiten*, Wien, 1963 (mimeographed), pp. C 11.

11. *Jugend in Wirtschaft und Gesellschaft, op. cit.*, Vol. II: *Lebensziele in der Pubertät*, Wien, 1963 (mimeographed), p. L 71.
12. *Jugend in Wirtschaft und Gesellschaft, op. cit.*, Vol. II, p. L 74.
13. *Jugend in Wirtschaft und Gesellschaft, op. cit.*, Vol. II, pp. L 29–L 33.
14. Rosenmayr, L., Köckeis, E., Kreutz, H., *Kulturelle Interessen von Jugendlichen, op. cit.*, p. XLVII.

girl friends are preferred to parents. *The discrepancy between reality and desire in relation to girl friends is more pronounced with students than with apprentices.* This is due to the fact that relatively more apprentices have occasional and casual girl acquaintances.[15] (Both groups are equal in going steady.) Moreover, they are not so much controlled. Frequently they carry their own keys and do not have to count on control questions concerning their evening activities, and they may relatively freely dispose of their money for satisfying their consumer wishes. Hence, they are able to invite girls more frequently to coffee houses or to dances, etc.[16] Comparative studies on leisure spending on two Sundays lead to results which fall in line with the above data. On the average, 50 per cent of the students spent the two last Sundays alone—this means, according to our schedule of leisure activities, at home[17]—or together with the family and relatives, while with apprentices the corresponding figure only amounted to 20 per cent.

Before concluding, let us briefly glance at some aspects of the differences in the structure of idols. Cinema actors, pop singers and athletes play an important role (they make up the relatively greatest group of idols) with apprentices, while with students they are less decisive and give way to the group of persons active in political, religious, creative and scientific work—a group which is absolutely missing in the consideration of apprentices.[18]

3. *Privileged Maturation: Variables Determining the Access to Symbolic Culture*

Summing up our results we may therefore say that students in secondary education experience a supported, *privileged puberty* in the following sense: elevated socialization methods of the parents (greater extent of control, more time spent on the children, different attitudes toward their learning and symbolico-cultural development, possibly

15. Kreutz, H. 'Jugend: Gruppenbildung und Objektwahl,' Dissertation, Wien, 1965 (mimeographed), Vol. II, p. 180.
16. Rosenmayr, L., 'Sozialbeziehungen und Milieu als Faktoren in der Pubertä männlicher Jugendlicher', *Österreichische Ärztezeitung*, Vol. 19, No. 7, April, 1964. Also cf. Rosenmayr, L., *Familienbeziehungen* . . . , *op. cit.*, pp. 107–116.
17. Rosenmayr, L., *Familienbeziehungen* . . . , *op. cit.*, p. 309, and further data of the Social Science Research Center which are unpublished as yet.
18. Detailed information is contained in unpublished materials of the Social Science Research Center of Vienna University.

more interest in the children, etc.) facilitate internalization[19] or, respectively, transportation of parental authority into the sphere of guiding images. Intensity and duration of socialization efforts leave their marks.

Thus, for example R. F. Winch also shows that functionality of a parent (i.e. the role a parent plays in socialization by means of interactions) correlates with identification, which again must be regarded as a form of internalization.[20]

A. M. Becker explains that persistent and continuous training promotes the ability to suffer actual frustration for the benefit of later advantage, or to resist actual attractions in view of later discomfort. This capacity has to be internalized *and* is trained, until a reliable control mechanism may be built up, so that given objectives can be reached by appropriate means. 'Such training', writes Becker, 'supplements drive-control guided by the viewpoint of purposive rational expediency, and—as this does not suffice for social life— may also install a control system of moral principles, based on common and general acceptance.'

The privileged puberty of students is also seen in their expectations of life objectives and in their attitudes towards occupation. Parental home and school act largely in the *same* sense. The driving forces are on the one hand the gratifications observed in the *level of the father's occupation* and also the recognition which parents receive on account of their status; on the other hand a certain *structure of ideals* becomes effective which is supported by the education afforded by the secondary school system.

Privileged puberty results in the *guidance and encouragement to solve problems in a specific way.* It supports the motivation to engage in *leisure activities, which satisfy culturally higher aims.* These processes might also be referred to as the development of the *cultural capacity to select.*

One of our studies demonstrated that the effect of schools—or, conversely, the absence of such an effect—is of great importance. It has been shown that with adolescent high school students, a privileged puberty gives them more numerous *chances of development* over a relatively long period. Apprentices, however, are both more

19. Cf. the theoretical studies of Claessens, D., 'Familie und Wertsystem', *Soziologische Abhandlungen*, Bulow, F., and Stammer, O. (eds), Vol. 4, Berlin, 1962.
20. Winch, R. F., *Identification and Its Family Determinants*, Indianapolis-New York, 1962, see especially pp. 140 and 151; in this study Winch is trying to use theoretical concepts for this complex of problems in connection with research.

exposed to and more influenced by those elements of popular culture,[21] which are directed toward quickness and ease of immediate wish fulfilment.

Privileged adolescents experience a differential development of cultural interests and an expansion of cultural activities, while the unprivileged experience *stagnation*. This explanation cannot—as several have shown—be disproved by saying that differential development is due to differential levels of intelligence.[22]

Intelligence does explain certain aspects of the differences in cultural and educational activities or interests. This certainly is a difficult problem as no intelligence tests free from socio-cultural factors have been developed[23] up to now. Environmental stimuli have influenced the use of intelligence from early childhood on; even prenatal influences cannot be excluded theoretically.

Findings from numerous studies in the sociology of symbolic culture and education permit us to form the hypothesis that *cumulative milieu stimuli are superadditive*. Thus, it is an often cited fact that children from the upper class, who have learned to express themselves well, not only are high academic achievers (which is frequently due to an environmentally conditioned motivation) but also, because of their ease and poise in communication, they achieve status among their classmates. This recognition adds to the child's self-confidence and assurance which, in turn, results in an increased admiration on the part of his classmates which may even influence

21. Cf. Rosenmayr, L., Köckeis, G., Kreutz, H., *Kulturelle Interessen . . .* , *op. cit.*, pp. 1–10.

22. Genetic intelligence, which can be separated from environmental intelligence by experiments with greatest difficulties only, does of course prevent or, respectively, promote the chances for access to environments or, respectively, differential levels of cultural stimuli.

23. Cf. Clausen, J., who, in a recently published paper, discusses the *deficiency* in correlation between intelligence tests carried out in infants and later measurements, in which language and conceptualization obtain great importance, both of which are highly dependent on milieu. (Smith, B., 'Socialization for Competence', *Social Science Research Council Items*, Vol. 19, No. 2, June, 1965, p. 19.) According to present day research, the influences of environment on intelligence, measurable by tests, are likely to start in the second or third year of life, since from the fourth year of life onward connections between intelligence and social origin have been ascertained; these connections, however, have been proved to be absent in the first year of life. Cf. also Bayley, N., 'Comparison of Mental and Motor Test Scores for Ages 1–15 Months by Sex, Birth Order, Race, Geographical Location, and Education of Parents', *Child Development*, Vol. 36, No. 2, 1965, p. 408.

the teacher. This assurance will then enhance parental attention and readiness for socialization, hence also the actual mediation of values and symbols, thus promoting the advantage over other children.

Inversely, an escalation of negative effect as described by Patricia Sexton may equally occur: 'The teacher learns that he (the student) has a low I.Q. rating and puts him into a slow-moving group where he is not expected to do much or be given much attention. He is bright enough, however, to catch on very quickly to the fact that he is not considered very bright. He comes to accept this very unflattering appraisal because, after all, the school should know. He is in his pigeonhole. He can't get out, and what is more, he doesn't try; he accepts his fate. His parents accept it, since after all, the school should know. Intellectually, he is lost. He has accepted this low appraisal of himself; and both he and society must suffer the consequences.'[24]

Our thesis says that the effects of two or more environments on adolescents, provided that they aim in the same direction, reinforce each other[25] by direct and feed-back processes[26] and are superadditive.[27] It may be assumed that the theorem, somewhat slackened, will also apply to adults.

This mutual preference and promotion could be ideally described by referring to speaking and reading behaviour, its social prerequisites and consequences. The learning of reading shows excellently the dependence of progress on the respective social stratum.[28] Connections between language and stratum,[29] spelling and reading behaviour, connections between the latter two and school marks may well be regarded as proven.[30] Reading behaviour

24. Sexton, P., *Education and Income*, New York, 1961, p. 52.
25. This conception is connected with terms from the field of cybernetics, especially with those of 'refundancy' and 'super-sign'; cf. von Cube, F., *Kybernetische Grundlagen des Lernens und Lehrens*, Stuttgart, 1965, especially pp. 56–59 and 105–110.
26. Cf. Poletajew, I. A., *Kybernetik*, Berlin, 1963, especially pp. 361–363.
27. This thought is highly speculative yet. Cf. Poletajew, I. A., *op. cit.*, p. 365.
28. Barton, A. H., and Wilder, D. E., 'Research and Practice in the Teaching of Reading: A Progress Report', in Miles, M. B. (ed), *Innovation in Education*, New York, 1964, p. 384.
29. Bernstein, B., 'Soziokulturelle Determinanten des Lernens, mit besonderer Berücksichtigung der Rolle der Sprache', in Heintz, P. (ed), *Soziologie der Schule*, Kölner Zeitschrift für Soziologie und Sozialpsychologie, Sonderheft 4, 1959, p. 52.
30. Cf. Rosenmayr, L., Köckeis, E., Kreutz, H., *Kulturelle Interessen . . .* , *op. cit*, p. 79.

can be understood only if it has been realized that learning patterns may also vary with socialization patterns or, respectively, with cultural patterns internalized in socialization.

The upper middle classes succeed in educating the child to a *communicative form of expression*. The formation of concepts, which the child learns at home and which places higher claims to the expression of the child, creates also a *specific kind of inquisitiveness and a desire for knowledge*. The perceptions which thus arise already contain perception mechanisms which make further information of similar level desirable. Thus, a child of the higher strata and more favoured environments will more rarely experience serious conflicts between his own expectations and his teacher's intentions.

## 4. *Cultural Poverty: System Effects of Underprivileged Maturation*

The socio-economic conditions under which our present day youth grows up are distributed over a broad spectrum, starting from a 'system of poverty caused by environment' to a 'society of affluence'.[31]

Poverty as a system, especially in the developing countries includes: a continuous fight for survival, unemployment, low wages, unskilled labour, absence of food supplies, insufficient possibilities for privacy, child labour and numerous forms of escapism such as alcoholism and drugs, etc. Oscar Lewis[32] excellently characterized the main feature of this system: *strong relationship* to the present[33] and the inability to defer gratifications.

It is our thesis that some traits of this attitude of *fatal immediacy*— as we would like to call it—are still present within the highly

31. Cf. Rosenmayr, L., 'Economic and Social Conditions Influencing the Lives of Young People', in *International Conference on Youth, Grenoble, 23rd August to 1st September 1964, Final Report*, UNESCO, Paris, 1964, Annex V.

32. Lewis, O., *The Children of Sanchez, Autobiography of a Mexican Family*, New York, Random House, 1961.

33. This 'short circuit' of the circle of experience and gratification as well as its limited radius can frequently also be demonstrated sociologically. D. Caplovitz wrote: 'In their famous study of the unemployed of Marienthal, Jahoda, Lazarsfeld, and Zeisal discuss the "proletarian consumer". They use the phrase "reduction in effective scope" to describe his shopping behavior. By this they mean that the blue-collar families limited their shopping to the immediate neighborhood; they were not particularly conscious of quality; they did not shop around before buying', in Caplovitz, D., 'The Problems of Blue-Collar Consumers', in Shostak, A. B., and Gomberg, W. (eds), *Blue-Collar World: Studies of the American Worker*, Englewood Cliffs, N.J., The Free Press, 1964, p. 112.

industrialized societies with *well-organized school systems*.[34] Many studies have proven that the lower social strata only in exceptional cases bring forth that type of family, for which Jean Floud[35] has coined this most appropriate term: 'famille éducogène'. This term refers to families which provide their children with an 'elevated care' by means of manifold educational and cultural stimuli adjusted to each other. Families who *know* about the value of education and continuously *perceive* the educational chances and institutions, will *strive* to a greater degree to make it possible for their children to take profound benefit from educational and cultural facilities over a long period of time.

The parental home in the lower social strata frequently does not provide for the spatial and factual prerequisites—for which, of course, the financial position is responsible to a large degree. The low income brackets have fewer musical instruments, books, pieces of art, pictures, collections of scientific or aesthetic value, etc.

In relation to learning and formal schooling, income is a forceful factor on the extremes of the economic distribution. It is powerful with the poor on the one and the wealthy on the other hand.

Yet *economic well-being does not automatically result in a higher cultural standard and in striving towards education.* Prosperity provides for funds, but also for possibilities of distraction. It does not, out of itself, breed the 'famille éducogène'. The better financial position alone does not suffice to enable the parents to mediate attitudes or knowledge *vis à vis* cultural symbols and values which they themselves do not possess. It follows from this that parents, having recognized negative influences as such and having succeeded in effectively averting them are frequently unable to shape and offer influences of higher value *to replace* the negative ones.

Furthermore, as has been demonstrated by R. Kaes,[36] the lower strata 'satisfy their cultural needs' only *after* their material demands have been satisfied.

34. Cf. Die unterentwickelten hochindustrialisierten Gesellschaften, Bergedorfer Gesprächskreis zu Fragen der freien industriellen Gesellschaft, Protokoll-Nr. 21, Hamburg-Bergedorf, 1966.
35. Floud, J., 'Social Class Factors in Educational Achievement', in Halsey, A. H. (ed), *Ability and Educational Opportunity*, Report of the Conference organized by the Office for Scientific and Technical Personnel, in collaboration with the Swedish Ministry of Education, in Kungälv, Sweden, 11th–16th June, 1961, p. 102.
36. Cf. Kaes, R., 'Les ouvriers français et la culture, Enquête 1958–1961, Strasbourg 1962', in *Population*, 1964, No. 4, p. 779.

Frank Riessman[37] tried to draw a schematical 'profile of the underprivileged': they regard themselves as outsiders and are, therefore, frustrated. They show no perseverance in the pursuance of goals which are important to them personally; in cases of failure they do not tend to blame themselves and they are direct in the expression of aggression. In their desire to ascend the wish 'just to make it' prevails over the objective to be successful. They prefer work promising security to such work as is connected with risks. Their ability to read is of little use, they are poorly informed in many fields; frequently they are open to suggestions but distrusting towards 'new ideas' and cling to traditional attitudes. They love thrilling experiences and want to escape the monotony of everyday life. News, gossip, new gadgets are therefore attractive to them. The actual search for new stimuli is frequently in opposition to their traditional attitudes.

Let us summarize some of our findings in connection with these generalizations.

The 'level' and quality of receptive and reproductive activities within the 'symbolic culture' of adolescents depends on their social environments created by family, school and peers—in this order of priority. Educational activities and interests of both parents and children are embedded within the whole complex of participation in values, norms and symbols. The process of socialization, especially with respect to elevation and consolidation of the level of the symbolic culture, is equally conditioned environmentally. It originates from there, yet in reception processes is 'tailored' socially. Admittedly, in the *genesis* of culture, socio-economic factors play an important role both quantitatively and qualitatively. Yet the selection processes in the reception of culture (the 'consumer side') —these included the receptive activities as studied by us—seem to be still more basically determined by socio-economic factors than creativity.

Culture generally depends heavily on its 'core': symbolic culture. In studying processes of socialization the opposite relationship has to be focused upon: the dependency of symbolic culture (and of the access to it) on the socially structured strata of cultural behavior.

We are confronted with several basic types of socio-cultural maturation during adolescence appearing with a certain regularity

37. Riessman, F., *The Culturally Deprived Child*, New York, Evanston and London, 1962, pp. 26–28.

because of certain variables of environment. Since, moreover, the connection between long duration planning, control, purposiveness of socialization on the one hand and the level of adolescents' socio-cultural activities on the other hand have been proven to correlate positively by a host of research material, we regard the theory of the two types of adolescence as not yet falsified.

# 10. The Poverty of Old People in Urban and Rural Areas

## Otto Blume

When I write about poverty, my understanding is that there is no generally valid definition of the concept of poverty which would be appropriate at all times and in all regions. In order to define the concept in operational terms, one must proceed from conventional assumptions. A person is described as poor if his total life situation lies below a subsistence level which is acknowledged as the minimum by the dominant public consensus. As in the case of the West German Federal Social Assistance and Youth Welfare Laws[1] the term 'poverty' is defined as a condition below a subsistence minimum. The term is applied when somebody is unable to achieve subsistence, that is, his requirements for food, clothing and shelter. This term is also used if he is unable to satisfy his cultural and social requirements e.g. if his ability to maintain contact with his environment is seriously impaired, on account of his inability to obtain essential material goods by his own strength and effort. It is not a necessary condition, however, for such an individual to regard himself as being poor. The term has to be defined independently of the subjective judgements of those concerned.

By old people I mean men and women who have completed their

1. Apart from financial help the Federal Social Assistance Law provides measures for: (a) preventive treatment of disease; (b) assistance in case of illness; (c) environmental aids for invalids; (d) assistance in case of tuberculosis; (e) assistance for blind people; (f) assistance if nursing is required; (g) assistance to run the household.

   Apart from the assistance guaranteed in the other regulations of the law, special assistance for old people is granted (under Section 75) in order to overcome the difficulties caused by old age and to prevent loneliness in old age. The following measures are permitted: (a) assistance in obtaining occupation; (b) assistance to get suitable accommodation; (c) arranging entertainment and activities which satisfy social and cultural requirements; (d) assistance to establish contact with relatives and friends.

   This assistance can be granted irrespective of income or private means.

sixty-fifth year of life. As physiological and chronological age do not coincide, it is entirely a pragmatic problem at what age one speaks about people as being old. The pensionable age of manual workers and of white collar workers in the Federal Republic of Germany is 65. This has become the conventional start of 'old age' on account of the fact that those who are employed have to leave their place of employment in almost all cases when they reach this age. This policy is the result of collective and other agreements governing the conditions of employment. This applies also to civil servants. They, too, are pensioned off at the age of 65, though at 62 in the case of poor health.

All the statements in this paper with regard to the situation of old people derive from the findings of empirical social research. Probability sampling methods have been used in these investigations. Between 1961 and 1966 sample surveys were undertaken in six large cities, in one highly industrialized rural area, in one less highly industrialized rural area, and in six predominantly agricultural rural areas. Interviews were conducted on the basis of standardized questionnaires. Certain groups of questions were not subject to any modification, especially those which concerned data about income and contacts with the social environment. Data was compiled on 11,000 punchcards, which form the basis of our analysis. The results are only representative for those urban and rural areas in which these investigations were carried out but may be regarded as valid for these areas. Almost 100 per cent correspondence was obtained in the results for the six large cities. Regional differences do not seem to have had an effect to any significant extent. (Tests were carried out in Bremen in the North, and Stuttgart in the South of the Federal Republic.) But as we shall show, there are greater differences between rural and urban conditions.

Why did we not conduct an investigation representative for the whole of the Federal Republic? In accordance with the Federal Social Assistance Law, responsibility for measures to support old people is vested in local government bodies, i.e. in urban and rural councils. This law has been in force since 1962. In the early 1960s neither rural nor urban authorities were in possession of adequate information (apart from routine statistics) concerning the situation of old people. Hence, it was not known how many old people were in need, nor the actual nature of their needs. The Federal Law had suggested various measures, but the authorities responsible for carrying out the law were insufficiently informed about the position of those who lived within their jurisdiction and might be eligible for support under the law. It would not have been practical to undertake an investigation for the whole Republic even with a sample of 10,000 informants, because people living in rural and urban conditions exist under very different social conditions and require different kinds of assistance and numbers in some categories would have been very small. For these reasons we based our investigations on representative samples which were derived from localities of different size and social structure.

## Two Subsistence Levels

The data refer to the year 1965. We need to deal with two minimum subsistence levels. The first of these amounts to DM 200,– for a person living alone. This is the sum which people above the age of 65 receive from Social Assistance funds if they are not in receipt of a pension or of insurance benefits of any kind and if they have insufficient private means to maintain themselves. This average sum includes any special allowance to which they may be entitled in respect of rent for accommodation. Social Assistance allowances are decided by the various States which compose the Federal Republic. At present they are the lowest in Bavaria (DM 120,–), and highest in Hesse (DM 132,–). In the case of persons above the age of 65, the above-mentioned sums are increased by 20 per cent. Thus they amount to DM 144,– in Bavaria, and DM 158,– in Hesse. In addition to these sums, Social Assistance pays their rents, and makes grants for clothing requirements. Together, these allowances reach an average of DM 200,– per person.

The second minimum subsistence threshold amounts to DM 300,– for a person living alone. This level has been established on the basis of empirical research and indicates the approximate income which is required if old people are able to participate in cultural activities and maintain social contacts. Our investigations have revealed that those whose income is below this sum are not in a position to make or receive visits, that it is almost impossible for them to take part in cultural activities, and that they are hardly in a position to take a holiday away from home. These people are uninterested in political affairs, and, compared with people with higher incomes, they participate least in the activities of their local church.

In view of the fact that it was the intention of Parliament in enacting the Federal Social Assistance legislation that old people should be able to take part in cultural and social activities, it would only be logical to grant to those concerned the financial means necessary for the realization of Parliament's intentions. These intentions were particularly specified in that section of the law which deals with measures for the welfare of old people. Thus we find that a subsistence level of DM 200,– applies only to the fulfilment of bare physical needs, but that a level of DM 300,– is required if social and cultural needs are to be included. These figures apply only to those old people who are living on their own. In the case of two old people living together e.g. married couples, the physical subsistence level amounts to DM 300,– and the socio-cultural one to DM 400,–.

## Results for Cities

How many old people have incomes which lie below the above-mentioned subsistence levels? To begin with we shall consider those who depend entirely on social assistance funds, who have no other source of income of any kind. In the large cities about 1 per cent of those above the age of 65 depend exclusively on Social Assistance, and another 1 per cent receive allowances to supplement extremely low insurance benefits. For example, if these benefits amount to DM 100,– Social Assistance will make a supplementary grant of DM 100,–. To translate these percentages into absolute figures, we reach the following results: if one takes a city with a population of 1 million, one finds that about 100,000 are above the age of 65. In a city of this size it will be found that about 1,000 persons above the age of 65 depend entirely on Social Assistance funds, and a further 1,000 receive supplementary allowances because their insurance benefits are inadequate for physical subsistence.

Who are these 2,000 persons above the age of 65, and what are their social characteristics? 90 per cent are women and 75 per cent of them are wives whose husbands had been self-employed as artisans, craftsmen, traders, or who had been in other occupations. These men were not subject to compulsory insurance, they had failed to make private arrangements to provide for their future, or —and this applies in the majority of cases—their private insurance premiums had been reduced to as little as 10 per cent of the original nominal value as the result of devaluation after the last war. Thus insurance incomes were enormously reduced and quite insufficient to provide an adequate pension for their widows. The remaining women are the widows of employees who died young. Their insurance contributions were consequently insufficient to assure their widows an adequate income.

At this stage it should be pointed out that men who have been employed continue to draw full insurance benefits even after the death of their wives. The wives, on the other hand, have not usually been employed, and on the death of their husbands, which in terms of statistical probability is likely to occur first, are only entitled to 60 per cent of the insurance benefits which they and their late husbands had formerly drawn together. This measure helps to explain why most old and poor people happen to be women.

In addition to these 2 per cent of people above the age of 65, living in large cities, and either entirely or partially dependent on Social Assistance, there are a further 20 per cent of women above 65 whose insurance benefits are below DM 200,–, but who do not claim any kind of Social Assistance at all.

What are the social characteristics of this group of women? We find the same social factors at work which determined the situation of the groups referred to above. Two-thirds are widows whose husbands had been self-employed, whose husbands had been employed for relatively short periods, had not paid adequate insurance contributions, or had lost their husbands when the latter were still quite young.

These women are reluctant to claim Social Assistance, although they are eligible for it. They include, first, persons who are in receipt of insurance benefits which fall only a little short of DM 200,–. These people are either too embarrassed or too shy to go to the Social Assistance Board for the sake 'of a few DM'. Second, there is a group of about the same size whose social prestige or self-esteem does not permit them to claim Social Assistance. Third, there is a group, the largest, which consists of those above the age of 65, who forgo making a claim because their children or grandchildren will be asked to refund any grants which they might have drawn from Social Assistance. Either because they want to avoid conflicts with their children (which arise frequently as a result of the latter's obligations to refund the Board), or because the children support their old mother of their own free will, the old people do not bother to apply for assistance. In as far as these old women actually live with their children, the sons or daughters pay the whole rent in about 50 per cent of all cases.

Absolute figures make the problem more evident. In a city with a population of 1 million one finds 100,000 above the age of 65. These 100,000 are composed of 60,000 women and 40,000 men. We found that in 1965 about 12,000 of the 60,000 women had incomes which were below DM 200,– (in addition to the 2,000 women who were in receipt of social assistance). By contrast there were only 1,000 men who were in a similar position.[2] Thus, altogether about 15 per cent of old people had incomes, excluding contributions from children, which were below the physical subsistence level.

The following data apply to the DM 300,– threshold: 42 per cent of women above the age of 65 (in a city with a population of 1 million their number amounts to about 24,000 out of 60,000) have less than DM 300,–. They consist almost entirely of widows, and include as many as 55 per cent of those whose husbands had been self-employed, and 30 per cent of those whose husbands had been unskilled labourers. On the other hand, less than 20 per cent of widowers have an income below DM 300,–.[3] To summarize: the poor in

2. According to an estimate of the Home Secretary (Bundesministerium des Inneren) approximately 60,000 households, whose head is above the age of 65, depend entirely on social assistance, while 75,000 families receive supplementary allowances because their insurance benefits are too low. A far larger group, however, are eligible as pointed out above, to claim social assistance. If we add the women and men whose income is below DM 200,–, and who do not claim any kind of social assistance, to the above-mentioned group, we then get a figure of approximately 300,000 people (not quite 5 per cent of the people above 65) who hardly reach the physical subsistence minimum.

3. As the interviews were conducted on the basis of standardized questionnaires, it is extremely difficult to make exact statements about the income of old people. For it is not easy to verify the answers given and some are not precise enough. 11 per cent of the informants refused to state their income. As this figure is relatively high, we tried to find out some characteristics of this group. From their other statements, we got to know their present or former job, their education and furthermore whether they possess a house, a car, a television or a refrigerator, etc. Analyzing these data we came to the conclusion that the majority of those who refused to state their income belong with great probability to the highest of our income groups (more than DM 600,–). By income we mean the net income per month of the elderly income unit of household, including all salaries, insurance benefits and so on. If the old people actually lived with their children in one household, the income of the children was not taken into consideration.

The following definition is given in Part 2 of the Federal Social Assistance Law 'Assistance toward Subsistence': 'The necessary subsistence comprises all food, shelter, clothing, physical culture, household necessities, heating and personal everyday requirements. These personal everyday requirements include social and cultural requirements as well to a certain extent.' Excluding those people who depend entirely on social assistance, there were in Düsseldorf

large cities are predominantly women living on their own, above all widows of men who were self-employed.[4]

## Results for Rural Areas

Only half as many persons depend entirely or partially on social assistance grants in rural areas, being only 0·5 per cent of those aged 65 and over. In as far as they do claim social assistance, one finds the same characteristics as were found in the cities. Assistance is claimed by women living alone, especially widows of men who had been self-employed. However, the number of those whose incomes are below DM 200,– per month is not lower in rural areas than in the large cities. The opposite is the case. Compared with 18 per cent of those aged 65 and over in the cities whose standard of living is below or very close to the 'subsistence minimum', there are 22 per cent in rural areas.

Why is so little use made of the Social Assistance Board in these rural areas? The characteristics of rural and farming life in the Federal Republic largely explain this reluctance. The eldest or the youngest son or daughter, as the case may be, inherits the farm or homestead. It is very frequent that an unmarried sibling (usually the sister) remains on the farm and assists in running it. They do this for many years and are highly appreciated for their work. In the majority of cases, however, no insurance contributions are paid for them by the siblings who inherited the farms. When these unmarried siblings reach old age they continue to live on the farm and receive their food from the present owners, but they receive no

---

and Stuttgart in the autumn of 1964:
  10 per cent with an income of less than DM 200,–
  15 per cent between DM 200,– and DM 299,–
  16 per cent between DM 300,– and DM 399,–
  16 per cent between DM 400,– and DM 499,–
  10 per cent between DM 500,– and DM 599,–
  22 per cent of more than DM 600,–
  11 per cent refused to state their income.
Altogether 26 per cent, including those receiving social assistance (that is, every fourth person of the age above 65) have an income of less than DM 300,– in these two cities. If we include the people receiving social assistance, 42 per cent of the women and 18 per cent of the men who live on their own have an income of less than DM 300,–. 20 per cent of the women and 10 per cent of the men living on their own have an income of less than DM 200,–.

4. The difficulties of old people correspond closely with their state of health. The greatest difficulties for the majority of old people above 65 do not seem attributable so much to low income as to decreasing health.

cash, or very little indeed. At this age they are tolerated rather than appreciated. It is, however, impossible under the sociological conditions of the village, for those above the age of 65 who are single and whose physical strength is very much reduced, to claim Social Assistance. The prestige of the present owner of the farm would not tolerate such an action. Should the old person ignore this and make a claim all the same, one of two things will happen: either the village burgomaster or mayor, or the parson or priest, will remind the farm owner of his obligations.

It is a mistake to assume that the situation of old people in rural areas is better on the average than it would be in large cities, because the multi-generational household is more frequent in the former than in the latter environment. The single and the widowed members of multi-generation families in rural areas have less cash at their disposal than their peers in the large cities. This is the least that can be said. Moreover, they have to put up with more humiliations, and feel more forsaken.[5]

5. The representatives of the welfare organizations in the Federal Republic of Germany hardly mention financial difficulties, but concentrate on the loneliness of old people. Very often the word 'loneliness' is used to characterize old age. Yet only rarely is there a distinct conception of this term. The question of friends and relatives dying is confused with the question of living alone. 'Living alone' does not necessarily mean feeling lonely. Even life within a family can create a feeling of loneliness due to insufficient contact and understanding in spite of the presence of the children. Old people who actually live with their children feel just as lonely as those who have a household of their own. The multi-generational household consequently does not alleviate the feeling of loneliness. 'Living alone' is an objective criterion, and is not necessarily of psychological significance. If we presumed that all people who live alone feel lonely, then the number of lonely old people would be very large, for about 50 per cent of the people above 65 have lost either their husbands or their wives, and this applies to large cities as well as to rural areas.

   As long as 'living alone' and 'feeling lonely' are considered to be the same, practical help will be very difficult. For the fact that people live alone cannot easily be altered. As many as 10 per cent of all women have lived alone for the whole of their lives and not only in old age, since they are unmarried.

   Our data show that very old, ailing and poor women who live on their own are most afflicted by loneliness. Those who are lonely are 2 per cent of the age group of 65–70, and 6 per cent of the age group above 80 (in both large cities and in rural areas). But this increase is largely explained by a decrease in the proportion of old people who are married. Six per cent of the informants who had an income below DM 300,– regarded themselves as lonely, but only 1 per cent of those who had more than DM 500,– at their disposal. Again, widowed status underlies these figures. Finally, we found correlations between loneliness and ill-health, and between loneliness and lack of education.

It is extremely difficult to make exact statements about income in rural areas, because most farmers are neither willing nor able to give precise information with regard to their incomes. We know only that the average number of those above the age of 65 who remain in employment after having reached this age, is higher in rural areas than in large cities (20 per cent compared with 10 per cent). We also know that 75 per cent of those over 65 in rural areas, live in homes which they own, compared with only 20 per cent in large cities. Seen in this light, home-ownership as well as longer employment indicate a higher standard of living in rural areas, provided one does not include those who are single and ailing to whom I have called attention above.

Another problem which is very acute in rural areas, particularly in Southern Germany, concerns agricultural labourers above the age of 65. Up to this age, they and their families receive board and lodging at their place of employment. After 65, or whenever they are unable to continue working, they are obliged to leave the farm. Usually they have been accustomed to receiving small cash wages, and consequently their insurance contributions have also been small. Accordingly, their pensions are small. They do not possess enough cash to buy their own furniture or pay the rent for accommodation of their own. In Southern Germany they receive preferential treatment with respect to accommodation in Old People's Homes. In certain rural areas of Bavaria 45 per cent of those above 65 live in Old People's Homes. The average in Bavarian rural areas is 15 per cent, compared with an average of 4 per cent in the large cities of the Federal Republic. On the whole, the achievement of socio-cultural subsistence levels is less likely under rural conditions than under those which are found in the large cities.

# 11. A Cross-National Study of Standards of Living of the Aged in Three Countries

## Dorothy Wedderburn

In this chapter I shall discuss five topics:

1. The evidence of poverty among the old.
2. The importance of conceptual problems in the definition of 'standards of living' for the old.
3. Why the old are so often poor; in particular the effect of retirement.
4. Whether there is a tendency for social security systems to provide benefits for the old which are close to the poverty line.
5. The diversity of economic circumstances, and the impossibility of speaking of a 'culture of poverty' among the old.

## 1. *The Old and Poverty*

Precise estimates vary, but most post-war studies of poverty in the United States and Britain have revealed a lot of poverty among the aged. As important, they have also shown the old to be a major group among the total numbers of poor in those countries. In a recent cross-national study, we made an estimate of the amount of poverty among the aged by applying generally acceptable measures of the poverty line to the income distributions obtained in the survey.[1] For Britain the poverty line was the equivalent of the 1962 National Assistance scale rate, plus a standard allowance for rent. In 1962 the National Assistance scale rate bore about the

1. This and all subsequent references to the cross-national survey are to a study of the social and economic circumstances of the elderly in Denmark, the United States and Britain. The field work was carried out in 1962, with random samples of people aged 65 and over in the three countries. The project was generously financed by the National Institute of Mental Health of the Public Health Service of the United States. See Shanas, E., Townsend, P., Wedderburn, D., Friis, H., Milhøj, P., and Stehouwer, J., *The Old in Three Industrial Societies*, New York, Atherton, and London, Routledge and Kegan Paul, 1968.

same relation to general income levels as the pre-war Rowntree Human Needs standard had to pre-war general income levels.[2] No poverty line was available for Denmark, because, in that country, the view was taken that such standards are meaningless. Comparisons had shown, however, that the general standard of living in Britain and Denmark was very similar, so the British standard was converted, at the current rate of exchange, and applied to the Danish income data. In the original study the standard used for the United States was one developed by the Social Security Administration.[3] Subsequently Miss Orshansky's estimates of poverty income criteria appeared and the present paper makes use of her economy levels for single and two-person households where the head is 65 or over. Moreover, as a small refinement the farm economy levels have been used for those income units, in the United States, where the head described his last occupation as farm owner or labourer.[4]

The United States non-farm poverty levels were $1,470 a year for a single person aged 65 and over, and $1,850 a year for a couple. The British levels were £196 a year for a single person and £290 a year for a couple. It is interesting to note that the income levels for couples were 34 to 35 per cent of male average earnings in manufacturing industry in both countries. We might say, therefore, that relatively speaking the two poverty levels are roughly equal, although in real terms the United States line represents a higher standard of living than does the British. It is also worth noting that the British standard makes no assumption about older people having lesser needs than younger ones. Approximately 30 per cent of the couples, 47 per cent of the men and 60 per cent of the women had incomes which were below the minimum poverty level in the United States. This represented a total of 42 per cent of all elderly income units.[5]

2. For a discussion of this argument and hence that this was, in 1962, a minimum poverty line, see Wedderburn, D., 'Poverty in Britain To-day—The Evidence', *The Sociological Review*, Vol. 10, No. 3, 1962. A line 25 per cent above the scale rate was used for the calculations of the amount of poverty in that article. A higher line was used by Abel-Smith, B., and Townsend, P., *The Poor and the Poorest*, London, Bell, 1965.

3. Epstein, L. A., 'Retirement Income and Measures of Need', *Research and Statistics Note 2*, Washington, D.C., Social Security Administration, Division of Program Research, 1964.

4. Orshansky, M., 'Counting the Poor: Another Look at the Poverty Profile' *Social Security Bulletin*, Vol. 28, No. 1, 1965, Table E. p. 28.

5. An income unit is a married couple, or single or widowed man or woman.

In Britain the corresponding percentages were 23 per cent of the couples, 29 per cent of the men and half the aged women; that is a total of 37 per cent of the elderly income units, with incomes which were below the poverty line. Although among each type of income unit, that is men, women and couples, there were fewer below the poverty line in Britain than in the United States, the overall percentage is not so far below that in the United States because there are relatively more single and widowed women in Britain, among whom poverty is greatest. In Denmark, 20 per cent of the couples, 16 per cent of the men and 12 per cent of the women had incomes below the minimum standard, that is about 16 per cent in all.[6] In other words the Danish aged appeared to be absolutely much better off than their counterparts in Britain and relatively better off than their counterparts in the United States. In both the latter countries significant proportions of the aged were found with incomes which were inadequate to meet minimum requirements, the estimates varying from over a third upwards to nearly a half.[7]

For estimates of the importance of the aged in the total numbers of the poor, we have to turn to other evidence. One United States study suggested that 28 per cent of all income units in the country (20 per cent of families) had less than the minimum income. A third of these were income units where the head was 65 or over.[8] Miss Orshansky's own estimates are similar although relating to families or households. 'Of the 12 million households with 1963 incomes below the economy level, 4 million were headed by a person aged 65 or older'.[9]

6. Even this figure may over-state the amount of poverty because a lower farm poverty level would be appropriate in Denmark. In Britain the farm population is so small that it would make no difference.

7. These figures may be compared with other estimates using in many cases slightly different definitions of the poverty line and independent income data.

　　(a) Morgan, J. N., David, M. H., Cohen, W. J., Brazer, H. E., *Income and Welfare in the United States*, New York, McGraw-Hill, 1962. Table 16—3, p. 194 shows 48 per cent of income units with aged heads below the poverty line.

　　(b) Orshansky, M., 'Who's who among the poor: a demographic view of poverty', *Social Security Bulletin*, Vol. 28, No. 7, p. 12 estimates 38 per cent of all households with aged heads to be below the poverty line.

　　(c) Wedderburn, D., *op. cit.*, 1962, estimates 44 per cent of income units with aged heads to be below the poverty line.

8. Morgan, J. N., *et al*, *op. cit.*, 1962. Tables 16–2, p. 190 and 16–4, p. 195.

9. Orshansky, M., *op. cit.*, July, 1965, p. 12.

One British study suggests that in 1960, 14 per cent of individuals ($7\frac{1}{2}$ million persons) had incomes below the poverty line, and that 3 million of them were elderly, that is 40 per cent.[10] In both countries therefore the aged are a major group among the poor. To quote Miss Orshansky again, 'The aged population accordingly exhibits a smaller degree of economic security than any other age group, despite the fact that more of the aged than of any others currently draw some support from a public program'. But the aged are relatively more important among the total population of the poor in Britain than in the United States. Moreover, for the elderly, as with other groups in poverty, there seems to be much more spread of income downwards from the poverty level in the United States than in Britain, where most people are clustered only a relatively small way below the poverty line.[11]

## 2. *Interpretation of 'Standard of Living'*

It is not the purpose of this paper to stray back to topics discussed earlier at this conference, in particular the conceptual problems involved in the definition of poverty. Nevertheless some references must be made to these matters because the interpretation of the preceding discussion of measures of poverty among the old depends very much upon such questions as whether income is a satisfactory measure of resources, and whether the 'income unit' or the 'family' is the appropriate grouping to use for the analysis of poverty.

The argument for using a wider concept of financial resources than income, at least when studying the standard of living of the old is a strong one. There is a widespread belief that, in so far as people are financially able to, they will save while they are working in order to have some assets to use in old age. There has also been widespread speculation about whether old people with assets do in fact use them when they retire, or whether they have not, by this time, acquired a habit of irrationally clinging to what savings they have. The information about the value of asset holdings obtained in the cross-national survey was rather scanty. Linking it with what we know from other studies, however, we can draw certain conclusions.

10. Abel-Smith, B., and Townsend, P., *op. cit.*, 1965, p. 65.
11. For the United States, Morgan, J. N., *et al*, *op. cit.*, 1962, Table 16–2, p. 190, and Table 16–3, p. 194. For Britain, Wedderburn, D., *op. cit.*, 1962, Table 1, p. 265. The cross-national income distributions also suggest this.

First, in all three countries, but more particularly in Britain, there remain considerable proportions of old people with no liquid assets, or with assets of such low value as to be insignificant. Between a quarter and 45 per cent, varying as between men, women and couples, in all countries, had no or very small amounts of liquid assets. There is also a high correlation between income level and asset ownership, particularly in Britain and the United States. Although there may be individuals with low incomes and large assets, it is mostly the people with incomes above the poverty levels discussed here, who are the owners of large assets. It can be argued that for a study of poverty it would be more satisfactory to devise some means of combining income and liquid assets into a single economic indicator. (Not owner-occupied houses or life insurance because these are so often non-realizable assets).[12] It has been suggested that the assumption should be made that individuals will consume what assets they possess, evenly over the remaining years of life expectancy. Income levels would then be raised by an appropriate share of assets. But Morgan *et al* who have made such a calculation report that 'Adult heads over 65 with inadequate incomes receive on average only $135 or 0·7 of their average budget requirements from investment of their capital in annuities.'[13]

But a wider definition of assets than a purely financial one may also be of particular relevance to discussions of poverty among the old. On the one hand it is sometimes argued that the 'needs' of old people are less than the needs of younger age groups because they are entering their period of low incomes, with a home which is already equipped, and with stocks of clothing and household linen built up during their working life. On the other hand it can also be asserted that poverty and low incomes, where they occur among the old, are long-term features of the old people's existence. Indeed this is one of the special characteristics of the elderly's poverty, that there is little expectation of moving out of the condition for the rest of their life. Within the framework of the cross-national study it was impossible to investigate such matters as stocks of durable goods, clothing, etc. This would, however, be a very fruitful area for

---

12. But if the object is to compare poverty among the aged with other groups of the population, then the treatment of these kinds of assets has to be handled with care. More old people will own their homes without mortgages and their life insurance policies will be worth more than those of younger age groups.
13. Morgan, J. N., *et al, op. cit.*, 1962, p. 190.

investigation, and specially on a comparative basis. Some work done on these lines in Britain suggests that at least in that country the low income groups are likely to have extremely low levels of stocks of many items of household equipment.[14]

Finally there is the question of help from the family to its older members. This involves not only the conceptual question of what is the most appropriate grouping for which resources should be measured—income unit, household or something wider still. It is also of relevance in assessing the role of the family in the 'culture' of poverty. First, however, it should be noted that our definition of income in the cross-national survey included all regular cash allowances received from any family members outside the dwelling. It did not include gifts in kind from such family members, because the questions were not asked in such a way as to enable us to put a money value upon them.

The cross-national survey established, however, that such help in kind was quite frequent, was probably not of great monetary value, and was sometimes two-way, that is from old to young as well as young to old. It makes very little difference to our estimate of poverty among the aged.[15] Intra-household transfers are a different matter, however. For, of old people with surviving children, 42 per cent in Britain live with at least one child and 20 per cent in Denmark and the United States. Moreover it is among the poorest, particularly the poorest single and widowed women, that sharing house in this way is most common. In the United States and Britain for instance, more than 70 per cent of the women in the lowest quartiles of the income distribution are living with relatives; in the highest it is only 40 per cent. The estimate of the amount of poverty among the old might, therefore, be changed if the income receiving unit was defined more widely to include all members of the household.

14. Wedderburn, D., *op. cit.*, 1962, p. 279. That study underlined the importance of understanding cultural differences in consumer spending habits. The indicator of adequate clothing for old women was taken to be the possession of at least one woollen dress or skirt. In some working class areas, particularly in Scotland, however, woollen dresses are not worn. The usual dress is a cotton one worn with a cardigan. Nor is possession of articles of clothing in good condition an adequate indicator. People change in size and shape and good garments become unusable.

15. Compare this finding with the results of an earlier survey in Britain where I did attempt to value help in kind, and where the same picture emerges. Cole, D., with Utting, J., *The Economic Circumstances of Old People*, Welwyn, Codicote Press, 1962, pp. 88–90.

But without detailed evidence of the financial position of the rest of the household no superficial assumptions should be made. For we also know that, particularly in Britain and to some extent in the United States, significant proportions of the elderly women were living with unmarried daughters who themselves may well not have had a very high income.

Is the importance of shared households for the poorest among the old of relevance to the discussions about a special 'culture' of the family among the poor? Or is it to be explained as straightforward economic response to the problems of poverty? First, we should note that in terms of general proximity and frequency of contact between the old and their families there were no significant social class differences in any of the three countries. In this sense family ties were close through all social class and income groups. Nor were there any such social class differences in terms of living arrangements in Denmark. In Britain and the United States however, the working class elderly were more likely to live with children than were the white collar elderly. A possible explanation of such differences is the differences in the size of families of the white collar and other classes. Certainly in Britain a high proportion of the elderly who live with their children have always done so. This may also be linked with housing problems.[16] We do not know whether this is also the case in the United States, where only relatively half as many live with children anyway. But there is evidence in that country of a joint household being formed for specifically economic reasons.

## 3. *Causes of Poverty among the Old—the Effect of Retirement*

The only undisputed claims to a share in the gross national product, which are recognized in capitalist society, are those arising from the provision of one of the factors of production on the market. If there is no labour-power to sell, no land or capital to provide, there is then no automatic right to income. It follows that since the vast majority of the population have only labour-power to sell, those who, for one reason or another, are unable to work are likely to be particularly exposed to the risk of poverty. The older people are, the less likely they are to work. In so far as the old are poor they are not, therefore, primarily poor because they are old, but because they are unable to work.

The association between 'labour-market participation' and

16. Cole, D., with Utting, J., *op. cit.*, p. 27 and pp. 34–36.

poverty among the old is well illustrated by an examination of the characteristics of those among the old who are at the bottom of the income distributions. In the cross-national survey in all three countries, we found that the retired, single and widowed women, and the over-seventies were all over-represented at the bottom of the income scale. A strong link between the three groups was provided by their work experience. Single and widowed women had low incomes in old age, both because very few indeed were likely to be working after the age of 65, and because very few had worked when younger. Their entitlement to occupational pensions, in particular, therefore, was limited. Then, again, the further people were past the traditional retirement age in their country, the less likely they were to be working.

There was some suggestion, however, that even among the retired the older were poorer. This was the only indication that age might be a factor. But in societies where real income levels of the active population have risen, and where price levels have also been rising, this finding is not surprising. The very old, having had lower real and money work incomes, will have had less opportunity to accumulate savings; to the extent that their pension levels are based upon their individual earnings levels in work, the longer retired will also have lower pensions; and the real value of any fixed income will be eroded by inflation. The conclusion of the study was, however, that such an indirect 'age effect' was very small when compared with the dramatic difference between the income distributions of those elderly who were working and those who were not.

In tracing the connections between poverty, old age and work, therefore, it may be relevant to pose the question to what extent are the old not working in industrialized societies because they are physically unable to do the jobs available to be done in those societies and to what extent is it because retirement and ageing are culturally linked. The cross-national survey shed some interesting light upon the influences of one cultural variable, the age of retirement. In the United States and Britain the age at which the government retirement pension could be taken was 65, although in the United States actuarially reduced pensions had been made available from the age of 62. In Denmark the pension age was 67.[17] The survey data showed that the labour force participation rates were about the same in the age group which succeeded the normal age for the pension, whether that was 65 or 67. In all three countries

17. This discussion relates to men only.

about one in two of all men retired as soon as they reached the age entitling them to a government pension. The conclusion was drawn, therefore, that the formal pension age had a strong influence in forming retirement norms. At the same time the data show poor health, or its variant 'the job was too tiring', as the major reason men give for retiring in all three countries. There is some conflict between the reasons individuals give for retirement and their score upon an index of incapacity. But as Professor Shanas, the author of this chapter in the cross-national survey, points out, first, the index of incapacity is not necessarily an adequate measure of capacity to work. Second, as other studies have suggested, it could well be that ageing does reduce man's capacity to work and that some men's health will actually improve after retirement.[18]

This discussion of the relationship between age, work or non-work, and health may seem rather remote from the subject of the culture of poverty. Yet there is an interesting phenomenon here which we still do not understand sufficiently. Low incomes and poverty are the consequences of retirement. Retirement in old age is partly due to physical changes; it is also partly due to individual choice. This in turn is influenced by the values of a society which legitimizes retirement from work at a particular age. At the same time there are also cultural elements in the society which may even make retirement compulsory at a certain age. The interplay between these factors is a complex one; but it results in poverty for many individuals.

### 4. Social Security Benefits and the Poverty Line

But, it may be argued, in countries like Denmark, Britain and the United States which, in theory at any rate, all have comprehensive systems of government pensions, retirement could produce a necessary, but not a sufficient condition for poverty. Poverty becomes a possibility then only if (a) there are groups outside these so-called comprehensive schemes, (b) the levels of retirement pensions are below the poverty standards. On both of these counts Denmark, where we saw there was little poverty by comparison with Britain and the United States, scores well.

18. For a review of earlier literature together with some fresh evidence which 'points to compulsory retirement being associated with a reduction in the incidence of serious illness' see Martin, J., and Doran, A., 'Evidence Concerning the Relationship Between Health and Retirement', *Sociological Review*, Vol. 14, No. 3, November, 1966.

In Denmark the pension system in operation at the time of the field work covered all resident citizens, and provided a small minimum pension irrespective of income. Over and above that, a full pension was provided, linked to a cost of living index and subject to an income test.[19] Most old people over pensionable age and not working were drawing a retirement pension. In Britain, and more particularly the USA, where contributory systems were in operation there were still significant groups among the old in 1962 without entitlement to a pension because of failure to satisfy contribution conditions.

As for the levels of pension, the full pension in Denmark for a couple in 1962 was 6,456 D. kroner a year; that is 40 per cent of average earnings in manufacturing industry, and actually above the poverty level we used. In theory the income test worked in such a way that no one should have been below the poverty line. But a few people may not have applied for supplementation, and there was the further possibility that among farmers money earnings could have been below the poverty level. In Britain the contributory pension scheme provided a basically flat rate pension which, for a couple in 1962, was £240 or some 29 per cent of earnings in manufacturing industry and only 86 per cent of the poverty line.[20] In theory supplementation was available from National Assistance to bring people up to the poverty line.[21] But in practice many old people with entitlement did not apply.[22] In the United States the picture is even more complicated because the contributory pension scheme provides minimum and maximum levels of benefit, but between these limits the level depends upon a worker's average monthly wage in covered employment but weighted in favour of those with low earnings. Hence there is a range, but in 1962 the average benefit in payment was $1,536 a year for a couple. This again was 29 per cent of earnings in manufacturing industry, and about 80 per cent of the poverty line used. These characteristics

19. Developments since 1964 have (a) abolished the income test for the full pensions and (b) introduced a contributory supplementary pension.
20. Small but insignificant increments to the flat-rate pension could be earned by continuing to work past retirement age and, since 1959, as a result of a small measure of wage-relation.
21. It will be remembered that our measure of the poverty line was in fact National Assistance scale rates plus rent.
22. See Cole, D., with Utting, J., *op. cit.*, p. 98, and the results of an official inquiry: Ministry of Pensions and National Insurance, *Financial and Other Circumstances of Retirement Pensioners*, London, HMSO, 1966, pp. 19–49.

of the various pension schemes relate directly to the experience of poverty among the old in the three countries. Moreover the Danish scheme, in addition to fixing relatively high benefits, also had two other important characteristics. It was linked to a cost of living index, and a special supplement was paid to the over-eighties. This together with its basically income-tested character served to concentrate resources upon the economically most vulnerable groups among the elderly, namely, the women and the very old. What is important for our discussion about 'cultures' of poverty is first, that in Denmark, unlike Britain and the United States, there seems to be no public feeling against an 'income' or 'means test'. Second, the Danish pension system at this time was not linked in any way, either via contributions or benefits, to past work experience.

## 5. *Heterogeneity among the Old*

So far we have concentrated upon the proportions of the old at the bottom of the income scale. But while in Britain and the United States these were a large group, there were also significant groups who were comfortably off by any standards. It is interesting, too, to find that quite a number of people in the United States said they had retired because they could afford to. It is precisely in the United States that differences of economic circumstance among the aged population are greatest.

Economic position in old age is, of course, related to economic position during working life. But the importance of poverty among the old to discussions about the 'culture of poverty' is that here is a type of poverty where there is little opportunity for a common culture to develop. The old who are poor may come predominantly, although not exclusively, from working-class backgrounds (and here the economic vulnerability of widows in all classes must specially be remembered). But these are not necessarily backgrounds of working-class poverty. The elderly's way of life, their values will have been shaped by their experiences during a working-life which for most was not spent in poverty. Most old people live scattered among ordinary communities, and this makes particularly relevant the question whether their frame of reference for judging the adequacy or otherwise of their economic position is their own past experience or that of their children and neighbours.

In the cross-national survey we did not ask the sample of elderly people to compare themselves financially with other groups of the population. But other studies in Britain, at least, have done this, and have suggested that whilst there is a widespread view among both older and younger people that the elderly have done rather badly financially, the old themselves have modest expectations:

> We have seen some evidence for the way in which the old have become a self-conscious membership reference group with claims to a re-distribution in their favour, and the evidence of the survey confirms the existence of a feeling among the old and poor that their needs after retirement are inadequately met. But their demands, when set against the gap between their incomes and those of others are modest ones.[23]

We did, however, ask our sample of elderly in the three countries to compare their financial positions at the time of interview with their position when they were 60 (age 55 was chosen in Denmark). Such a question is only an indicator of subjective feelings. It is most improbable that any realistic comparison could be made by people say, of 70 or 80, with their situation 20 years earlier. But one important dimension along which feelings of resentment or satisfaction may be developed is past experience. We found that between 34 per cent of the sample in Britain and 47 per cent in the United States said that they were getting along financially as well now as when they were younger. Over a half in Britain, over a third in the United States and only 17 per cent in Denmark said they were getting along worse. Around 14 per cent in Britain and the United States and 28 per cent in Denmark said that they were getting along better.

Two interesting points emerge from these results. First, that despite any general notions about how older people may be doing, there is a spread between individuals, who make positive and nega-tive assessments. Second, that these assessments, where we find the Danish old people consistently more cheerful and the British old people consistently less cheerful, agreed with our rankings of the relative economic position of the aged in the three countries, accord-ing to the objective economic data from the survey.

23. Runciman, W. G., *Relative Deprivation and Social Justice*, London, Routledge and Kegan Paul, 1966, p. 271.

# 12. Fatherless Families on National Assistance

## *Dennis Marsden*

---

This is a summary of a survey which I conducted in 1965–6 into the social situation and living standards in two areas of Britain of a group of fatherless families living on national assistance (as supplementary benefit was then called).[1] In this summary I have singled out the hardships of the unmarried. But the survey included also separated, divorced and widowed mothers, with legitimate and illegitimate children, and I refer to the whole group as 'fatherless families' or to the mothers generally as 'unsupported mothers'.[2] The inclusion of other groups of unsupported mothers along with the unmarried, permits a very rough comparison of living standards: in particular, comparisons may be drawn between the situation of unmarried mothers and the situations of widows who usually already have pensions as of right on which there is no means test.

Two points must be made about the scope of these survey findings. First, the groups discussed are not the poorest among the fatherless, since some families not receiving supplementary benefit are found to live below the benefit levels, while in other families where the mothers are working, outgoings in connection with work and child care will effectively lower their standards of living. Second, it will emerge that what is important for these families is their *relative*, not absolute, living standard: thus, while scale rates of supplementary benefit are higher now than national assistance rates in 1966 when the survey was carried out, so were wage rates. Today the situation

---

1. The full survey was published in 1969 as *Mothers Alone* (Poverty and the Fatherless Family), Allen Lane, The Penguin Press.
2. There were 116 families in all: twenty-six unmarried mothers (including six West Indians); plus forty-one separated, thirty-five divorced, and fourteen widowed mothers, twenty-eight of whom had had illegitimate children. The average family size was two children, but the unmarried mothers and widows tended to have fewer, and the other mothers more, children than average. The mothers were those who replied to a set of circulars sent out to a random selection of fatherless families who were receiving national assistance in 1965, the final response rate being about 60 per cent. The survey took place in a northern industrial town and a south-eastern market town.

of fatherless families relative to other families in society will probably be substantially as described here.

## Findings: The Incomes of Fatherless Families

A measure of the economic handicap of the fatherless family, compared with a family where the father is present, is provided by Table 1.

TABLE 1

*The incomes of a fatherless family with two children compared with the average income of a married couple with two children* (1966 values)

| Type of family, and income (with family allowance) | Weekly income | As a percentage of national assistance allowance‡ |
| --- | --- | --- |
| *Fatherless family*, with two children, and income from: | | |
| (i) average woman's wage (net of National Insurance)* | £9 14 6 | 115% |
| (ii) basic national assistance allowance | £8 10 0 | 100% |
| (iii) national assistance plus £2 maximum part-time earnings | £10 10 0 | 123% |
| Average income of a married couple with two children (net of tax and National Insurance)† | £22 3 6 | 202% |

\* *Ministry of Labour Gazette*, August 1966, HMSO, Vol. LXXIV, No. 8 (figure for April 1966).

† Ministry of Labour, *Family Expenditure Survey for 1965*, HMSO, 1966, pp. 83, 87.

‡ The national assistance allowance includes an amount for each person in the household, according to status and age, and an allowance for rent. For the purpose of this calculation the children are assumed to be aged 5 to 9, and the rent to be £2.

The unsupported mother of two children, working full-time and earning the average woman's wage, can make less than half the income of the average married couple with two children. Indeed, her income is only slightly more than the national assistance allowance to which she is legally entitled should she give up work. And it is actually less than she could get on assistance working part-time and retaining the permitted £2 of her earnings.

This means that if a mother is completely unsupported and has only average work-skills she will find it difficult to rise above the state subsistence level, even assuming she can overcome the problems and expense of having her children cared for while she works. Thus for half to three-quarters of the group of unsupported mothers whom I interviewed, living on national assistance was *economically* preferable to work, in that they had a higher income working part-time and drawing assistance than they could ever hope to earn if they worked full-time.

Yet this national assistance income level at which these families were pegged was only half that of the average two-child family in the general population (allowance being made in the comparison for the father's absence).

Although the fatherless families were all receiving means-tested benefits designed to provide a uniform minimum income level there was a great deal of variation. Taking into account many types of income[3] (which, of course, non-dependent families would also enjoy) the total incomes were only slightly higher than the basic assistance scale rate, an average of 123 per cent of scale rate. But eight of the families had total incomes below 90 per cent.

Unmarried mothers (at 118 per cent of scale rate) had income levels below the average for the whole group; while ten divorced or separated mothers with only illegitimate children had an average total income level of only 106 per cent, and as a group they were much the poorest. The explanation of the low income of mothers with illegitimate children lay partly in lack of help from relatives, in their inability to work because of young children, and in the likelihood that these mothers especially would have their assistance allowances reduced by NAB officers for suspected cohabitation. Widows had *relatively* less poor income levels (at 127 per cent of scale rate), chiefly because the NAB regulations permitted them to retain an extra 7s. 6d. per child from their widowed mother's allowance.

The unmarried mothers and mothers with only illegitimate

3. Such as permitted earnings, help in cash and kind from relatives and others, welfare benefits, etc. Some mothers had income from earnings, or pensions, which was disregarded wholly or in part by the NAB. Undeclared support from the children's father and undeclared earnings were only 1 per cent of income for this group, although there may have been a bias in selection of the sample and income may have been concealed, particularly among those who did not respond to our request for an interview.

children were also more dependent on assistance for their income, seldom having any other stable resources. Over half the illegitimate children received no support from their fathers, and for the one in four who were the subjects of paternity orders in no instance was there an award of more than £1 a week. As a result thirteen out of the twenty-six unmarried mothers would have had to earn £8 a week or more to become independent at a standard equivalent to assistance, and twenty-one out of the twenty-six would have had to earn £6 a week or more.

The widows on the other hand, were less dependent on assistance, in the sense that they received a higher proportion of their income from pensions. For this reason they tended to be dependent only temporarily, through ill health or because they had a number of young children. Such factors apart, they could more easily work and rise above assistance levels, eight out of the fourteen widows needing to earn £4 a week or less for independence. It is known that a smaller proportion of widows become dependent, compared with other groups of unsupported mothers.

### ACCOMMODATION[4]

Unmarried mothers and other women with illegitimate children also had relatively poorer accommodation than the average fatherless family. Over half the fatherless families who were seen lived in council accommodation. However, almost two-thirds of the unmarried mothers lived in much worse housing which was privately rented and for which they paid high rents—a factor further increasing their dependence on assistance. In general, the housing costs of these fatherless families were double the national average.

Half the fatherless families were overcrowded (compared with one in ten of all households in England and Wales). And again the unmarried mothers came off worst, three-quarters of them being overcrowded compared with one-quarter of the widows. Two in five of all fatherless families had not enough beds, and one in ten lacked bed space for two members of the household: thus an unmarried mother was sharing her single bed with a two-year-old child and a baby.

Fatherless families had fewer household appliances, with the possible exception of TV, than other urban families in Britain. (Table 2.) Again shortages were found particularly among the

---

4. The survey understates housing problems, since it did not include any mothers who were currently homeless, or any London families.

unmarried mothers. They lacked access to washing machines, refrigerators and telephones in the accommodation where they lived, and indeed fewer than half of the unmarried mothers (10 out of 26) had any furniture of their own. Such sketchy statistics cannot convey the enormous range of accommodation and furnishings in these homes, and a fuller inventory would reveal more clearly the relative disadvantage of the mothers of illegitimate children among such families.

TABLE 2

*Number and percentage of Fatherless Families and of All Households having Different Articles*

| Article | Marital Status of Mother | | | | All fatherless families per cent | Large and small urban areas per cent* |
| | Unmarried n=26 | Separated n=41 | Divorced n=35 | Widowed n=14 | | |
| --- | --- | --- | --- | --- | --- | --- |
| TV access | 20 | 34 | 31 | 13 | 84 | 81† |
| TV owner | 1 | 2 | 7 | 4 | 12 | — |
| Washing machine | 3 | 15 | 19 | 8 | 39 | 55 |
| Refrigerator | 1 | 6 | 6 | 5 | 15 | 30 |
| Telephone | | | 5 | | 4 | 16 |
| Furniture | 10 | 38 | 30 | 12 | 78 | — |

* *Source: Family Expenditure Survey, 1964*, HMSO, 1966. This was the only year to give breakdowns of possession of these items for large and small urban areas.

† The figures are not strictly comparable, since the Family Expenditure Survey figure is for licences rather than sets.

A lack of furniture represented an enormous potential drain on the resources of these families if they were ever to achieve a stable existence in their own homes.

LIVING STANDARDS

The conventional division of expenditure into 'essential' and 'non-essential' proved to be arbitrary and misleading. The families' current needs sprang at least in part from the style of life to which they had been accustomed and with which they were still to some extent in contact. Patterns of consumption were moulded by what the mother felt the community demanded of her, by the need for psychological well-being as well as material comfort, and by the standards set by the rest of the community. A few pointers can be given to illustrate the nature of the deprivations which these families were experiencing.

One in ten of the mothers had eaten literally no solid food on the day before the interview. In part this was a stress reaction to the situation, but also these and other mothers tended to go short of food themselves in order to balance the budget and give the children more: as one said, 'It's like the old saying, "In a poor family the mother gets nowt".' The diet of a larger proportion of mothers was unsatisfactory and boring. Although children of school age usually had school meals, their diets too were likely to suffer at weekends and during the school holidays. But this means that the mothers of young children, among whom are the majority of the unmarried mothers, were especially vulnerable. They had no subsidized meals, no man to cook for, and had often not acquired the skills and routine of preparing full meals for themselves.

Half the unsupported mothers never made any major purchase of clothing for themselves, and in almost a third of the families all the children's clothes were bought by relatives or passed on from some other source. Thus clothing tended to be distressingly unfashionable; but more important, the socially isolated families (among whom were a high proportion with illegitimate children) had greater problems with clothing and lived at an effectively reduced standard compared with families supported by relatives.

In certain respects the families showed how strongly their living standard was geared to that of the community. TV was regarded as a necessity: socially isolated mothers had no other company, and a separated wife said, 'I'm married to that thing now my husband's gone.' Partly because of the nervous strain of their situation, half the mothers smoked (the same proportion as in the general population) some of them going without food in order to do so. Twenty families still kept pets. The pets cost money to feed, but they were like members of the family and could not be discarded in hard times. Mothers were worried that their children did not get a holiday. Half the families had had no holiday, and in only one-fifth of the families had everyone had a holiday. The majority of those who had a holiday had been helped by relatives, friends or charities.

A measure of the mothers' social isolation was that three-fifths never went out in the evening—contrary to a popular stereotype only 3 per cent had been to bingo in the last fortnight.

The children were going to academically inferior schools, and children's lack of success was partly due to their being marked off from their schoolmates in a host of small ways. Mothers felt their poverty chiefly through the children, and spoke of them not having enough fireworks for bonfire night, not having a decent party dress, not being able to go to the Saturday cinema matinee or to the swimming bath, not being able to put money in the Sunday School collection, and not being able to join the cubs or brownies for lack of the uniform. Children without bikes could not go on outings with their friends.

At school, in addition to the embarrassments of free school meals and lack of school uniform, these children had problems in getting the full range of clothes for PE, sport and science. They could not go on school trips, and even cookery expenses created difficulties: one girl stayed away regularly when her mother could not give her the money, saying 'what will the other girls think? They'll think I'm a pauper.' School demands were growing, and the children in fatherless families were unable to keep up.

Although poverty was a spur to some families, the majority of children did badly at school. It seems probable that lack of money lowered the mothers' and children's aspirations, contributing to failure at 11-plus and to the early leaving of those who did pass for grammar school. One mother said, 'I'm worried to death in case she *does* pass the 11-plus'. With education now such an important factor in obtaining a good job, here was clear evidence that poverty was self-perpetuating, stretching into the children's generation.

FEELINGS OF DEPRIVATION

In spite of their obvious reluctance to say they felt poor—which some mothers felt to be tantamount to admitting themselves poor managers, or to asking for charity—two-thirds of the mothers said they felt hard-up. Of these half felt 'terribly poor', or said they were 'not living, just existing'. The remaining third said defensively that they 'managed' or that they were 'comfortable'.

The unmarried mothers most often felt hard-up, usually 'terribly poor', while the widows least often felt poor, two-thirds saying they 'managed'. Such feelings were evidently linked with the mother's total situation, and in particular with her degree of dependence on assistance.

## The Social Situation of Unmarried Mothers on Assistance

The unmarried mothers discussed here ranged in age from 16 to 50 and had up to five illegitimate children. One-third, the mothers who had only one young baby, were probably only temporarily on assistance until they could return to full-time work. However, there were also mothers with only one child whose self-confidence had been destroyed by the birth so that they felt they could not work full-time again. These were also larger families for whom the mother's return to full-time work was no longer economically feasible, since her earnings would be too low.

The mother's relationships with her parents were vitally important. Half the unmarried mothers still lived at home, and they often benefited from cheaper accommodation and concealed subsidies to their incomes (although psychologically living at home was not always the best solution).

A small number of mothers who had had to leave home, or who had previously lost touch with relatives, were so cut off from normal society that they might be described as an 'underclass'. Their only friends and support were other mothers with illegitimate children, and the only men they knew—regular soldiers and young highly-mobile West Indian workmen—were unlikely to marry them.

A small number of mothers still had some contact with their children's fathers, receiving minimal and irregular financial support. Occasionally a couple had set up a sort of 'marriage at a distance', living in separate dwellings but meeting regularly and maintaining a sexual relationship. It was economically advantageous for such couples not to marry—or under the cohabitation rule not to live together—but for the mother to live separately, supported largely by the state.

## Help from the Community

### (i) HELP WITH HOUSING

Although a large proportion of the families had been rehoused by the council, more help should have been given. Some of the families had been homeless or had suffered other severe hardships before strong backing from social workers or doctors had got them a house. Even so, the families tended to be rehoused in the roughest areas on the worst estates.

The most vulnerable mothers were the small group of mothers

with illegitimate children who had lost contact with their kin. They had low priority in rehousing, and frequent moves cut them off from the administrative machinery which might have helped them. In some fairly basic ways they did not want council accommodation, which would have brought official surveillance and would tend to confirm the status they preferred to regard as only temporary.

(ii) THE LAW

The legal situation of dependent mothers of illegitimate children (including divorced, separated and widowed mothers) represented the law at its least effectual, only a quarter of the children being acknowledged by a court order. Approximately half the mothers had taken no legal action because they feared the embarrassment of court proceedings and felt they could not prove paternity. The low level of the awards which were made (£1 out of a possible maximum of £2 10s.) appeared to be partly the magistrates' judgement of the mother's guilt, but also an acknowledgement that the Court was powerless to enforce payment of more than a minimal sum.

As we have seen, the failure of the law to secure an adequate income for illegitimate children robbed the unmarried mother of a valuable *steady* income upon which she might have built her independence. It follows that the level of state support cannot be considered in isolation from the adequacy of legal support.

(iii) NATIONAL ASSISTANCE (SUPPLEMENTARY BENEFIT)

These unsupported mothers were legally entitled to choose not to work but to draw assistance and stay at home caring for their children. The 1948 National Assistance Act thus represented in intention an important step forward in security for fatherless families. However, under the Act officers have very wide 'discretionary' powers, and the proportion of officers applying these powers in a manner contrary to the Act's spirit was high enough to undermine that security. For lack of any adequate public surveillance officers were using their powers to apply distinctions of 'less eligibility' to mothers with illegitimate children.

National Assistance was inadequately publicized, so that mothers found out about it too late (for example, the problem pages of women's magazines never mention it). It was felt by the mothers to be stigmatizing, and they were not reassured by their initial harsh reception in the NAB office, where they felt the officers were preoccupied with the prevention of fraud rather than the relief of need.

A proportion of the NAB officers evidently did not accept the mothers' right not to work. The psychological value of the unsupported mother doing a job, whether full or part-time cannot be over-emphasized. But the decision to work should be hers: that is, she should be aware of her rights and not be subjected to undue pressure from authority. Probably half the unmarried mothers and some of the mothers of illegitimate children had, illegally, been pressed to take full-time work and had been given the impression that they must seek work as a condition of obtaining assistance. Under such pressure, mothers were being forced off assistance and into full-time work when this was not the best solution to their problems.

A different aspect of the problem was that women who had been off work many years were presented once again, in their fifties, with the necessity of earning their living because their eligibility for assistance ceased when their child began work.

Part-time work for women was so badly paid and the earnings limit on the means-tested allowance was placed so low that had it not been for continual pressure from the NAB few mothers would have worked part-time. The earnings limit did not vary with family size, and the expense of child-minding was never taken into account by the NAB.

The NAB was understaffed so that to ensure that all earnings were declared, officers had to rely on anonymous letters.

Another major concern of the NAB was with cohabitation. Prosecuted cases of cohabitation amounted to only one in 300 of the unsupported mothers, yet officers treated a large proportion of the mothers suspiciously. The mothers I have called the 'underclass' were most frequently harried. But the discovery of almost any male acquaintance of a woman on assistance was likely to lead to suspicion of cohabitation. Again there was heavy reliance on anonymous letters. In their eagerness to obtain evidence, officers made frequent unannounced visits and in several instances were said to have entered houses without permission.

The 'offence' of cohabitation consists in 'living as man and wife', but it is nowhere spelled out clearly—and indeed in a pluralistic society it cannot be strictly defined. If the mother did not immediately surrender her allowance on the officer's discovery of her relationship with a man, questioning to establish the existence of cohabitation centred not on financial support from the man but on the possibility of sexual relations between the couple. It was usually doubtful that there was any financial support, so that stoppage of an allowance could bring great hardship to the mother and her children.

Certain of the officers also exercised discretion more often to reduce weekly allowances than to increase them. Fatherless families had evidently not been accepted as a group meriting extra allowances. Among families with low allowances, several were rent-stopped (i.e. did not receive their rent in full), and there was several times a move to treat as 'wages' the support from parents with whom the mother lived. In eight instances the mother's income appeared to be lowered for suspected, but not proven, cohabitation. Young mothers were paid at juvenile rates.

Lump sum grants, which were, theoretically, available for those with exceptional needs were scarcely ever made, despite the fact that the requirements of fatherless families often amounted to a whole new home. It was the apparent arbitrariness of the standards for awarding such grants, together with the presence of other equally obscure means-tested grants operated by bodies like the Education Committees, which caused mothers to feel the system was unfair.

The most disturbing feature of the situation was that mothers neither knew their rights nor believed themselves to have any power against the NAB. They had no written statement of how their allowance was calculated, nor was the code upon which officers work open to public scrutiny. Thus the Appeal Tribunals— intended as a countervailing force to officers' powers of discretion— were a dead letter. Mothers went to the Appeal inadequately briefed, not legally represented; if indeed they could overcome their mistrust of the Appeal machinery sufficiently to appeal at all.

With the change from the National Assistance Board to the Ministry of Social Security there has been a slight simplification of the discretionary rules. But the basic situation remains substantially as described, the same staff with the same powers and the same secrecy. The recent tightening up against fraudulent claims may have exacerbated the insensitivity of the system to the needs of fatherless families.

## Discussion

This small survey has illustrated the main areas of the problem. Fatherless families are poor because they lack a man's earning power and the mother's earning power is diminished by her children's needs for her care. In the long run therefore, the poverty and dependence of the fatherless family can only be eliminated by the attainment of sexual equality of social and economic status in society *and* by the provision of ancillary child care services. Until then many of the families will need a money subsidy from some source other than the woman's wage.

The families' disadvantage on the housing market also suggests that a rent subsidy might bring relief to this group in particular.

Money is not all that the families require. They suffer from different degrees of social ostracism which only the slow process of social education of the community can reduce. As a start we must attempt to bring into use some general description for all the families. There were numerous similarities and a degree of overlap between mothers of different marital status (for example, the birth of illegitimate children); and conversely between mothers of the same marital status there were vast differences, of age, marital history, family size and composition. The names 'fatherless families' or 'unsupported mothers' push aside the separate stereotypes we have formed of 'the widow', 'the unmarried mother', or 'the divorcee'. A single description would encourage us to think of what problems the mothers face in common. We and the politicians cannot properly discuss the problem until we have a less value-laden terminology.

Of course, this is not to say that we should never discuss separately the unmarried mother and her child. Of all the fatherless families, they are in the most acute need. But the ultimate aim should be to devise a common scheme for all the families in which the unmarried mothers and illegitimate children would share. Then it would no longer be possible for successive national budgets to discriminate, as they now do, between widowed mothers on the one hand and separated, divorced and unmarried mothers on the other.

How adequate is the present support system? Supplementary benefit levels are set in accordance with politicians' perceptions of what the community will tolerate as a minimum subsistence level for the poor. But both public and politicians may be remarkably ill-informed as to the actual standard of living of the poor, and it is to be hoped that there will be more surveys of how the poor live and how they view their living standards. In the present survey, inadequate incomes were causing a narrowing of aspirations and a restriction of social life, and it looked as though the children's future would be affected.

But it was not merely the level of income which must be criticized. Both the means test, and the mode of administration of national assistance were at fault. The aims of support for these families should be to encourage (or at least not to discourage) work, independence, and re-marriage. The example of the widow shows that independence and work can best be promoted by a fixed allowance given as of right. Bullying mothers to work is no substitute for a stable income on which the mother can build. Logically, since the income is to compensate for lack of earnings, there ought to be a means test. It must be remembered, however, that if a means test is to be fixed even at a generous level some form of *investigation* will be necessary; and however carefully this is conducted there may be a deterrent effect.

The question of relationships with men is probably the most difficult point in devising a scheme of allowances for families lacking male support. Allowances for the fatherless appear to undermine marriage. Greater support for fatherless families will certainly mean more fatherless families (more divorces, fewer re-marriages, more unmarried mothers keeping their children, fewer marrying their children's fathers). Facing this fact means publicizing allowances, and easing access to them. At the moment the public conspiracy of silence about support for the families, and difficulty of access, indicate ambivalence and a desire to protect marriage against erosion. Yet, in fact, marriage has never been more popular, and dissolving or preventing unhappy or hasty marriages can only enhance its status.

There is an important distinction to be spelt out between on the one hand encouraging marriage or re-marriage and on the other punishing deviations from an increasingly questioned conventional morality. At present the 'cohabitation' rules which deny a mother state support in certain degrees of relationship with a man are ill-defined and unenforceable. How is an officer to determine whether a couple are 'living as man and wife'? Is the officer to ask, do they sleep together or breakfast together, or does the woman wash the man's shirts and darn his socks? Is it the state's business to know whom she sleeps with as long as no financial support is involved? And should she and her children be punished by withdrawal of her allowance even if the man provides no support? The cohabitation rules appear to be defined principally to support marriage—but not to protect the child.

There is no easy solution to the problem of how to protect the

mother's and child's income, and yet permit the growth of relationships with men. As long as a mother is to lose some or all of her
allowance upon cohabitation or marriage there will be a financial
disincentive to legalizing any union. Moreover some kind of
investigation of the mother's relationships with men or of her
marital status will be necessary. One possible provision is that a man
who cohabits shall be liable to support only insofar as he is the
father of any children. Another is that the mother may retain a
portion of her allowance, say that for the children, if she remarries
or if she cohabits. This would make the allowance into a 'fatherless
child's allowance'. A rise in Family Allowances to equal subsistence
rates would remove a major element in the mother's disincentive
to remarry, and would constitute a sort of 'fatherless child's
allowance'.

What is more important here is that the role of social security in
relation to marriage should be explored much more thoroughly than
hitherto in the light of the mother's and child's needs.

So far the role of the father's payment has not been discussed.
This is deliberate, since the aim has been to emphasize the similarity
of these families and they differ chiefly in respect of previous and
present relations with the father. The problem of recouping the
money from the father and his ability to pay should be kept out of
a discussion of the *needs* of the mother and her child. There are a
number of suggestions, for fatherlessness as an insurable 'risk' like
widowhood, for collection through tax codes or National Insurance,
for state underwriting of court orders, all of which could and should
be worked out to a certain extent in isolation from the question of
support for the mother. However, it seems that there would be
problems in integrating an inadequate system of court orders with
other schemes. And there are also difficulties in making allowances
for families where the father has the capacity to pay more than the
minimum allowance.

I have not explored, either, the problem of equity between
families. How are we to encourage work and yet not open gaps
between the sick and the fit, those with small and those with large
families, the young and the old? Too great a concern with equity,
however, may prevent any advance in legislation.

Meanwhile, attention must be turned to improving the existing
means-tested structure upon which so many mothers depend. This
small survey revealed that there were defects and inconsistencies in
the secret code of allowances to which national assistance officers

were intended to work. But further than this, officers' behaviour departed from the code in making moral distinctions of desert among clients, and the officers' exercise of discretionary power worked on the whole to reduce the client's allowance. These restrictions could be removed by specifying the client's *right* to an allowance, which would entail publishing the code of allowances, giving the client a detailed written assessment of the allowance and strengthening the client's power of appeal. This would reduce the officer's power to withhold, and improve the client's power to obtain, the money the community intends the client to have.

But we must also learn more about the way officers' attitudes are influenced by the community, by organizational structures, and sometimes by the overwork, insufficient pay and poor surroundings which are consequences of the low status of this increasingly used residual service for the poor. Little gain can be made while the public and officers of these services are filled with suspicion of fraud, and the balance must somehow be shifted towards a greater concern to seek out and relieve need, even possibly at the expense of a rise in fraud.

Until the means-tested structure is radically altered we cannot claim to have eradicated the Poor Law from Britain.

# 13. Poor and Out of Work in Shields: A Summary Report[1]

## Adrian Sinfield

This study examines the impact of unemployment on a small group of men and their families. It was carried out in the North-East of England in 1963–64 after the sharp winter recession of the previous year. After the war the drop in the numbers of unemployed and legislation believed to provide a comprehensive system of social services and social security were often taken together as proof of the diminished burden of unemployment for the individual. This belief undoubtedly had an effect upon opinions about the unemployed but very little was known about what happened to those who did experience unemployment in post-war Britain.[2] This study was particularly directed towards the problems unemployment brings

1. The study summarized here was carried out with the guidance of Peter Townsend and Brian Abel-Smith and was financed by the Social Research Division of the London School of Economics—for a full account see *Unemployed in Shields*, Bell, London, forthcoming. It was one of four surveys carried out under Townsend and Abel-Smith as a preliminary to their major study of poverty and the distribution of resources in Britain: the other studies are Marsden, D., *Mothers Alone: Poverty and the Fatherless Family*, Allen Lane, Penguin Press, Harmondsworth, 1969; Land, H., *Large Families Living In London*, Bell, London, 1970, and a study of the chronic sick by John Veit-Wilson. In preparing this summary I have been particularly grateful for the help of Dennis Marsden, Susan Best and Dorothy Sinfield.

2. There have been very few studies of the unemployed since the war, and these have been mainly of the redundant. The major ones are Wedderburn, D., *White-Collar Redundancy* and *Redundancy and the Railwaymen*, Occasional Papers Nos. 1 and 4, Department of Applied Economics, Cambridge University Press, 1964 and 1965, and Kahn, H. R., *Repercussions of Redundancy*, London, Allen & Unwin, 1964, on car-workers in the Midlands. The effects of mine-closures in the North have been studied by House, J. W., and Knight, E. M., *Pit Closure and the Community*, and Knight, E. M., *Men Leaving Mining, West Cumberland, 1966–67*, Reports to the Ministry of Labour, Papers on Migration and Mobility in Northern England, Nos. 5 and 6, Newcastle, Department of Geography, University of Newcastle, 1967 and 1968. The impact of the 1952 recession in the textile industry was examined in PEP, 'Social Security and Unemployment in Lancashire', *Planning*, Vol. XIX, 349, 1st December, 1952.

the individual and his family and the effectiveness of the state services in meeting these.

Since the war unemployment has averaged about 2 per cent, a level much lower than that anticipated by Beveridge and the other planners of the 1940s. This persistently low rate has however been accompanied by markedly higher rates for the disabled, men over 55, the unskilled and those living in the regions furthest from London. There has been little evidence of any improvement in the geographical differential despite government legislation and activity to promote what are now hopefully called 'development areas'.

The long-term unemployment rate has remained high in comparison with many other industrial countries and one in four, often more, of the unemployed have been out of work as long as six months. Vulnerability to further unemployment is also high. Finally, another major expectation of the post-war planners has not been fulfilled. The role of assistance has not declined to insignificance by the 1960s: on average less than two out of three unemployed at any time receive unemployment benefit and more than one in three receives national assistance alone or as a supplement to insurance benefit.

SELECTION OF SAMPLE

The survey was limited to men only and based in the North-East of England where a higher incidence of unemployment made it easier and quicker to obtain a sample. North Shields, roughly the southern and Tyneside half of the county borough of Tynemouth, Northumberland, was chosen for the study because, although the unemployment rate there was still above the national average, it was lower than that for the region and opportunities in the local labour market were increased by an expanding trading estate. It was also convenient for study because only one employment exchange, National Assistance Board office and local authority were involved.[3]

A random sample of unemployed men was drawn by calling at every fifth house on the electoral register. A man was defined as unemployed if he said that

(i) he was registered for work at the employment exchange, or

(ii) he was out of work, available for and wanting work.

Only five men were included in the sample on the second condition alone.

3. Since the survey the government departments have been reorganized and renamed; the original names are used throughout.

92 men revealed as unemployed by the screening process—carried out by three third-year students of the Department of Social Studies, Newcastle University—were interviewed for an average of one hour by the writer between October 1963 and February 1964. More than two-thirds of the sample were reinterviewed before May 1964. Interview records were supplemented with five-year career histories from the Ministry of Labour employment exchange and data from the National Assistance Board: this information was obtained with the interviewee's consent and in 1968 the record of registration at the local employment exchange was brought up to date for the 75 men whose retirement, death or current labour force status was known. Central and local government officials, employers, trade union officials, the North-East Development Council and many others provided valuable background and supplementary information.

### THE UNEMPLOYED

There were 92 men in the sample, ranging in age from a boy of 15 just out of school to a fisherman of 74. Over half were under 40. Six men, all over 45, lived alone; 29, mostly young men, lived with their parents or with a brother or sister; the other two-thirds lived with their wives and 42 had at least one child to support.

The men had been out of work an average of seven and a half months at the time of interview. In the five years prior to the interview an average of one year and five months had been spent 'signing on at the dole', so the measure of current unemployment understated the extent to which the lives of these men were affected by unemployment. More than one-quarter of the last five years had been totally unproductive for the 92 men. The total length of this period of unemployment was over nine months for the 74 men for whom this data could be obtained: two of the men were still registered for work over four years later. More than half were back in work inside four months although over a third were unemployed at least six months.

Differences in the level of skill attained were closely related both to the duration and incidence of unemployment in the past. The skilled had on average been out of work just one month at the time of the interview, the unskilled one year all but three weeks. Over the previous five years the skilled had a total of under six months' unemployment, the unskilled one year and eight months. The semi-skilled fell between these two extremes together with men who had received a skilled or semi-skilled man's training but had last worked in an unskilled job.

Those who had suffered most unemployment recently and in the past five years were the disabled. Twenty-two said that they were disabled or suffered from poor health to the extent that it affected their ability to work, and fourteen of these were registered as disabled at the local employment exchange. These men had been out of work one and a half years since they last worked and altogether for half of the previous five years.

THE END OF THE JOB

More than two out of three men said they had been paid off by their last employers because there was no work and one out of four said that they had left their last job. The eight who left work because of illness, injury or disability were mostly older men, the fifteen who left for domestic or financial reasons mostly under the age of twenty-five. Four men said they had been sacked.

The pay-off usually came suddenly, most men receiving only one day's notice or less. Men said, if they had to be unemployed, they preferred the large-scale pay-off to a slow run-down of the labour force. The big pay-off from the shipyards guaranteed both status and sympathy in the community: the gradual reduction led to invidious comparisons and to rumours and speculations about certain men being paid off before others. The criteria for selection in a pay-off were rarely known.

The distinction between voluntary and involuntary termination of a job—so important in deciding eligibility to state benefits and public attitudes towards unemployment—was often a shadowy and arbitrary one. In industries with a high turnover it was easier to arrange to have oneself paid off; in some, such as the Merchant Navy, it was virtually impossible, whatever the family crisis, except at the end of a trip. Not only those who were paid off because of lack of work, but the leavers as well, were affected by the economic situation when they tried to find another job. How many others regarded their jobs as more than usually intolerable but decided to stay on because of lack of work elsewhere was, of course, not known.

THE SEARCH FOR WORK

The men's job-hunt was influenced very much both by their previous labour market experience and by prevailing demands for different occupations. In an area of high unemployment there was no way of testing a man's declared willingness to work; because of the large element of chance and the role of family and friends, finding work was no indication of the intensity of the search.

Although very few seemed to avoid any tension in looking for work, the skilled shipyard-workers expecting a recall when work returned were mostly saved the tedious and depressing trudge from shipyard to shipyard and from factory to factory made by those without a skill. There was less chance for these that they would be called back to their old jobs and the competition for jobs was much greater. Perhaps even more influential in moulding their attitudes and actions, there was no 'right way' to look for work and luck tended to dominate the job search. The value of informal contacts— family, friends or just a chance meeting in a pub—was even greater for the unskilled and was stressed time and time again in interviews.[4]

When illness or disability or the redundancy of a skill prevented men following their trades any longer, they faced special problems. However knowledgeable they might be about where to go, whom to see and what skills to display to obtain work at their old occupations, they now had to learn this all over again. They could not feel—as most of the others—that at least they were doing their best in the search for work, because they did not know what to do. Older men often despaired, alternating between frantic search and lethargy. More often than others they said it was no good looking for work: 'too old at 45' was often said by employers and trade union officials in the area as well as the unemployed.

Others who would probably have been able to get work comparatively easily in areas of labour shortage often found themselves vulnerable to prolonged unemployment on Tyneside. Men with a record of imprisonment or mental hospitalization said that they were acceptable only for the roughest jobs with the least security and were the first victims of any lay-off: in this way they were kept on the margin of the labour force.

4. There is no space in a paper of this length to discuss many of the problems in collecting data and evaluating response but the difficulty of evaluating the importance of different aspects in job search indicates a problem common to the survey. Men took for granted the help of family and friends and very rarely cited them when asked how they normally looked for work; they tended to say they 'just looked around'. Yet in answer to questions about how they found their last job, many said a relative or a friend had told them about it.

## MOBILITY IN THE SEARCH

It was difficult to obtain an accurate picture of people's attitudes to moving away to find work, and even more of how this related to action. Most said they had tried to break away from the dole queues and at least a half had worked outside Northumberland and Durham. Excluding those working away in the Merchant Navy (21) and doing National Service (5), at least one in four (23) had worked in other parts of Britain. Many had gone to a relative who had given them temporary lodging and often helped them find work. Usually this move seemed to be made before marriage, or during the first few years afterwards, and some of the younger men spoke of marriage as anchoring them to North Shields and to all the uncertainty of the labour market there. The major barrier to mobility cited by the men was housing, both its greater cost elsewhere and the difficulty of obtaining it, many local authorities setting residence requirements for council houses. (Of course the evidence for this is based mainly on men who had returned and may well be unrepresentative of movers, although a supporting picture was obtained from accounts of relatives who had moved out.)

## THE EMPLOYMENT EXCHANGE

The local Ministry of Labour employment exchange was the government agency with which the unemployed had most contact—all but 5 of the 92 men registered for work at the exchange twice a week. Perhaps because of this frequent contact, it was also the service with which most expressed chief dissatisfaction, their usually fatalistic and quietistic attitudes being discarded when talking about the exchange. The most vocal complainants—unskilled labourers—seemed on the whole to have received less benefit from registration; that is, if such a crude and ambiguous index as number of jobs obtained through the exchange can be taken as a guide to help received.

One in four of the jobs held during the last five years had been obtained through the employment exchange. Over half the jobs held by the skilled (mostly, though by no means entirely, 'recalls' to shipyards) had been found in this way compared with one in five of the rest. One in four of the skilled had obtained their last job through an exchange placing and only one in six of the rest.

There were 22 men who said they were handicapped by poor mental or physical health or injury or disability and fourteen of these were on the Disabled Persons' Register at the employment exchange. Although the fact that they were on a firm's statutory

3 per cent quota of disabled may have saved them from earlier pay-offs, once they were on the dole they experienced much greater difficulty in finding work again. (Nationally the registered disabled formed one in twenty-five of the male working population but one in four of men out of work over one year.)

Some of the disabled said they had refused to go on the Disabled Persons' Register as they believed this hampered them in competing in the open market and encouraged employers to consider them only for lower paid jobs. It also appeared to provide confirmation to assistance officers that such men, applying for aid for themselves and their families, should be wage-stopped (see below) without attention to previously high earnings. Most of the disabled and some of the older workers were registered at the exchange as 'light labourers'. In an area where men with a skill or training were having to take jobs as labourers and the number registered for this occupation far exceeded vacancies, this classification seemed tantamount to 'reject'.

The extent to which the employment exchange helped those with the handicaps of no skill, inexperience, old age and poor health or disability seemed severely limited by three factors—the economic situation in the area, the exchange's emphasis on its dependence upon the good will of employers and Ministry of Labour policy to submit those most industrially qualified for a job. It was the decision of the employer to notify, and to continue notifying, the exchange of any vacancies and many employers seemed to expect the exchange to save them some of the invidious problems of selection and rejection. If a firm felt the exchange was being too persistent in sending old, disabled or otherwise 'unsuitable' applicants for jobs, then it could discontinue notification of jobs and reduce the exchange's opportunity to place even its most suitable registrants. Obviously there was need for a delicate balance in relationships, but the existing balance seemed to be weighted heavily against the unemployed man.

Although a few employers believed that the exchange was trying to make them accept 'the dregs', this seemed unlikely. Employment exchange policy was to submit 'those most industrially suited' for a job and this is what it set out to do. The criteria for suitability became difficult when a clerk had to choose among many unskilled labourers with little knowledge of their employment experience to help differentiate them. It seemed likely that for want of other criteria those last out often became the first submitted, or some judgement of suitability in terms of personal appearance was made. Alternatively, if the clerk recognized the arbitrariness of such a decision, he might send them all for the job and both men and employers objected.

In the existing economic situation and without any change in policy, it seemed that little could be done to help those disadvantaged in the search for work. There was often a likelihood that such disadvantages might become more formally disqualifying factors for submission to work.

## The Reaction to Unemployment

The effect of unemployment on the life of a man and his family was hard to measure in one or two brief interviews. It was clear that men played down the impact while they were still unemployed. Once the crisis was over some of the more central issues were discussed more openly, an indication of how deeply unemployment could strike at a family's security. The laconic way in which men referred to their misfortunes seemed to be often due to the fact that unemployment was now part of their way of life and they had come to regard it fatalistically as 'just one of those things'.

Those who seemed to make the most adjustment in their days because of unemployment were of two kinds—the very recently unemployed who said they were confident of a swift return to work and those out of work over a year with little expectation of further employment. The first tended to regard the unemployment at least at first as a break or a chance to relax, or as one said, 'It gives you a chance to spend your money'. The second, all older or considerably handicapped, appeared to be gradually withdrawing from the outer community, some becoming highly suspicious of all with whom they had contact. When asked if he saw any friends, one man aged 60 and living alone said that he had his radio: it was better than bringing in people and kept him company.

The rest of the unemployed appeared reluctant to make even minor adjustments in their lives because they seemed to regard these as acknowledging that they might be out of work for many more months. The three effects of unemployment most commonly mentioned were depression, irritability and the problem of passing the time and these were often linked together. Married men rarely referred to the loss of income directly as their wives did, but they did complain about the loss of freedom this brought.

Arguments over 'little things' frequently arose (these were most often admitted in interviews after the return to work) but rows about money and the children appeared the most frequent. In winter only one or two rooms could be kept warm and the men had to share the kitchen with playing children. The majority of fathers found their control of the children diminishing with the length of unemployment and gave this as yet another incentive to get out of the house. At the height of winter the increased unemployment was evident from the numbers of men standing on corners, along the wall overlooking the river and outside the betting shop and the employment exchange, and from the men reading desultorily or slumped asleep in the reading-room of the public library.

## The Standard of Living

During unemployment all but three households were in poverty by the criteria used in *The Poor and The Poorest* (140 per cent national assistance entitlement plus rent).[5] More than one in three households had an income below their basic national assistance entitlement and one in two were only at the standard level or less than 20 per cent above it. By these standards, those with families to support were worst off; over a half of the unemployed with children had incomes below the basic assistance level compared with one-fifth without children. Eight out of the twelve families with at least four children were below the standard. Since all the unemployed but four were receiving national insurance unemployment benefit or national assistance, the efficacy of the social security system in meeting need must be questioned.

The median regular net income during unemployment was £5 a week, about one-third of the average worker's net wage—or 'take-home' pay—in the region at that time. While no one living alone or with his family of origin received more than £5, all but six of the forty-one families with dependent children were above the median, half of them receiving over £7 10s.

Three out of four experienced a drop in income during unemployment of over 40 per cent, two in five a drop of over 60 per cent. Those living alone or with their family of origin suffered the greatest percentage decline but even among those with children to support fewer than one in six had a drop of less than 20 per cent.

5. Abel-Smith, B., and Townsend, P., *The Poor and the Poorest*, London, Bell, 1965. 1965.

The actual money drop was great: in three out of five households the weekly income fell by over £5 and in one out of five by over £10. The terms 'acute' and 'chronic' are sometimes used to distinguish between the financial situation of those whose income has dropped considerably and those whose income is already low and has only dropped slightly. The experience of this group of unemployed suggests that the latter can be living at such a low level that the smallest reduction can precipitate the most acute crises in an already chronic situation.

Current hardship was made more severe by low earnings in the past for most men. Median 'take-home' pay in the last job had been £11–13 a week. The unskilled had the lowest wages, seventeen of the forty-one, mostly teenagers, earning under £9 a week. The disabled and the older men in poor health had often experienced a considerable drop in their earnings over the past few years.

Those with lower earnings in work tended to be those poorer out of work. More than two-thirds of those with a previous wage of £15 or more had an income over £6 5s. compared with less than one-third of those earning under £15. Most resources additional to social security payments were held by those with previously better earnings and smaller family responsibilities: income tax rebates and savings were both related to previous earnings and family structure.

Some needs could be deferred till the return to work while others, particularly children's clothing and shoes for the winter, could not. They had to be met more expensively, by buying on credit or by buying cheaply and having to replace sooner. For reasons such as these, families with dependent children more often had to face financial crises. Some idea of their standard of living can be provided by the answers given by wives to the question, 'What have you cut down on now that your husband's out of work?'— 'Well, we've never had many luxuries lately.'—'What do you mean by luxuries?'—'Oh, fresh or tinned fruit, biscuits and cheese'. Or 'Is there anything you bought while your husband was out of work that you felt you really shouldn't have because you couldn't afford it?'—'Oh, yes: On a Friday night when Jack collected his money at the dole, he would stop at the shop on the corner and buy us a pasty and bacon and eggs. I know it was extravagant, but we had to have something to cheer us up.'

The hardest pressed appeared to be those with four or more children to support, often existing on reduced assistance grants because of the wage-stop (described below). This group however received least sympathy and there was a widespread belief that they received unduly large grants: because of the operation of the wage-stop, the opposite was true. There was no evidence that larger families were more wasteful of their money than smaller. There were many indications that husbands in such families accepted that an even smaller proportion of their wage should be left them for their own 'pleasures', and wives resigned themselves to the fact that their clothes would have to last longer and their share of the meals be smaller.

Financial incentives and deterrents appeared to bear little relevance to the issues of persistent and recurrent unemployment, but financial support was essential for participation in society. For the man living by himself unemployment meant loss of company: lack of income restricted the search for company, but, with many more unemployed than jobs vacant, contacts were essential for finding work. The longer unemployment of the single, separated or widowed man, particularly as he got older, became connected with his isolation and meagre resources. With these handicaps, the incentive of a wage some 3 or 4 times above his present income could play little part.

## The Social Security System

National insurance unemployment benefit and national assistance were the main or only sources of income for all but four of the unemployed. Altogether 52 per cent were receiving unemployment benefit alone, 18 per cent benefit and assistance and 25 per cent assistance only. Well over half of those living with their family of origin had unemployment benefit only, while none of those living alone were drawing any benefit. One half of those with children to support were on benefit alone although this group was the hardest-pressed financially.

### NATIONAL INSURANCE

The skilled and better paid had a much stronger insurance position than the unskilled: all but eight of the thirty-one skilled and semi-skilled were receiving full benefit compared with less than half of the fifty-six unskilled.

Seven men had never qualified for benefit because they had never worked, or had not worked long enough. Fourteen had exhausted all their benefit because of persistent recurrent or continuous unemployment. Eight had their benefit withheld for up to six weeks and at least another ten had suffered disqualification in earlier periods of unemployment, usually because they had left a job 'without just cause'. Twelve men were receiving reduced benefit because their national insurance stamps had not been paid or credited—usually during earlier periods of disallowance.

In general those only temporarily unemployed with little previous experience of unemployment were best supported by unemployment insurance. This system seemed to envisage a single type of employer-employee relationship operating within an industrial, economic and social vacuum. It did not foresee the different economic experiences of workers in different industries in different regions: the result was the quicker exhaustion of benefit among workers in industries with recurrent or seasonal unemployment (shipbuilding and repair, building and construction). It often failed to adapt to the uncertain distinction between voluntary and involuntary termination of work described earlier, not differentiating the reasons for leaving a job beyond the 'just cause' provision. By denying credited contributions to those out of work because convicted and imprisoned, or merely accused and detained before trial—whether or not they were later found guilty—it administered its own punishment. It forbade all kinds of double social security payments without distinction: by the reduction of one benefit it penalized the man with a disability pension for himself and his dependants when he was out of work, and a husband who was unemployed when his wife was receiving maternity benefits. There was no evidence that the cost of childbirth declined with the man's unemployment.

A comprehensive system of national insurance based on contributions probably cannot provide for all; besides, in any scheme covering some twenty-four million workers there are bound to be some anomalies and some situations for which there can be no provision. The National Assistance Board, as it then was, existed to meet these 'unmet' needs.

NATIONAL ASSISTANCE

A programme aimed to meet unmet needs for those remaining in the labour market—traditionally and often euphemistically described as the 'able-bodied'—cannot avoid providing at least temporary, working answers to certain basic issues. In addition to deciding what needs shall be met, and to what extent, the relation between payments according to need and rewards available in the labour market must be determined.

Attitudes and beliefs about the discouragement of idleness and the need for incentive still had considerable force in the allocation of assistance to the unemployed, often conflicting with the Board's statutory obligation to promote the welfare of the individual. Some of these beliefs were explicitly supported in the Act, which forbade payments to those in full-time work however poor their wages, and the Regulations, which required the reduction of payments according to need to the level of the individual's predicted wage-potential (the wage-stop). Other beliefs appeared to gain strength from unpublished and internal instructions of the Board, and others still seemed to be derived solely from the attitudes of the officers of the Board. These often reflected their position in society and their own views of the just reward for different groups. One officer, for example, declared a grant 'enough for a labourer'.

Just over half of the unemployed in the sample were receiving national assistance payments, half of these as supplement to their unemployment benefit. Probably another nineteen of the remaining 45 (over one-fifth of the sample) would have received national assistance if they had applied for it.[6] Four of the 47 on assistance received grants above the regular scale and rent allowance and fourteen were reduced below the level laid down by Parliament as adequate 'to meet their requirements'. Altogether 23 of the 33 men below the assistance standard—whether on assistance or not—had a wife and one or more dependent children to support. Nine of these families had four or more children and were all actually on assistance.

Ignorance of their rights was the major reason for failure to apply for assistance by those apparently eligible. While many officials seemed to feel 'they know what to tell you and what to keep quiet about', the writer was struck by the general lack of correct information on the level of payments, the method of assessment, the possibility of special grants and the right to appeal on the part not only of those who had not applied but also of assistance recipients. Some thought they knew and were spreading wildly

6. Data for those on assistance was provided by the National Assistance Board; for those not on assistance the calculations are those of the writer after only brief familiarity with National Assistance practice in assessing need and resources.

inaccurate rumours; a few boasted of their knowledge while not realizing that their grants were being paid at a reduced level. Many said that they had been led to apply because others—a relative, friend or neighbour—had applied successfully. Ironically, the failure of insurance benefits to provide adequately which led more to seek assistance as well as benefit became a major eradicator of the stigma attaching to assistance grants.

Officers often seemed more anxious that they should not be taken in by a hard-luck story than that they should fail to meet any genuine need. In dealing with the unemployed the wide discretionary powers of the officers seemed to be most often exercised towards refusing or reducing assistance grants rather than adding to them or making special grants. Grants were reduced beneath insurance benefit level for those disqualified from benefit in order to reinforce the incentive to work.

### THE WAGE-STOP

One regulation appeared to conflict directly with the general intent of the Act to promote the welfare of the individual and his family. Instead, it tried to maintain an incentive to work believed to be provided by wages sufficient to meet the family's needs, even by the Board's own standards.

Eleven families, all with at least one dependent child, were wage-stopped—one-half of all the families on assistance with children to support. The intention was to ensure by the reduction of the grant that an unemployed man did not receive more on assistance than he would if he were working full-time in his normal job. What had been intended for occasional use seemed to have become a major instrument of policy. But such a regulation proved impossible to operate fairly in practice—what are 'normal' earnings if a man is just disabled or has not worked for eight years, or if ten firms pay different combinations of overtime, bonuses and flat-rate earnings? In such an arbitrary and unpredictable situation officers seemed apparently to 'play safe' by keeping payments low. The average deduction was 47s. a week and five families lost over £3 of their entitlement. Six of the families were wage-stopped below their benefit level and so received no assistance payments at all. These appeared particularly disadvantaged: a local social worker for example refused one family a grant because they were not on assistance and so he believed sufficiently well-off that they were ineligible. Some families had paid for medicines, not realizing that they would be eligible for a refund and two failed to apply for milk-tokens.

Nationally at that time the grants of one-third of all unemployed men with families on assistance were reduced and many more were probably discouraged from applying. The regulation had most effect in the depressed regions against those with restricted earning power (the disabled worker and the light labourer) and/or those with larger needs (the man with a large family or a high rent). It is important to note that those wage-stopped below their benefit level who received no assistance payments were not included in the statistics of the wage-stopped.

Many of the assistance officers met during the survey seemed to see themselves saddled, willingly or unwillingly, with the responsibility of ensuring that those who had no benefit continued to look for work and believed themselves caught in a dilemma—should they act to maintain the family's income or to maintain the man's incentive to take work? The employment exchange officers seemed to have a better understanding of local job opportunities and in general appeared less likely to put pressure on men to find work.

*         *         *

The contrast between the lives of the skilled and the unskilled in work continued when they were unemployed: in fact some of the differences became clearer in comparing their resources to meet such a crisis as unemployment. The position of the skilled was already stronger because of the greater demand for his work so he could expect to be unemployed less frequently and for shorter periods of time. So the skilled and the unskilled had different degrees of power and freedom in the labour market, different opportunities to exercise choice and different access to resources.

In looking for work the unskilled in particular were heavily dependent upon luck and informal contacts. Those most vulnerable in the labour market—the disabled and older worker—had little, if any, of their handicap lightened by the action of the local employment exchange. Within present policy it often seemed unable to do anything except perpetuate, perhaps even formalize, the odds already against them.

For the majority of these men the present period of unemployment was just one of many. Their earnings and security in work were so inadequate that they seemed trapped in permanent poverty or, at the best, ever on the margin of it. For them the operation of the existing social security system seemed to provide little benefit and in some households deliberately reduced the income below its previous low level.

In general the better a man's wages were in work, the better was the support out of work that he could provide for himself *and* could obtain from the social security system. The existing insurance programme coped best with those seldom and temporarily unemployed: those frequently or persistently out of work were dependent on national assistance. There was a conflict in the payment of assistance grants between the statutory obligation to meet need and a concern about the reduction of incentives which it seemed to be believed could be met by reducing payments. Those with families to support were most hard-pressed financially, both because of their more urgent needs and the greater restriction of assistance grants.

It seemed clear that, at least for these men and their families, the miseries of unemployment have yet to be dispelled. At present what public concern there is over unemployment is directed towards redundancy and there has been no recognition of recurrent unemployment.[7] Yet those exposed to repeated unemployment face problems as equally urgent and as potentially long-lasting as the redundant.

7. Analysis of legislation passed since the survey indicates that overall this has contributed to the general security of the employed and has benefited 'the élite of the unemployed', the relatively well-paid worker with little, if any, recent experience of unemployment, more than those who appear from national data and the sample to be the typical men out of work in Britain today.

# 14. Rural Poverty and Community Isolation

## Vilhelm Aubert

The income statistics of Norway suggest that poverty is to a large extent a rural phenomenon. Of the 50,000 who in 1962 were employees in agriculture, forestry and fishery, 32 per cent earned less than 4,000 kroner ($570) per year, and 27 per cent earned between 4,000 and 8,000 kroner. Exactly one half of a total of 7,800 providers who earned less than 4,000 and whose total household income was between 4,000 and 8,000, belonged to the agricultural occupations. The great majority of these providers were independent farmers and/or fishermen. Of those households whose incomes were less than 4,000, and where the poverty cannot be explained by youth, old age or disability, a large share were independent farmers or fishermen.[1]

The evidence on rural poverty is too fragmentary and insufficiently analyzed to permit safe conclusions. It must also be borne in mind that the same cash income lasts longer in a rural district than it does in a city. The production of milk, meat and fish for home consumption, as well as the greatly reduced building costs in the countryside, should be taken into account when rural and urban income levels are being compared. Nevertheless, it may be claimed that a large share of those whose major problem is poverty, are to be found in the isolated rural regions of Norway. There is reason to believe that for those who live in poverty in the cities, poverty is more frequently accompanied by other major problems. Mental illness, alcoholism or some other disability is very often a concomitant, or even a cause, of their underprivileged position.

The preceding does not imply that the Norwegian countryside is characterized by poverty. Rural poverty is not characteristic of any large region, but is found in relatively small pockets in the remote

1. The figures on low income groups are from Myklebust, P., *Personer med lave inntekter. Skattelikningen 1962*, Arbeidsnotater, Statistisk Sentralbyrå, Oslo, 1966.

mountain districts, on the west coast, and in the north. To some extent the poverty may be gleaned from the income statistics. Since these are organized on the basis of the municipality as the smallest unit, however, the smallest pockets of poverty are not easily located.

A special analysis of the income levels in the inland districts of the two northernmost counties, Troms and Finnmark,[2] has been undertaken by the Directorate of Labour. The analysis reveals incomes which are only half of the national average for taxpayers, and in some municipalities considerably less. In the whole area the *per capita* income is one-third of the income per taxpayer, and in one municipality down to one-fourth, while the *per capita* income for the nation is one-half of the taxpayer income. It means that substantially larger households must subsist on an income of less than half the national average.

Scarcity of natural resources is the basic cause of this poverty. The areas under scrutiny are hardly industrialized; farms are small and agricultural conditions generally unfavourable; communications are poor and distances very great. Although these factors are particularly powerful in Northern Norway, they are also present in many Southern Norwegian areas, where they sometimes lead to poverty, but often not. In addition to the poor resources, the inland municipalities of North Troms and Finnmark are characterized by a net increase of the population in recent years. More and more people have to subsist on the same meagre resources. Emigration has not in this region served as a safety valve as has been the case in many other non-industrialized rural regions. The Directorate of Labour's report explains this partly by the prevalence of Lappish-speakers in these areas, the Lapps being reluctant to leave their traditional habitat and community to seek employment under different and unfamiliar conditions. The language barrier is a crucial hindrance to emigration, but there are probably other obstacles to be overcome. We shall later return to this ethnic problem.

In other areas, the problems of rural low-income groups are being partly solved by immigration to cities and other industrial or commercial centres. The rate can be estimated on the basis of available statistics on abolished farms; during the last seven years 27,000 farms

2. *Indre Nord-Troms og Indre Finnmark. Næringsøkonomiske og etnososiologiske problemer*, Arbeidsdirektoratet, 5. juli, 1963. Christoffersen, T., 'Søkelyset på økonomisk svakstilte områder i Troms og Finnmark', *Arbeidsmarkedet*, nr. 7, Oslo, 1963, 6–11.

were abandoned due to a change of occupation. The reasons for the individual's movement from primary to secondary or tertiary occupations are not well known. It could be surmised that the smallholders who left their farms were poor or relatively near the poverty line. However, the decision to move does not depend upon economic need alone, but also on the ability to find work in a different occupation and to live in a strange locality. This may often favour the emigration of the relatively well-to-do. They are the most qualified to work in another occupation, they are better acquainted with job and housing opportunities, and they are more self-confident. Systematic studies in Sweden show that, among young people, the best educated and the more able and socially privileged seem to move more often from rural to urban areas than those who are less qualified.[3] It may thus be doubted that migration alone can solve the problem of rural poverty. The findings imply that the problem of rural poverty will, in most instances, take the same shape as in the cities, i.e. small pockets of poverty in isolated households.

Some rural groups are known to be particularly exposed to the risk of poverty, for example, forestry workers (lumberjacks). Here again a survey conducted by the Directorate of Labour is illuminating.[4] Two municipalities in Southern Norway were selected as representative of areas where forestry is economically important. Almost half of the forest workers earned a yearly income amounting to less than half of what an industrial worker earns. Between one-fourth and one-fifth of the forestry workers earned less than 5,000 kroner a year, an income which is below a reasonable poverty line. It emerges from the study that the low incomes are not caused by low pay per unit of time in the forest, but by seasonal unemployment. Forestry workers tend to own a small farm as well, and may also seek other types of seasonal employment. This situation is characteristic of rural areas with low income levels.

The study on forestry workers was motivated by a fear of falling recruitment to the occupation. Thus, migration and occupational mobility cannot simultaneously solve the problem of poverty and the problem of exploiting the forests efficiently. The situation is similar in certain coastal districts where representatives of the fishing industry fear difficulties in recruitment, while economic experts claim that there are already too many fishermen. This

3. Neymark, *Selektiv rörlighet*, Stockholm, 1962.
4. *En statistisk/sosiologisk undersøkelse av skogsarbeiderstanden i Brandval i Hedmark og Solum i Telemark*, Arbeidsdirektoratet, October, 1961.

paradox can be explained by the fact that it has not been possible to organize Norwegian fishery or forestry on the industrial model, with full time employment in large production units. There are many sources of resistance to such a development. The smallholder who is also a fisherman or a forestry worker may often doubt whether he has anything to gain by becoming a full time worker in these occupations.

The problems of unemployment most relevant to a study of poverty are probably those we have already touched upon: declared or hidden seasonal unemployment in economically undeveloped rural areas. In other regions the demand for manpower exceeds supply. What prevents a more adequate adjustment between supply and demand through geographical and occupational mobility? One difficulty is that country-dwellers would have to give up their property on migrating to more prosperous areas; their houses lose their value and cannot be sold in the event of depopulation. The quality of housing is reasonably good as there has been a great deal of public support for house building also in peripheral districts after the war. To abandon a good house and continue to pay interest and instalments on it, while at the same time setting up a new household in a city is not an attractive prospect. This explains a great deal of rural underemployment, some of which leads to incomes near the poverty line.

Official statistics on unemployment reveal its highly seasonal character.[5] By the end of December there are about four times as many recipients of unemployment insurance benefits as on the first of October. They are heavily concentrated in occupations related to fishing, forestry and construction work, which emphasizes that unemployment is, above all, a rural winter phenomenon, and especially in the three northernmost counties. The registration of unemployment is, however, difficult and the real situation may deviate considerably from the published statistics.

Among the poor peripheral communities in Norway, some of the poorest are those populated by Lapps. Most of the Lappish-speaking population are bilingual, and only a minority still work in the traditional Lappish occupation of reindeer herding. The Lapps have been undergoing a process of acculturation and assimilation for several centuries, and have also interbred extensively with the

5. Jonassen, Ø., 'Dødfødsler og dødsfall i 1. leveår og det lys de kaster over de sosiale forhold', *Tidsskrift for den norske legeforening*, Vol. 48, Oslo, 1964, pp. 1398–1399.

non-Lappish populations of Northern Norway, Sweden and Finland. However, they still constitute a clearly distinguishable minority in these districts.

Among the 300 reindeer-herding families in Finnmark, it is estimated that only 60 per cent own a herd which is large enough to support a family (200 reindeer). In 1960, the estimated income per taxpayer in Kautokeino, one of the predominantly Lappish municipalities, was no more than 42 per cent of the average for the country. Due to large families, the *per capita* income was a mere 32 per cent of the national average. There is no doubt that these figures imply a great deal of poverty.

Symptoms of poverty among the Lappish population of Finnmark can also be found in a socio-medical study of infant mortality in Finnmark, 1954–61. During this period, the mortality of infants during the first year of their life was 19·9:1,000 in the county, but 45·0:1,000 in the four predominantly Lappish municipalities of Finnmark (with a total population of 6,500). The mortality rate among illegitimate children in these Lappish districts was 79·6: 1,000.[6] Many factors contribute to the high infant mortality rate among the Lapps, but it can definitely be associated with poor housing and extremely low incomes.

In the survey conducted by the Directorate of Labour, it was established that *per capita* incomes vary inversely with the proportion of Lappish speakers in the twelve municipalities under scrutiny. To explain the remarkably high correlation, the population development was registered. In one of the most typically Lappish municipalities, Karasjok, the population increased by 100 per cent between 1930 and 1960, while the comparable figure for the nation was 28 per cent. In another municipality, Kautokeino, the number of men aged 20–29 increased by 41 per cent between 1950 and 1960, while the number of men in this age bracket in the whole of Norway decreased by 17 per cent during the same period. This latter finding is particularly important, since it suggests that the next generation are staying on in their home community, where they will be forced to subsist with their families on resources which have not expanded.

The conclusion of this study, as of a previous one,[7] is that there are certain barriers to the emigration of the Lappish population which

6. Jonassen, Ø., *op. cit.*
7. Eidheim, H., *Erverv og kulturkontakt i Polmak. Polmak og Manndalen. To samebygder. Samiske samlinger*, Vol. 4, Oslo, 1958, pp. 1–69.

contribute to the poverty found in these areas. One important barrier is the inadequate mastery of the Norwegian language, even among young Lapps; most of them attended schools where the teachers did not speak Lappish, and the children did not usually master Norwegian when they entered school. This has caused severe setbacks in their educational development. The fear of prejudice, especially among the non-Lappish population of Northern Norway, may have deterred the young from emigration. There are probably other contributory causes which have not been adequately studied.

The Institute for Social Research conducted an intensive, small-scale study of one Lappish community much further south (near Narvik).[8] The economic situation in this tiny community of 170 inhabitants is much the same as that which was found during the surveys of Finnmark and North Troms. Incomes are approximately one-third of the national average, housing is very inadequate, and many families are incomplete. A disproportionally high share of the population live on disability pensions. This seems to be true also of other isolated rural communities with a Lappish population. One study of a municipality near the city of Harstad, showed a proportion of disability pension receivers twice as high as the national average.[9] It is known that the proportion is considerably higher even than this in those districts within the municipality where the Lapps are concentrated. In these very poor communities the paradoxical situation arises that those who live on disability or old age pensions enjoy more economic security than do large families with a healthy provider.

Is any information contained in the studies referred to, which could elucidate the problems associated with the 'culture of poverty'? It is occasionally claimed that some of the poor groups, small farmers or fishermen, Lapps, and recipients of pensions, exhibit a certain 'mentality'. It is believed that at least some of the poor remain poor because they are backward in the sense that they irrationally reject modern production methods or have an aversion to city life, based on traditionalism and not upon a rational choice. We have found, however, that this apparently backward and irrational mentality of the poor in the rural periphery, is quite often an expression of a

8. It has, so far, resulted in a Master's Thesis by Lina R. Homme. Cf. also: *Tysfjord Kommune. Områdeanalyse,* 1964, pp. 39–53.
9. Andersen, T., 'Uføretrydgen', *Tidsskrift for den norske legeforening,* 1966, pp. 1543–1546.

rational choice in a practical situation which has been inadequately understood by the commentators.[10]

Observers of the Lappish groups have sometimes tended to believe that one of the reasons why many of them remain poor is their religion, a brand of Lutheranism (Læstadianism), which, rejecting luxuries and material wealth, should discourage entrepreneurship and economic initiative in general. This is probably an unwarranted inference. However, a recent anthropological article makes the point that Læstadianism may have served the function of explaining and justifying poverty or, at least, of making it bearable. It is presented as a religion for the underdog, separating him from his environment.[11] This could possibly be classified as an element in a culture of poverty, transmitted from generation to generation. If so, however, it demonstrates that there is no universal culture of poverty, applicable in all modern societies. The value structure of poor Læstadians is different on many points from the value structure outlined in Oscar Lewis's presentation of the culture of poverty based on Mexican data.[12]

The problem of disentangling cultural from situational factors in explaining the behavior of the poor, can be approached in several ways. In the course of a series of studies in isolated communities, we have come across two possible methods. One of them is to study the situational and motivational factors associated with migration from the poor communities. The second is to develop an action program, by introducing new capital and work opportunities into a community where it was assumed that the apathy and lack of interest of the population would prevent economic progress.

In a study of the first kind an attempt was made to compare the situation of the mobile and non-mobile population in two coastal municipalities near Tromsø.[13] Age and sex seemed to be important determinants of mobility, here as in the rest of the country, or even the rest of the world. The young have very few opportunities of gainful employment in the isolated rural community, and this is particularly the case for the girls. Among households, those who

10. Cf. Brox, O., 'Avvisning av storsamfunnet som økonomisk tilpasningsform', *Tidsskrift for samfunnsforskning*, 5, 1964, pp. 167–178.
11. Paine, R., 'Læstadianismen og samfunnet', *Tidsskrift for samfunnsforskning*, 6, 1965, pp. 60–73.
12. *The Children of Sanchez*, New York, Random House, 1961; *Five Families: Mexican Case Studies in the Culture of Poverty*, New York, Random House, 1959.
13. Aubert, V., and Karlsen, G., 'Flytting fra utkanten', *Tidsskrift for samfunnsforskning*, 6, 1965, pp. 182–212.

own a house and engage in some agriculture are more likely to stay on than those whose main income derives from fishery and who do not own a house and some land.

On the whole, the situational differences between the mobile and the non-mobile point in the direction of rational choice is a major explanatory principle. More specifically, when poor families decide to stay on in their home communities, this is very often due to an awareness that mobility would not lead to increased welfare for them within a reasonable time period. It does not seem necessary to search for factors related to culture or mentality in order to interpret the findings. However, one encounters certain attitudinal patterns in these peripheral communities which are related to their isolation and to the deprivations that go with their geographical location. Various superstitious beliefs in divination, reincarnations of the dead, miracle cures and witchcraft are more widespread and seem to be taken somewhat more seriously than in the cities. Rejection of city ways and a reaffirmation of the rural virtues of independence, tranquility and morality, occur also rather frequently in conversations. It seems, however, very doubtful whether it would be appropriate to classify these traditional attitudes as elements in a culture of poverty, and equally doubtful that they contribute much to explain economic behavior.

The second approach to the problem of disentangling cultural from situational factors in poverty is now being tried as an incidental product of a modest action program in a small, isolated and extremely poor community. The action program has three aspects: assistance in communicating with a wide range of public agencies who execute aid programs of various kinds; direct material help on a very limited scale to poor families; investment in a small fish-buying enterprise aimed at an increase in the productivity of fiord-fishing. The prediction of many experts, and of some local authorities, is that such an effort will fail to activate the population economically. This negative forecast is frequently coupled to arguments which seem to presuppose the operation of a culture of poverty in the community.

It is too early to report on the findings of this piece of action research. So far, the assistance that has been offered has either been forthcoming in response to a direct request, or has immediately been accepted and acted upon by the local population. For the first time, some kind of partnership has been established between the poor inhabitants of this remote fiord, and an outside agency. There have been many impediments to a realization of the action program, but so far none of these seem to be related to the culture of poverty. One negative consequence of the program has been a sharpening of a conflict between those who are most actively engaged in the program and some local leaders. This fission can be traced to a scepticism among local leaders, based partly upon 'nativistic' rejection of outside interference, but partly also upon a philosophy of modernization which favors migration and full assimilation. Exposed to these two types of attack an action program may flounder. The fact that a program of this kind calls forth such a dual, and quite contradictory, response may explain why some communities of poor are caught in a state of economic immobilism.

We have so far dealt with a few factors which may contribute to an explanation of why a family or a single community stays poor in a welfare society. Quite as important is the search for factors which impede the economic progress of the larger social categories to which these families or communities belong. The distribution of incomes and wealth in a modern 'welfare state' is influenced by a series of bargains struck between interest groups and by pressures exerted upon the political authorities. In this machinery of bargaining some relatively deprived groups have been less favorably placed than others. It is a question of to what extent the cause of poverty is related to organization-favoring or organization-impeding factors. We shall now proceed to an inspection of the formidable obstacles to organized action on behalf of the rural poor, and especially the Lapps.

These segments of the Norwegian population are relatively small and do not count for much in terms of political strength. The Lappish group is estimated to comprise somewhere around 20,000 individuals. How many rural poor there are outside this group is almost impossible to estimate. The lack of clarity in the criteria of rural poverty is in itself a reason why neither the rural poor themselves nor the political parties can look to this category as a source of important political pressure. However, in some municipalities the Lapps or other categories of rural poor constitute a sizeable minority or even a majority. I shall deal with this situation below.

The rural poor are dispersed over a large territory and live, almost by definition, in isolated parts of the country with poorly developed communications. For these groups to get together and discuss common problems they would have to make long and expensive trips. Besides, the network of communication is so organized that they primarily visit in cities when they travel. The old patterns of visiting and exchanging goods and services within a milieu of rural folk are vanishing. The major reciprocal relationships are now to be found between the inhabitants of the rural fringe and representatives of the local centres.[14]

The rural poor are a heterogeneous lot. There are fishermen, farmers, reindeer-herders, seasonal construction workers and others. In Northern Norway there are Lapps and non-Lapps. Within the Lappish population, there exist several major language groups and all gradations of mastery of the Norwegian language from those who speak only Lappish to those who count themselves as Lapps although they speak nothing but Norwegian. Concomitant with this one finds great differences in the intensity and the content of Lappish identification. Different occupational groups among the Lapps may have conflicts of interest, such as those between big and small reindeer-herders, and between reindeer-herders and farmers. To find a common political denominator, common demands around which the whole group might rally, is difficult. To this must be added that the very idea of the organizational weapon is alien to the traditional Lappish culture and social structure, which was characterized by extreme political decentralization.[15]

To be rurally poor or, even more, to be a Lapp is in many ways an ascribed characteristic, a born quality of the individual. The place of birth and the ancestry is initially decisive for membership in the categories under scrutiny. On the other hand, the individual is entitled to choose his own future, irrespective of these ascribed characteristics. Thus, any attempt to organize these categories of poor would have to cater for the needs of two groups, whose interests may diverge considerably; those who want to remain what they were born to be, and those who want to take advantage of their citizen's rights to move geographically and socially. To put it differently, organizational attempts will have to cope with the continuous loss of potential members and strike a balance between the claims made in favor of the good, traditional life and the demands of those who are prepared to break with tradition. It may not be impossible to strike this balance, but no one can doubt that extraordinary political skills are required of the leadership of an organization of rural poor.

14. Paine, R., 'Emergence of the village as a social unit in a Coast Lappish fjord', *American Anthropologist*, 62:6, 1960.
15. Vorren, Ø., and Manker, E., *Samekulturen*, Oslo, 1958.

It may even be very difficult to define the group which the organization is representing. Thus, there exists no clear-cut answer to the question: Who is a Lapp?

The rural poor have received little education, have limited experiences with organizational problems, and some of them are even set apart by language and cultural barriers. Thus, whatever organizations they establish would be handicapped by the difficulties of establishing well qualified leadership, especially on the lower, local level. This is one characteristic which the rural poor share with other poor, underprivileged, handicapped and disabled groups.

The rural poor and the Lapps have, in some instances, access to power on the local level. However, the tasks and the organization of the municipalities are such as to prevent a concerted effort on behalf of those particular interests which concern the rural poor or the Lapps. The major task of the municipal leadership is to cultivate good relations with the national government and to settle problems of distribution between districts within the municipality. The strength of the municipality is often frittered away on local conflicts over the location of public investments. And the need to establish links with the great political parties tends to make local policy subservient to wider party interests, to the neglect of the particular problems of these minorities.

As for the Lapps, their problems are today under consideration in the Lappish Board, an advisory body, appointed by the national government. Most of the members share ascribed Lappish characteristics, but have no base in an electorate of Lapps. Thus, they have neither decision-making power, nor a legitimate base as a pressure group. Neither can they appeal to public opinion, as their deliberations and recommendations are confidential. Although the Lappish Board is in a position to contribute to reforms in favor of Lappish interests, their strength is restricted by these circumstances. The existence of such a board may possibly reduce the likelihood that a truly representative leadership of the Lapps will emerge. The positions are, as it were, already halfway occupied.

The other side of this coin is that the Lapps have no governmental agency with which they can deal in matters which are of special interest to the Lappish population. There exists no 'Lappish Bureau' in the national government. In principle, Lappish problems are dealt with like all other problems, that is, according to functionally specific criteria and in terms of the expertise required to deal with them. If the Lapps as an ethnic minority want to deal with the government, their only chance to do so is on the cabinet level or through initiatives in Parliament. Obviously, such confrontations will be rare. In matters of detail, even very important details, decision-making is in the hands of civil servants whose responsibility and area of competency, is very restricted.

Granted that the rural poor and the Lapps are at a disadvantage in achieving adequate representation through organizations, their fate is, like that of the sick, old and disabled, completely dependent upon government initiative. Unfortunately, there exist important impediments to effective administrative action on behalf of the government in relation to the problems of the rural poor and of the Lapps. We shall now turn to these problems.

Most administrative decisions to aid small, specific groups of rural poor, need municipal sanction or recommendation. The municipalities where the pockets of poverty are found, are themselves usually poor by national standards. Thus, those comparisons most relevant to local decision-makers, are those between the really poor and other groups who, although better off, still live on a standard well below the national average. This makes it difficult to obtain municipal approval for special aid or development programs in the poorest districts. Either the municipal authorities prefer to apply principles of formal and automatic equality in settling questions of distribution, which will lead to unfavorable results for the very poorest. Or, they are guided by fiscal considerations and a desire for economic growth, which normally favors aid to, and investments in, groups and districts which are already relatively prosperous. Wealth attracts, and poverty discourages, investments, and also public investment. This is a major factor in the vicious circle in which the poor are caught.

The proliferation of governmental agencies and the dispersal of decision-making that is relevant to the problems of small territorial units, prevent the development of concerted action to aid a specific group of rural poor. The geographical location of problem-areas is to some extent taken into account, but mostly in terms of larger regions, leaving the small pockets of poverty unattended. School problems are dealt with by the Ministry of Education, farm-problems by the Department of Agriculture, social problems by the Ministry of Social Affairs, and so on. The contact between the various agencies is limited, and the process of passing information between the agencies is very time-consuming. It cannot unreservedly be claimed that the dispersal of functions is to the disadvantage of the rural poor. It may also prevent concerted action on the government's behalf in a direction which is considered undesirable by the local population. Thus, it becomes very difficult for the government to pursue a consistent policy of moving people from the isolated, poor regions to districts where the employment situation is assumed to be better.

The expertise of the administrative personnel and their demands for quality, constitute under certain circumstances an impediment to projects which might aid the poor. To the extent that experts develop plans consistent with similar plans in other, more prosperous areas, they may run into the difficulty that these programs cannot be implemented. Either the investments become disproportionally great in relation to the expected output, or the necessary co-operation from the local population fails to manifest itself. Programs of an inferior, less expensive, and less demanding kind may be rejected by the experts as contrary to their professional conscience, in spite of their potential to benefit the poor.

The lack of trust and a tendency to moralize often prevents action on the part of governmental agencies. By definition the poor have a defective record in terms of work, education and other conventional symptoms of moral worth. These deficiencies are often attributed to qualities of the poor, to the mentality of the rural poor and to the ethnic characteristics of the Lapps. The rising standard of living in the rest of the population makes it increasingly difficult for the average citizen, as well as for the relatively affluent experts, to understand and empathize with the practical situation in which the poor find themselves. The increasing distance between the poor and the rest of society may favor interpretations of poverty in terms of culture or mentality where a situational approach would have been more adequate.

A moral dilemma is a basic obstacle to effective programs to aid the rural poor and the Lapps, a moral dilemma which is closely related to the ambivalence concerning the status of Lapps and other people on the rural fringe. Is their status, and the concomitant deprivations, a consequence of ascribed characteristics, aspects of a fate which they could not influence? An affirmative answer to this question would imply that these groups have a secure place within a comprehensive system of social policy aids. However, it is also possible to interpret their situation as a consequence of a choice, or of a lack of willingness to make the choice to leave the poor community and apply for work where there is a shortage of man-power.

Whenever doubt can be raised about the imputation of will or causality to a human situation, social policies tend to waver between half-hearted aid and the application of sanctions to motivate the individual to get out of his predicament. This is nowhere more clearly seen than in the modern treatment of criminals. But one may see the beginnings of a 'criminalization' also of the rural poor. In a welfare state all citizens are entitled to certain minimum services, regardless of costs. This applies most clearly to education and medical aid, where the interests of the rural periphery are protected by legislation. Other rights are protected, not by legislation, but by moral and political principles which are invoked with considerable success.

This situation worries some civil servants in the central administration. Since the rural poor have very low cash incomes they contribute little to the internal revenue, and the government is under the impression that the rural communities on the periphery are being heavily subsidized. This situation, which is of post-war origin, explains why a new kind of 'theft from society' is being defined, namely that which consists in remaining in a poor rural community and insisting upon being granted full citizens' rights. The national policy wavers between an attitude of genuine willingness to aid and a posture which means, in effect: If only you would be sensible and move somewhere else, we should pay you the cost of travel, aid you to get housing and retrain you for a different type of occupation.

This ambivalent basis of policy leads in many cases to satisfactory consequences. But the policy is not particularly effective in relation to the poorest inhabitants of the rural periphery. For a variety of reasons these are unable to take advantage of the opportunities to move. Thus, a further impoverishment of the remaining population may result from this aspect of the policy. This is especially true in the districts with a Lappish-speaking population. The barriers to mobility are great. Geographical mobility implies simultaneously a decision to relinquish Lappish identity or to accept a lonely life without social support for the subjective feeling of still being a Lapp.

To the extent that government policy develops in the direction of more emphasis upon 'growth centres', with less willingness to subsidize districts and occupations which seem non-viable, the fight against poverty may turn into a fight against the poor. For, although poverty is deplored by most everyone, poor or non-poor, some of the conditions that go with poverty may still be cherished. Although the fact of being a Lapp and the fact of being poor are closely connected, the individual may not be willing to shed his Lappish identity as an entrance fee to the welfare state. And who is capable of guaranteeing him that the gains will outweigh the losses?

Whatever the probable consequences of relinquishing the traditional way of life, whether in a Norwegian-speaking or in a Lappish-speaking community, the question is whether a welfare state can permit itself to assume a posture which is beset with the ambiguities I have mentioned. To eradicate these ambiguities is no easy matter. It costs money and it requires great inventiveness in community development under difficult natural conditions. It also presupposes an ability to overcome the elements of moral aggression against the poor who seem to be clinging to an outmoded way of life. This aggression may have one of its sources in the fact that the existence of these groups challenge the very ideological foundation on which the welfare state is built. Rightly or wrongly, these isolated rural groups appear to scorn the attractions of the good, urban life. Although poor, they seem to be about as cheerful as the average city-dweller, and as much attached to their way of life as anybody else. The urge to move them away may, in part, be supported by a secret desire to eliminate the challenge to those values which form the very foundations of policy in a modern state.

# PARTICIPANTS IN THE INTERNATIONAL SEMINAR ON POVERTY, UNIVERSITY OF ESSEX 3rd—6th April, 1967.

*Professor Brian Abel-Smith, Professor of Social Administration, London School of Economics and Political Science, Houghton Street, Aldwych, London, W.C.2., England. Senior Adviser to Secretary of State for Social Services.

*Professor Vilhelm Aubert, Professor of Sociology of Law, Institutt for Rettssosiologi og Forvaltiningslære, Universitetet i Oslo, Fuglehauggt 6, Oslo 2, Norway. Research Director of the Institute for Social Research, Division of Sociology, University of Oslo.

*Christopher Bagley, Research Officer, Centre for Social Research, University of Sussex, Brighton, Sussex, England.

Dr William A. Belson, Head, Survey Research Centre, London School of Economics and Political Science, Houghton Street, Aldwych, London, W.C.2., England.

Miss Sheila Benson, Fieldwork Organiser, National Survey on Household Resources and Standards of Living in the United Kingdom, London School of Economics and Political Science, 13 Endsleigh Street, London, W.C.1., England.

*Dr Otto Blume, Director, Institut für Selbsthilfe und Sozialforschung, e.V., Universitat Koln, 5 Koln, Aposteinstrasse 9, West Germany. Lecturer in Social Policy, University of Cologne; Chairman, German Consumer Association.

Mrs M. Cooper, Research Assistant, Department of Sociology, University of York, York, England.

Professor Richard Downing, Ritchie Professor of Research in Economics, University of Melbourne, Australia.

Henning Friis, Director, Danish National Institute of Social Research, 28 Borgergade, Copenhagen K, Denmark.

*Professor Herbert J. Gans, Professor of Sociology and Planning, Department of Urban Studies and Planning, M.I.T. Faculty Associate of the Joint Center for Urban Studies of M.I.T. and Harvard University, Cambridge, Mass. 02138, USA.

* Contributor to this volume.

Leonard H. Goodman, Senior Research Associate, Bureau of Social Science Research, 1200 17th Street, N.W., Washington D.C. 20036, USA.

Per Holmberg, Secretary, Governmental Commission into Low Income Groups in Sweden, c/o Afa, Fack, Stockholm 19, Sweden.

Miss Hilary Land, Research Officer, Department of Social Administration, London School of Economics and Political Science, Houghton Street, Aldwych, London, W.C.2., England.

Tony Lynes, Family Casework Organiser, Children's Department, Oxfordshire County Council, The Moors, Kidlington, Oxford, England. Formerly Director, Child Poverty Action Group, 1 Macklin Street, London, England.

Miss Alison MacEwen, Lecturer in Sociology, Department of Sociology, University of Essex, Wivenhoe Park, Colchester, Essex, England.

*J. C. McKenzie, Market Information Manager, Market Research Department, Allied Breweries Ltd., St John Street, London, E.C.1., England. Formerly at the Department of Nutrition, Queen Elizabeth College, London, England.

*Dennis Marsden, Lecturer in Sociology, Department of Sociology, University of Essex, Wivenhoe Park, Colchester, Essex, England.

*Professor S. M. Miller, Professor of Education and Sociology, New York University, Washington Square, New York, N.Y. 10003, USA.

Professor Dr Stephanie Munke, Professor in Social Policy and Sociology, Free University, Spindelmuhler Weg 35, 1000 Berlin 45 (Lichterfelde), West Germany.

Gunnar Olofsson, Assistant Secretary and Sociologist, Governmental Commission into Low Income Groups in Sweden, c/o Afa, Fack, Stockholm 19, Sweden.

*Professor Martin Rein, Professor of Social Work and Social Research, Bryn Mawr College, Bryn Mawr, Pennsylvania, USA. Consultant to the Office of Economic Opportunity.

*Miss Pamela Roby, Research Sociologist, School of Education, New York University, Washington Square, New York, N.Y. 10003, USA.

* Contributor to this volume.

*Professor Leopold Rosenmayr, Chairman of the Department of Sociology and Director of the Social Science Research Center, Institut für Soziologie, Universitat Wien, Dr Karl Luegerring 1, Vienna 1, Austria.

*Dr Alvin L. Schorr, Professor of Social Policy, Brandeis University, Boston, Mass., USA. Director, Income Maintenance Project, 818 18th Street N.W., Washington D.C. 20006, USA. Formerly Director of Research and Planning, Office of Economic Opportunity.

*Adrian Sinfield, Lecturer in Sociology, Department of Sociology, University of Essex, Wivenhoe Park, Colchester, Essex, England.

Miss Olea Smith, formerly Assistant Secretary, Child Poverty Action Group, 1 Macklin Street, London, W.C.2., England.

Professor Koji Taira, Associate Professor of Economics, Department of Economics, Stanford University, Palo Alto, California, USA.

Professor Richard Titmuss, Professor of Social Administration, London School of Economics and Political Science, Houghton Street, Aldwych, London, W.C.2., England. Deputy Chairman of the Supplementary Benefits Commission and formerly a member of the Royal Commission on Medical Education.

*Professor Peter Townsend, Professor of Sociology, Department of Sociology, University of Essex, Wivenhoe Park, Colchester, Essex, England.

John Veit-Wilson, Lecturer in Social Administration, Rutherford College of Technology, Ellison Place, Newcastle-upon-Tyne 1, England.

Mlle. Alwine A. de Vos van Steenwijk, Director, Association 'Aide à Toute Détresse', Institut de Recherches et de Formation aux Relations Humaines, 107, Avenue Général-Leclerc, 95 Pierrelaye (Val-D'Oise), France.

*Mrs Dorothy Wedderburn, Lecturer in Industrial Sociology, Imperial College of Science and Technology, Exhibition Road, London, S.W.7., England.

Dr Ian Whitaker, Reader in Sociology, University of York, York, England.

Dr Harriett Wilson, Senior Research Associate, Centre for Child Study, School of Education, University of Birmingham, Birmingham, England.

* Contributor to this volume.

# Index

Page numbers in italic figures indicate references in footnotes only

43; & education 168; & expenditure in Britain 100–12; a factor in social honour 138–40; & food choice in Britain 80–1, 84–5; in kind 25, 26, 47, 111; measure of resources? 196–9; measures of 100–12; & television 169; surplus 7; tax allowances 87; tax rebates 110; *see also* assistance; benefits; capital assets; pensions; resources; savings; social security; subsidies; tariffs; wages; windfalls
India 9, 15, 16, 33, 35, 39
Indians (expatriate) 36
Indonesia 33
industrialization 32, 146
industry 11, 37–9, 42, 44
inequality: concept of poverty 46, 47, 124, 143; non-economic aspects of 144; sexual 216; social 16, 125; *see also* class
injury 233, 225
insurance, national: benefits 86, 88, 218, 230–1
intelligence 23, 178–9
International Committee on Poverty Research vii, x
International Labour Organization 3
International Union of Family Organizations *120*
investment: by municipal authorities 247; in housing 121–2; overseas 11
isolation xi, 236–50
Italy 14

Jackson, E. F. *20*
Jahoda, M. *180*
Janowitz, M. *134, 141*
Japan *50*, 95
Jews 36
Job Corps (USA) 145
jobs: *see* employment
Jonassen, O. *239*
Joseph, Père 139
justice (legal) 47, 48, 133, 213

Kaes, R. 181
Kahn, H. R. *220*
Karlsen, G. *242*
Kelly, K. D. *20, 23*
Kemsley, W. F. F. *101*, 108
Kenya 13, 37, 39
Keyserling, Leon H. 62
Klanfer, J. *ix*
Knight, E. M. *220*
Köckeis, E. *168, 175, 178, 179*
Koestler, F. A. *117*
Kolko, G. 138
Kriesberg, L. *153*
Kreutz, H. *168, 175, 176, 178, 179*

Labbens, Jean 161
Labor Statistics, US Bureau of 51, 59, 91, *129*

Labor, US Department of *129, 132*
labour: *see* employment
Lagos, G. *1*, 10, *11*
Lamale, Helen H. *51*, 62
Lampman, Robert J. 62
Land, Hilary x, *220*, 252
Landecker, Werner S. *1, 20*, 22, 27, 29
Lapps (in Norway) 239–50
Laslett, Peter *18, 19*, 31
Lansing, J. B. *16, 43*
Laos 4
Lasswell, H. D. 4
Latin America 9, 32–3, 41, 122
Lazarsfeld, P. F. 173, *180*
League of Nations 90
Lebanese 36
Leibenstein, H. *32*
leisure 6, 7, 42–3, 162, 166–83
Lenski, G. E. *20*, 27, *129*
Lerner, D. *3*
level of living 6, 7, 48, 87, 95, 97, 99, 111; *see also* living standards
Lewis, Hylan *114, 146*, 147, *148*, 153, 160, 161
Lewis, Oscar *44*, 147, *148*, 150, 155, 157, 161, 180, 242
Lewis, R. *114*
Liberia 33
Libya 4
life-styles xi, 28, 138, 140–2, 146–64
Lipset, S. M. *129, 130, 133, 136*
literacy 3, 4, 8, 9, 35
living standards 86–99, 104, 123, 193–9, 209–11, 216, 228–30
Lockwood, D. 23, *140*
Logan, W. P. D. *74, 75*
London School of Economics 25, 29, *112*
loneliness *184, 191, 192*
lower class: *see* working class
low-income countries: *see* developing countries
Luck, J. *51*
luxuries 82, 92, 108, 229
Lydall, H. *16, 43*
Lynes, Tony *57*, 252

MacEwen, Alison 252
McKenzie, J. C. v, xi, *1*, 64, 252
MacKenzie, N. *130*
MacLean, R. 75
Malaysia *8*
malnutrition: *see* nutrition
Malthus, T. R. 142
Manker, E. *245*
Mannheim, Karl *146*
Manniche, E. *ix*
market: labour, & social security xi; & well-being 128–32, 133, 199–200
Marks, J. *71*, 72
marriage 30, 217–18, 225; *see also* family
Marsden, Dennis vi, vii, x, *205, 220*, 252